The Rise of
the Urban South

The Rise of
the Urban South

LAWRENCE H. LARSEN

//

THE UNIVERSITY PRESS OF KENTUCKY

Copyright © 1985 by The University Press of Kentucky

Scholarly publisher for the Commonwealth,
serving Bellarmine College, Berea College, Centre
College of Kentucky, Eastern Kentucky University,
The Filson Club, Georgetown College, Kentucky
Historical Society, Kentucky State University,
Morehead State University, Murray State University,
Northern Kentucky University, Transylvania University,
University of Kentucky, University of Louisville,
and Western Kentucky University.

Editorial and Sales Offices: Lexington, Kentucky 40506-0024

Library of Congress Cataloging in Publication Data

Larsen, Lawrence Harold, 1931-
  The rise of the urban South.

  Bibliography: p.
  Includes index.
  1. Urbanization—Southern States—History—19th
century. I. Title.
HT123.5.A13L37 1985   307.7'6'0975   84-25596
ISBN 0-8131-1538-8

Contents

Tables

Preface

This book is a study of the dynamics of southern urbanization in the Gilded Age. It is part of a larger project started well over a decade ago designed to analyze the sectional aspects of urban growth. The first volume, *The Urban West at the End of the Frontier*, appeared in 1978. Monographs on the Midwest and Northeast are yet to come. The decade of the 1880s was of crucial importance in shaping the American urban network and forging a national economy. Yet, the country was not yet a "nation of cities." Although there were similarities between communities in all parts of the land, sectional antecedents continued to have important political, economic, and social implications.

In the February 1950 issue of the *Journal of Southern History*, the Southern Committee of Ten, discussing research possibilities in southern history, singled out the urban South as a fertile field of investigation. "Urban life and development offer many suggestive topics for exploitation," they noted. "Among these are towns as trade centers, as cultural centers, and as county seats. The Southern town has an important enough history behind it to justify study. It is interesting to contemplate results of studies which approach southern urban development as it complements agrarian life on the one hand and it competes with a staple-crop agrarian system on the other" (p. 59).

In the years since then, several scholars have answered the call. Of special note have been the contributions of Blaine Brownell, Leonard P. Curry, David R. Goldfield, and Howard N. Rabinowitz. They and other pioneers in the field of southern urban history have contributed to a better understanding of the subject. Until recently, however, the main thrust of historiography has been in other directions. Of the rich body of scholarly material available on the nineteenth-century South, only a relatively small amount deals directly with the urbanization process. Despite a few excellent suggestive essays and studies on specific subjects, little in the way of comprehensive analysis exists on the early stages of city building in Dixie. The object of this book is to help answer that need, and at the same time to stimulate research in southern urban history.

The South, with all its distinctiveness and contrasts, has always been a region in slow motion. The southern urban mosaic was not built in a short span. Rather, it evolved in relationship to the resources and needs of an agrarian and commercial society. Southern leaders patiently constructed layers of cities. They eschewed the unrestricted promotional frenzy that led to the raising up within a few decades of cities in the Midwest. Even after national events drastically altered the course of American urbanization, southerners continued to pursue an orderly policy. The Civil War and Reconstruction disrupted their plans. The "New South" movement (as distinguished from wider applications of the term) raised false hopes at the same time it sought to sustain faith in southern traditions. Racial controversy wasted human resources. The question of whether to welcome or oppose outside developers continued as a constant source of debate. As cities in Dixie grew in size, an increasingly uniform response to municipal problems threatened their individual characteristics. Agricultural deficiencies checked the creation of prosperous urban hinterlands. Through it all, the South's city builders persevered, continuing to erect an urban network suited to their requirements.

A serious discourse in thought and action about the need for southern cities occurred in the antebellum South. The discussion continued through the Civil War, the Reconstruction period, and the Gilded Age. The New South visionaries and the arguments they articulated deserve serious attention. The impact of their views is another matter. Patterns of urbanization developed in the South that evolved over the course of the nineteenth century. The cities differed only in degree from those elsewhere in America. Even so, judgments about progress in urbanization and industrialization require measurement by southern as well as national standards.

The urbanization of the South has to be considered on its own terms. In that context, the story of southern city building in the Gilded Age is not one of failure. Rather, against a backdrop of defeat, discouragement, and disillusionment, it is an uplifting account of a limited victory: a triumph that in many ways contributed to the making of the great alabaster cities of the twentieth-century South.

I started working on this project more than a decade ago. Over the years so many people have helped me that it is impossible to acknowledge all of them. Needless to say, I appreciated their concern and aid. Fredrick Marcel Spletstoser and Barbara J. Cottrell read and commented with great care on various versions of the manuscript. Spletstoser's observations on the New South movement were especially valuable. W. Bruce Wheeler also read and commented on several draft chapters. Helping in a variety of ways were several of my colleagues at the University of Missouri-Kansas City. They included Stanley B. Parsons, Herman M. Hattaway, Richard Elrod, James Falls, Jesse V. Clardy, William R. Brazelton, Richard McKinzie, and George Gale. Dean Eldon Parizek of the UMKC College of Arts and Science provided a scholarly environment. Roger T. Johnson of *Milling & Baking News* fished with me and discussed agricultural economics. Douglas McLennon, Sam Wallace, John Finger, and Lawrence Christensen offered valuable criticism. Among other contributors were William Petrowski, Patrick McLear, William Pratt, and R. Christopher Schnell. James and Marian Cottrell provided an island in Canada. Barbara LoCascio and Claire Hildebrand typed the manuscript.

Of course, though both custom and prudence demand it be said, I am responsible for errors of fact or interpretation.

To Ruthie

1

A Wider Field
Both for Virtue and Vice

In 1980 enthusiastic promoters predicted a magnificent future for the urban South. Census statistics indicated that many southern towns had grown significantly in population through a time when numerous old industrial centers in the North had experienced marked declines. Publicists claiming that a new age of racial harmony and enterprise had dawned below the Mason and Dixon line portrayed Dixie's cities as good places in which to live and invest money. At long last, buttressed by a network of metropolises, the South would assume its rightful place in America. Even the use of the term "South" was passé in some circles, replaced by "Sunbelt," which had broader connotations.[1] "Sunbelt" blurred racial considerations by linking the destiny of southern cities with that of entirely different historical traditions in the Southwest and on the Pacific coast. It was a public relations triumph of the first degree, worthy of the best of Madison Avenue. Fortunately for southerners, the claims of a coming urban millennium had more substance than was indicated by the promotional froth. Population trends, coupled with economic indicators and quality of life studies, appeared to give the predictions considerable validity. The problem was that it was an old refrain. Equating the interests of the South with those of other parts of the country or glossing over racial disharmony were not new concepts.

Was the new South of the 1980s simply another manifestation of many past new Souths that had failed to see dramatic progress? Cynics noted that after any period of activity and bold talk the South always remained several decades behind the rest of the nation. After all, in 1980, New York City, for all its perceived troubles, had a metropolitan area population more than ten times larger than that of Atlanta. Nevertheless, at long last, urbanization in the South seemed to be becoming a reality.

There is a continuity to southern history, as has often been pointed out.[2] In the 1980s advocates of a new urban South included such diverse groups as Gulf State real estate salesmen, corporate bankers in Atlanta, and integrationist politicians all across the region. Although differing in many of their views, all agreed that even as the South developed considerable urban dimensions, it would remain unique, its people and institutions distinguished by geography and temperament. Whether or not they realize it, these modern visionaries share a bond with southern leaders of the distant past. In the early days of the republic, when the nation first began to develop into an urban society, serious students of life in the South pondered the desirability of cities. They recognized the need for commercial and cultural centers but feared the consequences of rapid urbanization. A central philosophical question was how to build an urban system without upsetting the existing agrarian order.

Thomas Jefferson reflected the conflicting opinions about cities held by many plantation owners. His views changed markedly over the years, affected by a combination of his own moods and experiences, changes in prevailing scientific theories about the prevention of disease, and the exigencies of the international situation. In the 1780s he asserted, "The mobs of great cities add just so much to the support of pure government as sores do to the strength of the human body,"[3] and warned that abandonment of agrarian principles would corrupt the country.[4] Jefferson believed that cities provided an unnatural atmosphere for human life, an assumption strengthened by the yellow fever epidemics that swept through American cities in the 1790s. Yet by 1805 he concluded that building cities on a "more open plan" would alleviate health problems. At this point he decided that it was necessary and practical, in light of threats from overseas, to place "the manufacturer by the side of the agriculturist." Shortly before his death he again reevaluated his position. In 1824, equating cities with "vice and wretchedness," he called New York a "Cloacina of all the depravities of human nature."[5] Coming full circle, he was a man of his times, mirroring the shifting attitudes of his fellow countrymen toward urban institutions. In Jefferson's day "urban" and "rural" were not standard categories of thought. People viewed both town and country as "normal." They appeared to have the same characteristics, except that some problems—disease, vice, and crime—seemed more concentrated in cities.

Rapid urbanization resulted in changing conceptions. Census figures indicated that between 1820 and 1860 cities grew at a rate of 797 percent, against 226 percent for the nation as a whole. New statistical information on a wide variety of subjects further accentuated differences between rural and urban areas. Many promotional writers extolled the virtues of cities; conversely, reformers wrote tracts attacking various aspects of urban life. At the same time, many citizens of the South became increasingly concerned about the position of their section in the federal union. Once they accepted the proposition that cities were more than simply extensions of a rural society, they began to question their own values. Most of the new urban growth was occurring outside of the South. The realities of increasing city populations and the resulting changes in intellectual conceptions caused white southerns to think of their region as a unique agrarian society.[6]

Champions of the Old South used Jefferson's statements in various ways to support their own contentions about cities. Some agrarian extremists claimed that the absence of many towns augured well for the rise of a separate southern civilization. They dismissed existing towns as agrarian dependencies, of small consequence beyond their traditional roles as receiving and distribution points. The rapid building up of cities in the North led to charges that cities not only subverted Jeffersonian ideals but were evil places that menaced Christian moral values. The assaults intensified as the nineteenth century progressed, fueled by fears that grubby commerical and manufacturing centers, where crude "lords of the loom" would oppress workers and unscrupulous merchants would gouge buyers by selling shoddily produced goods at inflated prices, might rise in Dixie. In 1849 a pro-agrarian commentator contended, "In a city the temptation to indulgence is incessant, because almost every object of desire is in market, and desire itself is inflamed not only by opportunity but by rivalry."[7] It followed that the South, rural in residence and temperament, did not present the temptations, the opportunities for sensual gratification, or the ruinous waste of human life that supposedly characterized northern metropolises.

Many southern statesmen, however, of all philosophical predilections, became increasingly reconciled to the need for cities. Andrew Jackson was an official of the town company that established Memphis. Henry Clay worked to advance the fortunes of his home, Lexington, Kentucky. John C. Calhoun envisioned a great southern commercial empire based on large cities. Jefferson Davis wanted towns and railroads to serve as means of welding the South into a nationalistic entity.[8] In general, though, conflict continued to characterize thoughtful deliberations about the course of urbanization. In 1843 George Tucker, a Jeffersonian theoretician and professor of moral philosophy at the University of Virginia, said that demographic trends made the future growth of cities inevitable and that therefore the positive side of city life should be stressed and means found to control potential unsavory elements. "In the eyes of the moralist," he said, "cities afford a wider field both for virtue and vice; and they are more prone to innovation, whether for good or evil.[9]

Actually, antiurbanism was a national as well as a sectional concept supported or rejected in direct relationship to the needs of a given situation. Since the early days of settlement in North America, religious leaders had attacked towns as places where lust, vanity, and conspiracy thrived. Novelists portrayed cities as representative of the evils that affected all human nature. Popular writers expanded on livid themes about the pitfalls of urban life. The editors of agricultural journals warned rural youths about the evils of the city. New England transcendentalists, including Henry David Thoreau and Ralph Waldo Emerson, praised nature and questioned whether urban materialism actually meant progress. But while a flood of promotional literature exhorted people to build cities, the vast majority of citizens, North and South, accepted the original Jeffersonian premise that the nation should remain agricultural.[10] Faith in the desirability of agrarianism grew in direct proportion to the movement of Americans into cities.

The doctrine of antiurbanism had a practical side. Few outside commentators had anything good to say about New York, the nation's most successful city. In the first half of the nineteenth century, the Empire City garnered the money power and became the nation's primary distribution and receiving center. Its command of credit rates and commercial prices caused both admiration and hatred. Especially in the South, New York was a symbol of exploitation. An editorial in the *Vicksburg Daily Whig*, written on the eve of the Civil War, summed up prevailing attitude: "New York, like a mighty queen of commerce, sits proudly upon her island throne sparkling in jewels, and waving an undisputed commercial spectre over the South. By means of her railroads and navigable streams, she sends out her long arms to the extreme South; and with avidity rarely equalled, grasps our gains and transfers them to herself—taxing us at every step and depleting us as extensively as possible without destroying us." Similarly, *DeBow's Review*, the leading southern commercial journal of the 1850s, denounced New York and all its works: "Southern toil and labor . . . has been showering down gold for fifty years into her lap amounting to countless millions. The patronage of the South has furnished its full quota towards supplying the means to rear that immensely wealthy city. Unsuspecting Southern liberality has done its utmost to feed and pamper this monster city."[11] On another occasion, a commentator in *DeBow's* accused New York of fostering the slavery system. Such was the price of success in antebellum urban America.

New York's ascendancy was one part of the changes that within a few decades threw city building and relations between the sections out of kilter. A gradual approach to urbanization came to an abrupt end. No actual economic conspiracy against the South existed. The success of the urban North resulted from the ability of entrepreneurs to read trends correctly, to make plans, to obtain financing, and to make use of technological innovations. In that context, the South was the loser in the construction of cities in the pre–Civil War period. But the differences resulted from another reality. Using the rules that had governed urban needs over the previous 150 years, southerners had done a fairly good job of creating cities. Antiurban attitudes had little to do with the South's failure to develop great cities. Rather, the rush of events overwhelmed the builders of a carefully constructed urban network. Events outside of the region placed the South at a distinct economic disadvantage. On one level, southern urbanization can best be approached on its own terms, inside its own history. On another, broader level, an understanding of the larger picture is essential. In short, urban developments in the South cannot be considered in a vacuum, any more than they can be considered within the context of hypothetical musings about the nature of cities.

Urbanization in the colonial South had been a reasonably logical and orderly procedure.[12] In the early days natural advantages had taken precedence over entrepreneurial considerations. The first settlers sought sites with good harbors, defensive positions, and easy access into the interior. Many later attempts by authorities to designate town sites, notably in Virginia and the Carolinas, for the most part failed miserably. The South required only a few major cities until well into colonial times. Tobacco growers in Maryland and Virginia shipped from their own docks; Charleston served the needs of the Carolinas. Baltimore, which grew as a tobacco port after planters used up coastal lands, triumphed over a number of competitors in the upper Chesapeake Bay region. From the start, however, southern town-building activities seldom overreached. Instead, they developed in reaction to the needs of the society, thereby establishing important precedents.

The United States entered the nineteenth century as a maritime and agrarian nation. A few cities were sufficient to serve the needs of the republic. Following the War of 1812 the United States turned inward. The breaking of Indian power east of the Mississippi River provided an opportunity for the quick settlement and exploitation of hundreds of thousands of square miles of potential farm and plantation lands. A popular political proposal, the American System, based on the hope of developing a self-sufficient economy, spurred interest in interior markets. As people poured into the newly opened areas, both North and South, New York capitalists responded to the changing conditions. On one plain, coastal schooners that carried freight from New York to southern ports stopped deadheading on return trips. Instead, they carried cotton for transshipment out of New York to overseas ports. On a larger plain, New Yorkers strongly supported the building of the Erie Canal. Its success started a race between New York and its East Coast rivals for western markets in the old Northwest Territory. [13]

The South was unprepared to respond to the sudden dash for western markets. In the first place, the section's Atlantic coastal cities had to contend with horrendous geographical obstacles—forbidding and rugged mountains that separated the ports from the interior. North of Georgia, the easiest way through the mountains was the Cumberland Gap, but even that route, which was followed by the National Road, passed through difficult territory. [14] To the south, the great valleys of the Shenandoah, the Cumberland, and the Tennessee all ran northeast to southwest, rather than east to west. Given the underdeveloped transportation technology, the best way was to go around, which meant swinging south through north central Georgia, through foothills and hollows. More lines of mountains ran east to west across Kentucky and Tennessee. It was easy to project communication lines from the Atlantic to the Ohio River; realizing those lines was much different. In 1836 leaders of the Tennessee Valley town of Knoxville were at first elated when coastal interests projected a railroad from Charleston to Cincinnati running through their community. When they learned that the line was to go straight over the mountains, they knew it would never be built. [15] Critics chided Charleston planters for not supporting the project, claiming it would have enabled the city to compete on an equal basis with New York. In this instance, the planters were simply being realistic.

Until much too late, the southern Atlantic seaboard cities failed to obtain transportation lines that could challenge New York. The National Road lost importance. It handled less than two hundred thousand tons of east-bound commodities annually, at a time when the Erie Canal carried several million tons. Despite geographical problems, Baltimore interests made a bold move—they undertook construction of a four-hundred-mile-long railroad from their city to Wheeling. Building started in 1828, well in advance of existing railroad engineering. No one knew whether tracks could be laid through the mounains beyond the Cumberland Gap. Work progressed so slowly that the line did not reach Wheeling until 1853. It gave Baltimore access to the Midwest, and, after the Civil War, trunk connections to St. Louis and Chicago. These routes enabled Baltimore to compete successfully for the growing Midwest grain trade. [16] Some southern interests claimed that because it had built tracks outside the section Baltimore was no longer a true southern city. [17] But the city's railroad strategy, even though overly ambitious, demonstrated that some southern capitalists were ready to take calculated risks. At a time when its basic hinterland lay entirely below the Mason and Dixon line, Baltimore had penetrated Yankee territory, an achievement of no mean magnitude.

Places to the south of Baltimore were unable to do as well. Baltimore was a wealthy seafaring city, with enough sources of credit to spend $15 million on railroad projects in the antebellum period. No other town could raise that much money. In an age of gerrymandering, urban underrepresentation, and property qualifications for voting, promoters had to go hat in hand to rural-dominated state legislatures. Although legislators were frequently sympathetic to proposals, they were reluctant to make appropriations, award franchises, or authorize bond issues. Even partial funding was hard to come by, unless a project had demonstrated local significance, in which case planters and merchants frequently supported bond subscriptions.[18] A favored promotional tactic linked railroad proposals to the moving of cotton, which was much more attractive to southern elites than nebulous visions of midwestern grain markets.

Limited achievements were the general rule. A Norfolk scheme to build a railroad to the Ohio River died almost at its inception, blocked by opposition from Richmond in the Virginia legislature. In retaliation, Norfolk interests successfully opposed railroad lines and canal extensions desired by Richmond. On another level, Richmond and Norfolk combined to stop the internal improvement plans of other cities in the Old Dominion, notably Alexandria and Lynchburg. Washington promoters were more successful than many of those inside the state in dealing with the Virginia legislature. In the 1820s Washington canal builders received money from that body and its counterpart in Maryland to dig the Chesapeake and Ohio Canal from the Potomac to the Ohio. Congress also contributed funds, convinced that the project could be integrated into a national defense plan to assist the movement of troops through the Appalachian Mountains. The canal was a total failure, never progressing beyond the Cumberland Gap. In North Carolina, officials in a number of small ports could only wish for money to undertake big schemes. During antebellum times, they did well to construct several local railroads, including one that was 125 miles long. There was no money to accomplish more in an undeveloped agricultural state. Down the coast in South Carolina, Charleston interests concentrated upon securing local lines and extensions into Georgia for the primary purpose of carrying cotton.[19] Undeterred by Charleston's plans to build rail lines in Georgia, Savannah interests had conceived a magnificent integrated ocean and land transportation network. Its capitalists, with money raised in New York, paid for the construction of the *Savannah*, which in 1819 made the first partially steam-powered voyage across the Atlantic.[20] The ship was a financial failure, so the Savannahans retrenched. With considerable success, they thrust roads and railroads into Georgia, challenging Charleston's plans. By the Civil War none of the cities below Baltimore had direct connections with the Midwest, but they had built lines to the jumping-off points into the underdeveloped southern interior. The basis had been laid for a sound policy of future development, well suited to the needs of an agrarian order.

As the trans-Appalachian West opened for settlement, economic experts pondered which was more profitable, grain or cotton. Both could raise empires, but it was easier to open up grain than cotton fields for cultivation. Grain, basically strains of weeds, was a renewable resource that could be grown almost anywhere. The crop predominated along the frontier in the early days of settlement. Until the nineteenth century, the chief wheat-growing region in the country was in Maryland and Virginia. By the 1830s it had moved to the Genessee Valley in upstate New York. During the 1840s it had shifted to the Maumee River Valley in Ohio. In the ensuing decade, Illinois emerged as the number one wheat state and, ten years later, Wisconsin.[21] The upper Great Plains became "America's breadbasket" following the Civil War. In the antebellum Midwest grain production rose tremendously because the vast prairies and easily broken soil made agricultural settlement relatively uncomplicated. So many people went to the area from New England that some leaders in that section worried about depopulation. These developments seemingly harked well for the South, given the often-stated belief that the Midwest would forge strong economic ties with New Orleans.

The course of development in the Midwest upset calculations about the creation of ties with the South. Promoters carried on a frenzied speculation in town sites. Land sharks platted thousands of paper villages.[22] The Panic of 1837, in part nurtured by overextended city building, only temporarily checked the speculative spiral. Most towns failed, but the "forced-draft" effect of a combination of successful urban promotions and agricultural progress gave the Midwest numerous "instant cities" by the Civil War. The settlement of the antebellum Midwest demonstrated that people could raise up cities in a hurry, a development alien to southern experiences and practices.

Great regional power changes affected the sectional struggle. Cincinnati and St. Louis leaders, instead of looking south, concentrated on garnering new midwestern markets. Louisville authorities, unable to corner markets north of the Ohio River, shifted their concerns to building railroads in Kentucky and Tennessee. Chicago strategists soon developed and carried out a railroad policy that led to further alterations of the emerging urban network. Most of Chicago's gains came at the expense of its arch rival St. Louis. By the Civil War, Chicago was the rail center of the Midwest. The rapid advance of Chicago—it gained a reputation as the "Wonder City of the World"—further darkened hopes for a cautious national urban policy. Northeastern "plungers" rushed to invest money in Chicago lines. This was all very frustrating to southerners used to operating within the constraints of an older and more equitable structue that was no longer valid.[23]

In the decade and a half before the Civil War, writers in *DeBow's* carefully framed their arguments favoring urbanization in terms of threatened northern domination, sectional disparities, and the historic role of cities. Virginia economist William Burwell contended that railroads could quickly build towns in the South, restoring the section to preeminence. The publication's editor, J.D.B. DeBow, agreed, stressing the need to counter the achievements of railroad builders in the North with "corresponding weapons." To reinforce the point, DeBow published an article by Jesup Scott, a wealthy Toledo, Ohio, capitalist with a reputation as an authority on railroads and urbanization trends. Scott claimed that rail networks would soon create monster cities of ten million people. Consequently, he argued that the South would be left far behind the rest of the nation if it continued to place faith in an outmoded agricultural economy.[24] Other commentators, after studying national patterns, asserted that geographical inevitability dictated the rise of towns along the Mississippi and Alabama rivers. Metropolitanism was equated with progress; cities were said to be beacons in mankind's long search for knowledge, humanity, and light. Advocates of urbanization insisted that enormous southern communities would be unlike those elsewhere, for they would pose no menace to prevailing norms. They discounted fragmentary evidence of the incompatibility of slavery and urbanization. As DeBow stated in 1860: "Once Baltimore, Richmond, Charleston, Savannah, Mobile, and New Orleans will supply all goods foreign and domestic, how easily we might cut off all dependence on the North."[25]

Dixie's antebellum urban centers contained men who perceptively recognized that despite cotton prosperity the South was in danger of losing its economic position in the American Union. DeBow, Hinton R. Helper, William Fitzhugh, and other intellectuals believed that an agrarian society could not hope to avoid outside domination. So they called for the development of manufacturing, direct trade with Europe, promotion of railroads, and programs designed to attract northern investment capital. Southerners to the core, these otherwise farsighted individuals were white supremacists, who, with the exception of Helper, believed that slavery was a necessary labor system and an essential agency for the maintenance of racial harmony. DeBow claimed that "the negro was created essentially to be a slave, and finds his highest development and destiny in that condition."[26] But, DeBow and other

economic activists achieved only limited success. Although they received a wide hearing, they were virtually powerless in a South that
was under the political and intellectual control of a planter aristocracy.

Helper and Fitzhugh had strikingly different views about the
"peculiar institution." Fitzhugh, a widely known Virginia sociologist,
used human skulls and other evidence to attack the concept of a free
society and to prove what he considered the innate racial inferiority of
blacks. Fitzhugh, in equating slavery with high civilization, felt that
cities further enhanced the human experience. "Cities are but human
hives and honeycombs," he asserted, "and as much the natural residence of man as the latter are of bees. . . . The vitality of cities has been
as remarkable as their influence on human destiny."[27] Helper, a brilliant but alienated North Carolinian, believed that slavery retarded
economic growth. In his controversial 1857 book, *The Impending Crisis of
the South: How to Meet It*, he demanded the establishment of a gigantic
southern metropolis. He alleged that sinister manipulations by the
slavocracy enabled northerners to draw away from the South more
than $120 million every year, drastically changing the sectional bal-
ance. "Now, instead of carrying all our money to New-York, Philadelphia, Boston, and Cincinnati," he speculated, "suppose we had
kept it on the south side of Mason and Dixon's line—as we would have
done, had it not been for slavery—and had disbursed it in the upbuild-
ing of Norfolk, Beaufort, Charleston, or Savannah, how much richer,
better, greater, would the South have been to-day!"[28] He implied that a
plot prevented the growth of cities in the South. Although his dark
thoughts about a far-reaching conspiracy seemed improbable, they
received a wide audience in the North, adding fuel to the fires of
sectional controversy.

Southern nationalists had little interest in competing with northerners to see who could build cities in the shortest period of time. As long
as cotton was king the few voices for urbanization in the South were
unable to bring about a dramatic change in policy. In 1858 an English
tourist, Hiram Fuller, caught the prevailing mood of the dominant
groups when he wrote, "Mobile is a pleasant cotton city of some thirty
thousand inhabitants—where people live in cotton houses and ride in
cotton carriages. They buy cotton, sell cotton, think cotton, eat cotton,
drink cotton, and dream cotton."[29] Railroads into unchartered territory, risky manufacturing ventures, and diversified agriculture had no
place in the antebellum South. In that context, white southerners
appeared a shiftless lot of racists, dedicated to supporting a cruel
system of exploitation based upon human slavery at the expense of
their own self-interest. Few northerners cared about city building in
the prewar South. They were interested in New Yorkers creating a
national urban system and Chicagoans plotting a railroad strategy.

These developments, compressed into less than half a century, changed the direction of the national experience. By comparison the plans of southern urban innovators paled to nothing.

The Civil War hurt all the southern cities. Even those that sustained no military damage had to contend with ravaged hinterlands and disrupted commerical connections. As late as 1879 *New York Tribune* reporters who toured the South concluded that "tried by Northern standards, there are only a few cities between the Potomac and the Rio Grande that can be said to be growing and prospering." They thought Mobile "dilapidated and hopeless," Norfolk "asleep by her magnificent harbor," and life in Wilmington and Savannah "at a standstill."[30] The victors were far from generous. Exploitation of the South continued as before the war. There was no scheme—such as the Marshall Plan after World War II to help Western Europe—to raise up the prostrate South.

During a period of defeat and humiliation, the plight of the South was such that urban promoters found a far more receptive audience. DeBow used the pages of his revised commercial magazine to call for a postwar policy that emphasized industrialization, diversified agriculture, immigration, and attemps to obtain outside capital. DeBow had served the Confederacy as the chief overseer of the cotton trade, adding to his impeccable sectional credentials. He wrote in 1866, "*We have got to go to manufacturing to save ourselves*. We have got to go to it to obtain an increase of population. Workmen go to furnaces, mines, and factories—they go where labor is brought."[31] This was "old wine in new bottles," to be sure, but it helped to bridge the gap in the southern experience caused by the Civil War. In the 1870s the call for an urban and industrial South intensified. By the end of the decade it had been codified into the New South creed.

Some of the most articulate New South spokesmen were newspapermen: Henry Watterson of the *Louisville Courier-Journal*, Richard Edmonds of the *Manufacturers Record*, Francis Dawson of the *Charleston News and Courier*, Walter Hines Page of several different journals, and, above all, Henry Grady of the *Atlanta Constitution*.[32] In an era in which political leaders were unable to represent the section, either because of their past loyalty to the Confederacy or their activities during Reconstruction, journalists more than at any other time spoke for the South. Perhaps under different circumstances, some of these men would have become statesmen on a par with John C. Calhoun, Henry Clay, and the presidents of the Virginia dynasty. But the older America no longer existed at the dawning of the Gilded Age. Southern politicians had little national credibility. Prominent journalists, although certainly not above politics, could, by the nature of their work, take a higher ground on economic matters. They were able to present apparently nonpartisan, progressive, and rational answers to the problems of the day. Southern newspaper editors of such weekly publications as the *Yorkville Enquirer,* the *Sparta Ishmaelite,* and the *Troy Messenger* gave them a wide hearing by reprinting their commentaries, as did important northern newspapers. Some small southern papers worked out joint selling arrangements with larger publications.[33] The subscribers of the Alexandria, Louisiana, *Town Talk* had the option of receiving Grady's *Atlanta Constitution.* When the journalistic advocates of change sallied forth on the lecture circuit to preach their doctrines, they went not as representatives of the Lost Cause but as skilled communicators who articulated programs that they claimed would bind sectional wounds.

The purveyors of the nostrums were all relatively young men. Watterson, born in 1840 and the son of a Tennessee lawyer, had edited the *Rebel,* the most widely read of wartime papers in the Confederacy. Following hostilities, he did a quick about-face. Under his editorship, the *Nashville Banner* supported reunion, forgiveness, and drastic changes in the southern way of life. He moved to Louisville because he claimed it had a more cosmopolitan outlook than Nashville. Edmonds, born on a Virginia farm in 1857, became convinced as a youth that misguided economic policies kept the South in poverty and prevented the exploitation of its natural resources. His regional journal, which he founded in 1881 in Baltimore, supported southern industrial progress with missionary zeal. Dawson, an Englishman imbued with the right- eousness of the southern cause, had enlisted in a British port in the Confederate navy, going to sea on a commerce raider. Twenty-five years of age when the war ended, he settled in Charleston and became a newspaperman. Under his editorial direction, the *News and Courier* lashed out at the Republican carpetbag government of South Carolina, clouding his role as an advocate of urbanization. His career ended tragically in 1889, when he was killed in a quarrel over a woman. Page, a North Carolinian, was only four years old at the beginning of the Civil War. In 1878, after attending three colleges, including the Johns Hopkins University in Baltimore, he drifted into newspaper work. He soon became a writer for national magazines, including *Harper's Weekly.* His main role was as a critic who told northern readers about the inferior economic condition of the South and called for a redress through the building of cities. He eventually became a part owner of the *Manufacturers Record* but then moved on, capping his career by serving as Woodrow Wilson's ambassador to the Court of St. James. Page was thoughtful in his analysis of the post-Reconstruction South, placing problems in a national context. He believed that southerners needed to exert more energy to change conditions. Edmonds saw factories as a sectional panacea. Dawson and Watterson were zealous urban promoters of a classic American mold. Dawson wanted to make

Charleston the "Liverpool of America." Watterson called Louisville a "Railroad Bismarck."[34]

If Dawson and Watterson had been editors of the *Racine Journal-Times* or the *Cedar Rapids Gazette* they would have been considered typical town boosters. At best, they might have been grouped in the same class as Robert T. Van Horn of the *Kansas City Western Journal of Commerce*. Believing that Kansas City's future lay to the west, he extolled the Kansas hinterlands as the "Garden of the World" rather than as the official designation of the "Great American Dessert." Van Horn entered public life and served as mayor of Kansas City and as a United States congressman.[35] Dawson and Watterson, however, were editors of southern papers, and they made judgments within a larger framework than that of town promotion. Henry Woodfin Grady operated under the same restraints.

Grady had perfect credentials. Certainly a friend of this courtly and uncommon man did not do him justice when he wrote gushingly, "Mr. Grady's love was an organic force, with eyes to see and brains to plan and hands to execute. While, like the sun, it shed its cheering beams on every side, it was so individualized and focalized that it specially touched and inspired everyone within its range, shining alike on the evil and on the good, and distilling its beneficent dews upon the just and the unjust."[36] Despite such hyperbole, Grady seemed almost too good to be true. Born in Athens, Georgia, in 1851, he was the son of a successful merchant. In a class-conscious society in which roots counted for a great deal, tradesmen were not at the top of the social scale. His background could have been a liability to a prophet of urban destiny. But, Grady's father joined the Confederate forces and died in the field during the last days of the war. The citizens of Athens raised a monument in his honor, providing his son with a tangible link to the Lost Cause.

Henry Grady graduated from the University of Georgia. After broadening his horizons by spending a year at the University of Virginia, he became a journalist. He worked for several newspapers, serving for a time as the southern correspondent for the *New York Herald* before joining the staff of the *Atlanta Constitution* in 1876. Four years later he bought a quarter interest in the paper with $20,000 loaned by New York business leader Cyrus Field, who had long cultivated southern commercial ties. Grady edited and published the *Constitution* until his sudden death in 1889.[37] At the time he was among the best-known southerners in the nation.

During his short adult life, Grady gave a number of major speeches on "enemy soil" in the North. He took great pains to appear moderate and a bit apologetic on the race question, assuring his listeners that a new era of progress lay ahead. In 1886 he told a New York audience, "I am glad that the omniscient God held the balance of battle in His Almighty Hand, and that human slavery was swept forever from American soil—the American Union saved from the wreck of war."[38] With considerable eloquence he talked of the bond between southern whites and blacks, describing in moving terms how slaves had shielded the bodies of their fallen masters on the battlefield. Grady expressed the belief that northerners, who, he said, came from a section with a poor record in dealing with Indians, had out of ignorance and inexperience blundered badly in handling southern blacks. A favorite Grady theme was that once northern humanitarians left the South, southern blacks and whites would work together to achieve racial harmony. He said, "I want no better friend than the black boy who was raised by my side . . . I want no sweeter music than the crooning of my old 'mammy.' "[39] This reasonable view received reinforcement in the *Constitution* through Joel Chandler Harris's "Uncle Remus" stories, which stressed blissful black and white relations. Through such means, Grady spun myths about slavery acceptable to the very northerners who had destroyed the system.[40]

Few northerners, at least those eager to invest in what they accepted as a reformed South, saw, or wanted to see, another side of Grady's racial views. He talked much differently on the subject when addressing his fellow white southerners. He bluntly told an audience: "But the supremacy of the white race in the South must be maintained forever, and the domination of the negro race resisted at all points and at all hazards, because the white race is the superior race. This is the declaration of no new truth; it has abided forever in the marrow of our bones and shall run forever in the blood that feeds Anglo-Saxon hearts."[41] The words about slaves protecting the bodies of wounded masters or about the love of white children for their black nursemaids were strictly for northern consumption.

Watterson and Edmonds displayed similar dualism on the race question. Edmonds wrote movingly about the "progressive evolution from the darkness of slavery into the fullness of freedom." He saw blacks rising toward true manhood by using their physical and moral powers. "In all history," he averred, "there has been no similar instance in which the ruling race has so nobly and unremittingly aided its former bondsmen to rise to the highest levels of which they were naturally capable." Although arguing that the "troublesome race question" would vanish in the New South, he accepted the superiority of the Anglo-Saxon "race" and claimed that the development plans of the "white men" would be executed through the use of the "strong muscles of industrious negroes."[42] Watterson observed that only poor judges of human nature would believe that the well-being of blacks did not lie in the South, where they would be protected by their former owners. Indeed, he lashed out at the Ku Klux Klan and fought successfully in Kentucky to allow blacks the right to testify in court. But he said in print that blacks were "barbarians" and "ignorant and degraded" people hardly removed from the wilds of Africa.[43] Statements by New South leaders on racial matters depended upon the audience and the time and place.

The proponents of an urban renaissance in the South told northern investors what they wanted to hear: that the Civil War had mooted older attitudes and that white southerners regarded northerners as brothers under one flag. As such, the defeat of the Confederacy was a blessing for the entire country. Hundreds of thousands of men in blue and gray had died gloriously to give birth to a New South that deemed Abraham Lincoln a hero. The section offered unparalleled opportunities to those who would help it became economically integrated. Crying out for industrialization, potential metropolises such as Birmingham and Atlanta promised untold fortunes to any capitalist willing to take reasonable risks. Race was no longer an issue in the new urban areas. Speaking of blacks, Grady wrote, "The love we feel for that race you cannot measure nor comprehend."[44] Conversely, New South spokesmen had little trouble convincing southerners that they had been ruthlessly exploited by northern interests for generations before the Civil War. To achieve independence, Southerners needed to build factories and develop transportation systems. Abundant raw materials and a more than adequate black labor force were at hand. Cities like Atlanta and Birmingham needed to attract northern capital and technical expertise so they could vie with Pittsburgh and Chicago.[45] Everyone, North and South, had something to gain from the rise of southern cities.

The very concept of the New South moved leaders of the cause to offer extravagant praise. When Grady promoted southern economic development, he portrayed the entire section as a harmonious and stable land abounding with business opportunities. He conjured up visions of a South totally integrated into a gigantic nationwide industrial complex. "As I think of it, a vision of surpassing beauty unfolds to my eyes," he claimed. "I see a South the home of fifty millions of people; her cities vast hives of industry; her country-sides the treasures from which their resources are drawn; her streams vocal with whirring spindles; her valleys tranquil in the white and gold of the harvest . . . sunshine everwhere and all the time, and night falling on her gently as wings of the unseen dove."[46] Edmonds wrote, "Who can picture the vast, illuminate future of the glorious sunny South?" After waxing eloquent about the advantages of the region, he proclaimed, "The more we contemplate these advantages and contrast them with those of all other countries, the more deeply will we be impressed with the unquestionable truth that here in this glorious land, 'Creation's Garden Spot,' is to be the richest and greatest country upon which the sun ever shone."[47] Watterson put the situation more bluntly: "The South, having had its bellyful of blood, has gotten a taste of money, and it is too busy trying to make more of it to quarrel with anybody."[48] Surely, the arguments went, the South presented northern capitalists with untold opportunities not only to make money but to participate altruistically in building a land of milk and honey. Glory awaited all who wanted to help the South realize its true potential.

The spokesmen for the New South creed were fairly convincing.[49] Their efforts attracted northern investments that resulted in industrial development, a significant expansion of the rail network, and considerable urban progress. They also uplifted the spirits of southerners at the end of a very dismal period in the section's history. Even so, because in reality little had changed, the area neither became integrated into the nation as a whole nor acted as a magnet for northern dollars. Outsiders quickly learned that for small initial investments they could pay low wages, engage in exploitive labor practices, buy politicians, charge high interest rates, and realize lucrative profits while reinvesting little. For unenlightened and ruthless capitalists willing to tolerate lethargic laborers, corrupt politicians, racial segregation, and hostility toward outsiders, the South was a land of opportunity.

The South did not start to rise economically to the level of the rest of the nation until a combination of the boll weevil and the cotton-picking machine revolutionized its agriculture. World War II and the black migration to northern cities helped to undermine segregation. Federal policy makers following Franklin D. Roosevelt pledged that in the postwar world blacks should have equality in return for supporting the war effort. The civil rights movement, led by a black Atlantan, Martin Luther King, Jr., received bipartisan support in the North and from the federal government. Court decisions and legislation made the South an integral part of the American Union, ending a period of alienation extending back to April of 1861. The election as president in 1976 of James Earl Carter of Plains, Georgia, a former segregationist and son of a small-town merchant, indicated the national impact of the changing status of the South. In the election of 1980, Ronald Reagan of California routed Carter. He did not, however, lose either as a Georgian or a southerner. Rather, he lost as an American. His defeat did not signal a new exclusion of southerners from national politics. In a sense, the election and subsequent defeat of Carter represented a culmination of the efforts started by the New South leaders a hundred years earlier to bring the South in line with the rest of the nation.

A New South resembling that extolled by Grady and his colleagues failed to emerge until after the attitudes of the region and its leaders had moderated their opinions. Only after significant cultural and population interchanges between the major regions of the country had occurred did Atlanta and other cities move ahead. A chief reason for the delay between the predictions of the 1880s and the progress of the 1980s was the reality of the nineteenth-century southern urban network. The concept of a New South built on urbanization and industrialization demands revision. Did the South, even with northern help, have the capacity to achieve sectional parity quickly? Was there a significant urban base upon which to build? Had the antebellum South developed a sound policy for constructing cities? To what extent was race a factor in city building? These and other questions cry out for exploration and analysis. The South in the Gilded Age must be viewed from a new perspective, for during that era the doctrine of the new urban South was born.

The Civil War and Reconstruction totally upset southern hopes of catching up with the rest of the nation through an orderly system of urban growth. Exceptional circumstances required extraordinary action. The war prevented the quick rise of the South's interior cities and eroded the national position of its old inland and ocean ports. No southern city could reach a "takeoff" point from which a New Orleans or an Atlanta might have overtaken Chicago and other northern metropolises. The aftermath of hostilities left the South with a fractured urban network. All that remained were communities with small and dispirited markets. The older, logically built cities were in disarray. Dreams of a southern civilization lay in ruins. Advocates of the New South claimed to know how to reverse the situation. As Henry Watterson proclaimed in the *Louisville Courier-Journal:* "The South! The South! It is no problem at all. The whole story of the South may be summed up in a sentence: She was rich, she lost her riches; she was poor and in bondage; she was set free, and she had to go to work, she went to work, and she is richer than ever before."[50]

Watterson and his colleagues preached doctrines designed to move the South to prominence within the American Union. They envisioned urban jewels named Louisville, Atlanta, Charleston, Baltimore, and Birmingham glittering in the afternoon sun. But to succeed, they needed to overcome southerners' conflicting feelings about cities that extended back to the philosophical musings of Thomas Jefferson. Whether such a dream could be achieved remained to be seen.

2

A Victory of Plenty

Part of the antebellum urban South died on 15 November 1864 as General William T. Sherman watched his troops burn Atlanta. A military band serenaded him with "Miserere" from *Il Trovatore*.[1] Rebirth came a few days after the start of the brutal March to the Sea. Atlantans returned to their stricken city and started to rebuild. "From defeat and utter poverty were to be wrought victory and plenty," an emotional Henry Grady wrote. He told how people used the roofing of destroyed buildings to make five hundred shanties and described the revival of the downtown. "Four posts," he said, "were driven up—iron sheeting tacked about them, a cover laid, a door cut, and in these, with pitiful huckstering, was established the commercial system that now boasts its palatial stores, its merchant princes, and is known and honored the Republic over."[2] The destruction of Atlanta and the aftermath melded together. Despite the devastation and dislocations caused by the Civil War, an essential continuity remained. New structures rose upon the ashes of the old.

Throughout their more than two-hundred-year history, cities in the South had survived fires, floods, plagues, and wars. In 1619 Indians attacked and destroyed several settlements in Jamestown Colony. A fire burned over much of Charleston in 1796. In 1832 a flood inundated Louisville's business district. The terrible yellow fever epidemic of 1853 ravaged New Orleans. Calamities were an accepted part of urban life. Viewed against this background, the Civil War and Reconstruction were simply interruptions similar to those that had occurred before. Yet this is hardly to suggest that the era of defeat was not a great watershed. No justification exists for a reperiodization of southern studies based on the urban experience. Cities throughout history—Rome, Athens, Berlin, Hiroshima, and hundreds of others—have overcome holocausts. A remarkable feature of urbanization has been the ability of important cultural, political, and economic sites to regain their former status following a disaster. The Civil War did not eradicate private property titles. In Atlanta, the land beneath the burned-out buildings in the commercial districts near the railroad terminal remained of prime value. People with a strong spirit and sense of community had the capacity to rebuild a city quickly. Grady's moving words about the rebirth of Atlanta were true. Indeed, cities all across the South recovered and advanced, their citizens hardened survivors with the will to endure.

The differences between what happened during the Confederate years and at other times of crisis were matters of degree. Surely, occupied New Orleans suffered under the military rule imposed by Benjamin "Beast" Butler. Yet were conditions worse than during the frequent epidemics in the Crescent City? Without question, the Civil War and its aftermath were terrible times for the southern people. The South was not on the verge of an urban Golden Age, but there was no doubt about the ability of southerners to build cities.

In 1880 the boundaries of the South were somewhat different from those of the Confederacy. With few variations, traditional sectional lines prevailed. The border states of Kentucky and Maryland were integral parts of the region. They held two of the section's major metropolitan areas, Baltimore and Louisville. Both localities were major ports of entry into Dixie. All goods and produce that passed through the two cities by rail needed transshipping, because northern and southern railroads had different gauge tracks.[3] The resulting bottlenecks, which slowed the movement of goods, accentuated the roles of Baltimore and Louisville as unofficial border crossing points.

Two other states, Delaware and Missouri, had no important southern cities. Rural Delaware was in Baltimore's immediate hinterland. The Blue Hen State's only major city, Wilmington, was an industrial center with close ties to Philadelphia that extended back to colonial days. Although Delaware had been a slave state, with a very small number of human chattels, it had stayed in the Union in 1861. In Missouri, however, the rural Boot Heel and Little Dixie supported the rebel cause. A prosouthern governor tried unsuccessfully to take Missouri out of the Union. Only quick federal military action prevented St. Louis from falling into Confederate hands. All during the war, Kansas City, which had many southern sympathizers, was for all practical purposes an occupied town. Postwar times were bittersweet in Missouri. Unionists tried to deny the civil rights of alleged Confederates. The Jesse James gang received widespread support in western Missouri by claiming to avenge the wrongs done by Yankee invaders. There was a distinct rural-urban split in the Show Me State. In 1880 the major cities, unlike the countryside, were not southern in character. St. Louis, as before the Civil War, saw its destiny in the Midwest and in southwestern trade. Kansas City boomed after the opening at the city in 1869 of the first permanent railroad bridge over the Missouri River. As the composition of Kansas City's population changed, it became a regional metropolis with a western outlook and few southern connections.

A sectional shift had changed the western borders of the South. Arkansas, an underdeveloped Confederate state with few railroads, maintained its strong southern ties. The Arkansas River was the main commercial artery, trying the economy more closely than ever to the states bordering the lower Mississippi. Old natural lines still loomed as more important than artificial ones. A much different situation existed in Texas. Southerners had founded the Republic of Texas. A southern president brought Texas into the Union. Texans fought and died under the Stars and Bars. Drastic changes followed the Civil War. Texas gradually become a predominantly western rather than southern state. To complicate matters, the great cattle drives up the trails into the Kansas and the building of trunk railroads from the North into Texas changed economic ties. By 1880 the growing cities of the Long Horn State were western towns.

The heartland of the urban South was east of the Mississippi River and below Kentucky and Maryland, encompassing former Confederate states and the District of Columbia. Many southerners had mixed feelings about Washington, as did people from other parts of the nation. In the early 1870s midwestern congressmen had claimed that Washington did not represent the interests of the people and that the seat of government should be moved to a central site. Washington had been a southern city since the day of its founding. It was older than many other southern cities, far more representative of sectional traditions than the new industrial center of Birmingham, Alabama.

Washington was not the only southern city called atypical or said to belong in a different section. Unreconstructed agrarians viewed cities as representative of Yankee values. Like the advocates of the creed of the New South, they found it convenient to forget that cities had existed and served important purposes in antebellum times. Furthermore, urban boosters emphasized the differences among southern communities. New Orleans leaders stressed the cosmopolitan aspects of their city. Grady and others carefully tried to demonstrate that Atlanta was vastly different and more progressive than its rivals. Promoters in Chattanooga went farther, calling for industrialists to come south and revitalize the city along northern lines. Charlestonians considered their genteel cultural traditions superior to those in interior places such as Macon and Montgomery. Virginians took credit for building a smoothly functioning system of cities, which served the needs of an agrarian civilization. About the only thing most people in the former Confederate States of America could agree upon was that Baltimore and Louisville had helped northern philistines humble the

Southland. Was there a typical southern city? Probably not. Just as all around the country, there were American cities. They shared certain economic, political, and social values, yet remained different from their neighbors, even within the same section.

The 1880 federal census reports raised important questions about southern urban prospects. The data showed a serious erosion of the South's urban position in the Union. In the nineteenth century experts considered a population of 10,000 or more the determining figure in assessing the relative importance of a city. Places below that mark were not thought to have attained a true urban dimension. There were obvious flaws in this definition. "Town" governments in New England frequently consisted of one or more densely populated bodies, along with a scattered rural population. Some fairly large cities contiguous to larger centers were primarily suburban in nature. The census labeled New York City and four neighboring jurisidications as "The Metropolis." In some other parts of the nation relatively small communities, Tucson and Bismarck for example, had regional significance disproportionate to their size. Still, the 10,000 figure was generally accepted and, within understood limitations, served as a convenient measure.

Between 1870 and 1880 cities with more than 10,000 inhabitants increased nationally from 165 to 228, but only from 26 to 30 in the South. The number in the Northeast rose from 86 to 113, in the Midwest from 43 to 62, and in the West from 8 to 23. These figures presented a discouraging picture to advocates of a southern urban destiny.

Other 1880 statistics further reflected the South's urban plight. Of 580 American towns with populations over 4,000 only 63 were in the South. Of 99 communities over 20,000, only 17 were in the South. Of 20 metropolises over 100,000, only 4 were in the South. To phrase it another way, the South had 13 percent of the nation's towns over 4,000, 13 percent of those over 10,000, 17 percent of those over 20,000, and 20 percent of those over 100,000. The figures reflected developments outside the South: the building of a great railroad network, the growth of secondary industrial and agricultural centers, and the consolidation of markets by regional metropolises. Considering the depressed economic conditions that followed the Panic of 1873, national progress had been amazing.

Advocates of the New South creed had a point when they told investors about the region's potential. As Grady once asked northern capitalists, "Why remain to freeze, and starve, and struggle on the bleak prairies of the northwest when the garden spot of the world is waiting for people to take possession of it and enjoy it?"[4] Potential investors not only worried about their welcome—the word carpetbagger carried unfortunate connotations,—but weighed chances of mak-

Table 2.1. Southern Cities and Their Populations, 1880

City	Total Population	City	Total Population
Alabama		Maryland	
Mobile	29,132	Baltimore	332,313
Montgomery	16,713	Cumberland	10,693
Arkansas		Mississippi	
Little Rock	13,138	Vicksburg	11,814
Dist. of Columbia		North Carolina	
Georgetown	12,578	Wilmington	17,350
Washington	147,293	South Carolina	
Georgia		Charleston	49,984
Atlanta	37,409	Columbia	10,036
Augusta	21,891	Tennessee	
Columbus	10,123	Chattanooga	12,892
Macon	12,749	Memphis	33,592
Savannah	30,709	Nashville	43,350
Kentucky		Virginia	
Covington	29,720	Alexandria	13,659
Lexington	16,656	Lynchburg	15,959
Louisville	123,758	Norfolk	21,966
Newport	20,433	Petersburg	21,656
Louisiana		Portsmouth	11,390
New Orleans	216,090	Richmond	63,600

ing more money elsewhere. With profits in the range cattle industry said to average over 40 percent per annum and speculative Colorado mining stocks seeming to offer unlimited returns, few plungers expressed more than passing interest in the South. More tangible considerations further clouded possibilities for vast influxes of outside money. Atlanta, publicized as the "Chicago of the South," added close to 16,000 people in the 1870s, an increase of over a third. By southern standards, this was an impressive gain. But Chicago, despite the terrible fire of 1871, grew from 299,000 to 503,000 people. Obviously, it would take considerable salesmanship to persuade northern interests to pour large amounts of money into the South. If the section was to avoid permanent colonial status it desperately needed investment capital.

The best product the South had to market was an existing urban network of thirty cities with more than 10,000 people (see Table 2.1). The towns were part of an urban system rendered obsolete by the city-building methods used in the Northeast and the Midwest in antebellum days. At first glance, there was not much to sell. Hence overblown, impassioned, and optimistic statements about future prospects hid very practical considerations. A New Orleans editor talked of a coming "commercial evolution unparalleled in the annals of American progress."[5] Another writer proclaimed that "wealth and honor are in the pathway of the New South."[6] Both observations reflected the need aggressively to counter arguments about the decadence and slow pace of southern life. Fortunately for the region, there was a base upon which to build.

Some experts produced statistics that indicated the urban South lagged at least half a century behind the rest of the country. But there was an easy reply: in 1830 the emerging Midwest had trailed the settled parts of the nation in development by roughly two hundred years. The opening of the region led to spectacular progress. Why could not the South experience similar growth over the next few decades? "The promise of her great destiny," Grady proclaimed, "written in her fields, her quarries, her mines, her forests, and her rivers, is no longer blurred or indistinct, and the world draws near to read." He spun tales of cities "growing as if by magic"[7] in every county—the rise of a great southern urban system was preordained.

There were several layers of southern cities.[8] The first included the Atlantic coastal towns. The second consisted of the old frontier posts roughly along the fall line from Virginia to Georgia. Third came the spearheads of settlement in the New West. A fourth stratum consisted of the former French and Spanish towns along the Gulf Coast. Fifth were the inland river ports and railroad centers that served the cotton trade. The future of the South depended upon the cities within these five layers.

The Atlantic coastal towns had histories that reflected faded glories and renewed hopes. Baltimore was the South's only large commercial and industrial city, a true late-nineteenth-century American metropolis. Since the Civil War, Washington had more than doubled in size, its growth related directly to that of the government. The nation's capital overwhelmed two older nearby commercial towns, Georgetown and Alexandria. Norfolk's prospects seemed bright. As at so many points in its history, prosperity appeared just a few years away. Its neighbor, Portsmouth, had little hope of ever being more than a satellite city. A town without serious rivals, Wilmington faced an age-old problem of trying to build a hinterland in an underdeveloped agricultural state. Savannah, as since its earliest days, had aggressive leaders but no resources to carry out broadly based plans. Charleston, a symbol of secession in the North, was a special target of wartime Yankee wrath. It had little chance of regaining its former luster.[9] For the Atlantic coastal cities in 1880 hopes ranged from very bright to extremely dark. Yet it was on the seacoast that southern community building had started in 1607 when English adventurers had founded Jamestown. Although the experiment failed, the cities built at later dates along the coast had helped raise up the South. Whether they could do so again in the Gilded Age was certainly a moot point.

In 1880 the lesser southern Atlantic coastal towns had few immediate prospects. Only three had more than 4,000 people. Annapolis, Maryland, with 6,600 people, had not been important as a port since the Revolution. Were it not the state capital and the site of the United States Naval Academy, Annapolis would have been little more than a fishing village. New Bern, North Carolina, had 6,400 inhabitants. Located on the Neuse River near where it emptied into Pimlico Sound, New Bern had never enjoyed more than limited prospects. A visitor in 1879 thought it "at a standstill."[10] Jacksonville, Florida, twenty-five miles from the mouth of the St. John's River, was a relatively new town and had been a village until after the Civil War. In 1880 the city had a population of 7,700, equally divided between whites and blacks. It was a lumber shipping point and enjoyed some tourist business. Unlike Annapolis and New Bern, Jacksonville appeared to have possibilities. "Its relative importance in a state so sparsely settled as Florida is very great," an official commented. "It is, and from its favorable position will probably long continue to be, the commercial metropolis of the state, the lumber and cigar industries taking the lead."[11] As northern Florida developed, Jacksonville seemed sure to benefit. Until then it would remain unimportant.

During the colonial period, southern pioneers founded many backcountry posts. Most had only limited purposes as either transportation junctions, exploration points, or temporary agricultural settlements. Some survived for only a short period. Waxhaws Settlement, along the North and South Carolina line, the birthplace of Andrew Jackson, disappeared entirely. A number, however, achieved permanent status. In 1880 fifteen had populations over 4,000, providing a second layer of cities, running from Maryland to Georgia. Frederick (8,700) and Hagerstown (6,600) were two Maryland commercial and railroad towns. Virginia had a network of interior cities that had risen in the age of antebellum sectionalism, when numerous observers thought that an emphasis on agrarian values had stifled progress in the Old Dominion. The most successful was Richmond (63,000), located at the head of navigation on the James River, roughly seventy miles from Norfolk. Another James River town, Lynchburg (16,000), aspired to be a factory center. So did Petersburg (21,700), on the Appomattox River. Secondary towns included Danville (7,500), Staunton (6,700), Manchester (5,700), Fredericksburg (5,000), and Winchester (5,000). North Carolina had two towns with potential as textile centers, Raleigh (9,300) and Charlotte (7,100). In South Carolina, Columbia (10,000), at the fall line on the Congaree River, had impressive waterpower for industrial use. Greenville (6,200) was a road junction near the Great

Smoky Mountains. Augusta (21,900), a little over a hundred miles up the Savannah River from Savannah, had long been a transportation hub, and it appeared on the verge of acquiring a large manufacturing dimension. To the leaders of the old interior posts, factories appeared to be panaceas that would bring prosperity at a time when agriculture seemed on the decline. Mills would take the place of hinterlands.

Factories required large capital investments. Southern banks, unable to fund existing programs, especially in agriculture, lacked the large amounts of mortage money necessary to finance industrial establishments. Nor did potential southern manufacturers have sufficient resources to convince northern bankers to loan them hundreds of thousands of dollars. Only northern industrial interests with good credit lines had the ability to obtain the money needed. Building new plants meant accepting further domination by northern banking and industrial interests—a high price to pay for limited progress, for it meant absentee owners, low wages, and poor working conditions. Nevertheless, advocates of the New South creed urged northerners to invest in southern factories. Richard Edmonds of the *Manufacturers' Record* wrote, "The El Dorado of the next half century is the South. The wise recognize it; the dull and timid will ere long regret their sloth and their hesitancy."[12] Mill towns patterned after those in New England were thought to be the wave of the future. Yet none of these ideas were new. The horsepower potential of the waterpowers along the fall line was widely known. In 1845 William Gregg started an experimental textile mill at Graniteville, South Carolina. By the Civil War, even though few planters heeded Gregg's advice to put money into manufacturing, South Carolina had mills capitalized at $1 million. Throughout the 1850s a number of promoters advocated building textile plants in North Carolina. In late antebellum times, leaders in the interior towns accepted the contention that industry was the wave of the future. They saw no other way of countering the effects of a decline in agriculture, caused by soil exhaustion.[13] Places from Richmond to Augusta sought to become the "Lowell of the South."

In the last half of the eighteenth century, southerners had moved into the New West, forming a third layer of urban communities. Rugged individualists, Daniel Boone, John Donelson, and others, fought Indians by day and planned inland empires at night. Neither the Proclamation Line of 1763 nor fierce Indian resistance stopped American penetration. Kentucky entered the Union in 1792 and Tennessee in 1796. Settlers moved through the Cumberland Gap and over the Great Smoky Mountains. They established a number of towns that had more than 10,000 people in 1880. Cumberland, Maryland (10,700), one of the first settlements on the western side of the Appalachians, was a railroad center. Two Kentucky communities, Covington (29,700) and Newport (20,400), had grown because of their proximity to Cincinnati. Cumberland, Covington, and Newport grew at a late date and at first were relatively unimportant compared to other localities. The early centers in the New West were Knoxville and Nashville in Tennessee and Lexington and Louisville in Kentucky.

Being first did not necessarily spell success. Knoxville started fast and then faltered badly. It was off the beaten path of east-west communication and never developed more than local markets. In 1880 the city had a listed population of 9,700. About half as many people lived in the immediate area, along creeks and turnpikes. Nashville took the state capital away from Knoxville in 1817 and became a river and railroad center. Its population in 1880 was 43,400. In that year, Louisville, the only larger southern river port west of the Appalachians, boasted 123,800 persons. It had eclipsed its old Kentucky rival, Lexington, which had 16,700 inhabitants.[14]

The fourth layer of cities in the South was along the Gulf Coast. In 1880 four cities had more than 4,000 people. Two of these were in Florida. Key West, with an important naval station, had 9,900 people. Key West, far removed from the main currents of southern urbanization, had a distinct Spanish character. Pensacola in the Florida Panhandle had 6,800 inhabitants. It had a naval yard and was a lumber port. Further to the west, Mobile, Alabama, remained, as before the Civil War, a cotton-shipping port and potential railroad terminal. The population was 29,100. The metropolis of the Gulf region was New Orleans. It had 216,100 residents. Although New Orleans had failed to achieve predictions that it would be the greatest city in North America, it was the nation's number one cotton port. There were those who believed that the city's glory was yet to come, but this was a selective judgment.[15] Such advocates of the New South as Henry Watterson of Louisville, Francis Dawson of Charleston, and Henry Grady of Atlanta pointedly ignored New Orleans, which they viewed as a rival of their communities.

The hopes of the postwar South rested with the interior river and railroad cities, which had started either as road junctions or as cotton shipping points. An integral part of the prewar southern urban system, they had served the needs of local plantation owners and of merchants in Louisville, Augusta, Mobile, and New Orleans. Businessmen in those places thought of them as part of their hinterlands. Thus Louisville railroaders thought of Atlanta as part of their growing systems. Augusta interests believed Macon a satellite. Mobile agents took for granted close relations with Montgomery. New Orleans leaders assumed they controlled upriver towns. Many of the interior cities had suffered grievously from the war. Because of their role in the cotton and plantation economy, they seemed to embody the values of the Old

South. Yet they were cities of the mid-nineteenth century, just as were their counterparts in the Midwest and West. Most of the southern interior cities had just started to grow in the years immediately before the war. In 1880 the census definition no longer considered them part of the frontier, but because of the vicissitudes of war and the destruction of the old agricultural system, these cities were frontier communities. Their prospects had to be evaluated by different standards than those used for the older and more settled southern communities, many of which had grown conservative and had long given up hopes of major urban success. If similar reasoning prevailed in the newer places, if their leaders looked only backward to perpetuating the values of the Lost Cause, the chances of building a new urban South were bleak. The spokesmen of the New South creed would see their hopes dashed as badly as those of the Confederate statesmen. The South would suffer another defeat.

In 1880 sixteen cities of 4,000 or more were in or near the cotton belt. Athens, Georgia (6,100), was a college and market town. Natchez, Mississippi (7,100), was a fading river city. Jackson (5,400) in Tennessee, Jackson (5,200) and Meridian (4,000) in Mississippi, and Shreveport (8,000) in Louisiana were transportation points. In Alabama, Huntsville (5,000) and Selma (7,500) had potential as manufacturing centers. Two of the large cities, Columbus (10,000) and Macon (12,800), both in Georgia, hoped to expand their roles as cotton centers. Vicksburg (11,800) already lived in the past. Little Rock (13,100) was the only place of importance in a developing area. Chattanooga (12,900) and Montgomery (16,700) hoped to grow as manufacturing centers. Memphis (33,600) had been set back by a terrible epidemic. Atlanta (37,400) looked ahead to metropolitan status. The odds were long against building an urban empire from this group of cities. New promotions faced equal difficulties. There was no guarantee that either Birmingham or Bessemer, both of which appeared well financed and situated, would advance beyond village status. In the eyes of promoters, however, the southern interior towns had as promising chances as their counterparts on the far western frontier. After all, in 1880 Los Angeles had 11,200 people, San Diego had 2,600, and Seattle had 3,500.

Opportunities to build cities continued to exist. The western half of the country was just opening for settlement. Promoters sung the praises of the North Dakota "banana belt" and the "Rocky Mountain Empire." William Gilpin developed elaborate theories based on the "axis of intensity" and "isothermal zodiac" in an attempt to prove that great cities would rise throughout the West.[16] The advocates of the New South creed never developed formal systems, but Grady claimed, "Surely the basis of the South's wealth and power is laid by the hand of the Almighty God, and its prosperity has been established by divine law."[17] Furthermore, he said, "It is an axiom in our new iron region that, 'An iron furnace is like godliness. Have that, and all the rest shall be added unto you.' From this theory the 'magic cities' of the South have sprung."[18] The key, of course, was attracting capital. Entrepreneurs had to be persuaded to invest in Columbus, Atlanta, or Montgomery rather than in Los Angeles, San Diego, or Seattle. Here was the bottom line. What did the South have to offer?[19]

The band of men who promoted a South of cities and industry emphasized the opportunities that awaited outside investors. The South Land was "Creation's Garden Spot," one of "Nature's Wonderful Blessings."[20] Henry Grady claimed in 1884 that the South had surpassed the West. "The time will come," he said, "when there will be an amendment to the shibboleth, 'Westward the star of empire holds its sway.' "[21] Yet conditions in Dixie were not promising. The section had a network of cities adequate to the needs of a plantation economy based on King Cotton. City builders had avoided the excesses of uncontrolled urban speculation. And the past histories of leading southern cities provided strong evidence of an entrepreneurial spirit, which could not be hidden by northern propagandists hoping to deter investors and ridicule southern ways. Of course, there was never a master plan for building cities in the Old South, nor did one exist in the New South. There was only rhetoric. The postwar southern cities had little to sell except dreams. The cities competed against each other in the midst of a depressed region. It was no coincidence that the most successful southern cities had commercial ties outside the section.

The South entered the 1880s with an agricultural system unsuited to the needs of a free market. Land barons and country merchants presided over a fragmented economy. Sharecropping and crop liens stifled individual enterprise. Temporarily inflated cotton prices were a snare and a delusion. New sources of supply clouded the world price picture, let alone that in the Cotton Belt.

Many southern cities sought industry to compensate for conditions in the rural South. Southern urban populations had swelled since before the war, but much of this growth was unrelated to progress. Most of the migrants were blacks who had left plantations, and they not only complicated life for white southerners but added to employment problems. The means were unavailable to transform the southern economy overnight. So the urban South that arose from the ashes of Atlanta, Richmond, and Columbia was similar to that of antebellum days. Civil War and Reconstruction compounded matters. The quest for manufacturing brought new problems. More and larger cities were not the answers to the waning of the Old South civilization. Cities could be calculated to make the South more like the rest of the nation.[22]

They functioned as a common denominator that overrode sectional considerations. Yet there was no need for more of them in the South. What needed to be done was to shore up the existing urban network. Under the circumstances, that was not going to be an easy task.

3

Cogs in the Great Machine

In the North, the Lost Cause, sacred to generations of southerners, was a subject of mockery. Southerners' lack of contrition hardened northern attitudes toward the region. Following Reconstruction, the spirit of reconciliation engendered by the "reunion" was threatened by northern politicians, who played on the emotions of their constituents by attacking everything about the Confederacy. The "bloody shirt" prevented the South from rejoining the United States on equal terms. The continuation of feelings of hostility made it all the more difficult for the men of the New South creed to carry out their dreams.[1]

Few northern whites admitted that they had turned their backs on southern blacks. Instead, they blamed the dismantling of the gains won by blacks during Reconstruction on the Ku Klux Klan and the Knights of the White Camellia. In truth, racial equality could not have been achieved without the continued presence of northern bayonets. The later Supreme Court decisions, notably *Plessy* v. *Ferguson* (1896), which promulgated the "separate but equal" doctrine, formally ratified an already accomplished reversal of national policy.[2]

Northerners in all walks of life felt uncomfortable about the South. Even the word "redemption," used by white southern orators to signal a return to an older order of race relations, carried discomforting connotations. Northerners viewed the South as a land of racial hatred and violence inhabited by rednecks and blacks, all living in log cabins and denied advancement by the oppressive sharecropper and croplien systems. Southern country store owners and city merchants, on the other hand, blamed the economic plight of rural southerners on continued northern economic exploitation.[3] Above the Mason and Dixon line, the South was widely thought to be dispirited and decadent. In short, the South seemed to many outsiders to radiate an aura of failure.

Edward King, a well-known northern journalist, tried to paint a far different picture of the South, particularly its urban components, for northern readers. During 1873 and 1874 he made an extensive tour, visiting all parts of the region. His "Great South" series appeared in *Scribner's Monthly*, a popular national magazine.[4] King displayed many of the characteristics of a typical urban promoter of his day. At times he got carried away and waxed eloquent about towns that had limited prospects at best, although he found that in Beaufort, South Carolina, a "silence as of the grave reigned everywhere," and he described Mobile as "tranquil and free from commercial bustle." Yet, on the whole, he praised southern cities. His predictions were not always borne out, for example, his contention that Wedverton, Maryland, would one day flourish as a gigantic manufacturing center and that Strasburg, Virginia, would become a place of "great importance."[5] Neither town ever advanced beyond the village stage. Despite his fallibility, King reported with considerable accuracy on the significance of cities in the South. He depicted them as vital economic and social organisms. In detailed descriptions he showed how they fitted into a whole, implying that the future course of southern development depended upon urban progress and prosperity. His major theme was that investment opportunities abounded in the cities of the South. An advocate of the New South creed could hardly have been more positive.[6]

Even though he was writing during Reconstruction and depression, King accentuated the positive. He said, "Augusta's excellent railroad facilities and her advantageous situation, have made her an extensive cotton market." The city exhibited a "life and energy worthy of the brightest of Northern cities of its size." Savannah's prospects appeared even better. "As we walked," he wrote, "day by day, through the Savannah streets, late in autumn, we were amazed at the masses of cotton bales piled everywhere. . . . The huge black ships swallowed bale after bale; the clank of the hoisting-crane was heard from morning till night." Central to King's analysis was that the Civil War had not permanently impaired southern urban prospects. He predicted that Charleston would recover like a "veritable phoenix" because "her businessmen have an elastic spirit and a remarkable courage, which reflect the highest credit upon them." In addition, "Commercially, Wilmington has every reason to hope for great development." He thought that Columbus, only recently removed from the frontier, had the potential of becoming a great industrial town. "After riding all day through regions where the log-cabin was oftener seen than the frame-house, and where the forest still held possession of nine-tenths of the land," he observed, "it was refreshing to come upon a town of such energy, activity and prospects as Columbus." Lynchburg, he thought, had almost unlimited potential: "Lynchburg's great natural advantages of situation will, in a few years, increase it from a city of 12,000 population to a huge overcrowded railway centre." King believed that "Richmond is chief among Virginia cities, no less because of its proud

position as the capital than because of its enterprise and rapid growth."
Other places had equally promising claims to future achievements.
Louisville was "springing into vigorous life." In New Orleans a
"throng of speculators" surrounded the cotton exchange. The "march
of progress" had started in Chattanooga.[7] A great future lay ahead
throughout the length and breadth of the urban South.

King concluded that the same forces that had built northern cities
were at work in the South: natural advantages and entrepreneurial
leadership, coupled with commercial progress in the country as a
whole. He felt that the end of slavery had swept away the old values
and brought new attitudes. Like Hinton R. Helper at an earlier date,
King thought slavery an oppressive system that had hurt trade and
urban development. He attributed Louisville's progress to the end of
slavery in Kentucky.[8] He was convinced that following the Civil War
"one of the most remarkable revolutions ever recorded in history"[9] had
transformed the South, making it much like the rest of the nation. He
sought a spirit of accommodation and reconciliation between the sections. Northerners, he explained, should look with sympathy on the
problems faced by white southerners in regard to the race question. He
called on people outside the South to place the changes going on
within the section in proper perspective. Few answered. The times
were not right. King was a voice in the wilderness of sectional divisions.

In 1886, over a decade after King's tour, Henry Grady went to New
York to address the prestigious New England Society. Some 360 businessmen had assembled in the banquet hall at Delmonico's, one of the
most famous restaurants in America. Grady spoke after William T.
Sherman had made short remarks and the orchestra had played a
spirited rendition of "Marching through Georgia." It was an unlikely
and unusual platform for an Atlanta editor, but Grady rose to the
occasion. His opening remarks received wide notice throughout the
nation: " 'There was a South of slavery and secession—that South is
dead. There is a South of union and freedom—that South, thank God,
is living, breathing, growing every hour.' These words, delivered from
the immortal lips of Benjamin H. Hill, at Tammany Hall, in 1866, true
then and truer now, I shall make my text tonight." Few at Delmonico's
had heard of or cared about the "immortal lips of Benjamin H. Hill," or
whether Grady quoted him correctly, which he did not. But they did
respond to the rest of Grady's speech, alternately cheering and weep-
ing. Grady, always a master orator, played to his audience to perfection.
He even placed the best possible light on the burning of Atlanta.
"Somehow or other," he claimed, "we have caught the sunshine in the
bricks and mortar of our homes, and have builded therein not one
ignoble prejudice or memory."[10] Perhaps Grady would have found

something good to say at his own public hanging. But at Delmonico's he had a specific purpose: as in his other speeches, he wanted to attract northern resources to the South. Advocates of southern material progress were hindered by the persistent belief that the South's way of life was anachronistic and out of step with the rest of the land.[11]

Grady preached his doctrines of a changed South during a period of urban boom in America. The 1880s saw the completion of the basic elements in the nation's urban mosaic. Chicago was the fastest-growing town in the world, within a decade its population increased from 500,000 to one million. The Windy City's stockyards, packing plants, and railroads were visible evidence of its growing power in the Midwest.[12] On the edge of the Great Plains, Kansas City and Omaha emerged as regional metropolises, fueled by huge quantities of outside capital. The rapid settlement of the central plains led to countless opportunities in agribusiness. Even greater riches could be found on the Pacific coast. San Francisco was a dynamic and flourishing city with the sobriquet "Monarch of the West." One of the greatest land booms of the nineteenth century was under way in Los Angeles where thousands of speculators were throwing money to the wind and some lots changed hands several times in a single day. In the Pacific Northwest, the arrival of eastern rails touched off a spiral of land speculation. Tacoma, Seattle, and Everett vied with one another, igniting a struggle for control of Puget Sound.[13] A spirit of progress was abroad from Maine to California. Encouraged by a series of probusiness presidential administrations, the county appeared poised on the brink of becoming an urban and industrial society. The ideal of an agrarian republic was a faded vision of the past.

The continual rise of New York had followed almost naturally. The city's business community emerged stronger than ever from the depression that followed the Panic of 1873. In a period of consolidation of wealth, the money power centralized as never before in the Empire City. Great investment banking houses benefited from a wave of mergers and stock transactions that made trusts and monopolies an integral part of economic life. In many ways, the worst fears of antebellum southern statesmen had materialized. With the South in an inferior position and agrarianism vanquished, there was little to check the concentration of wealth in New York. The attacks on Wall Street by Populist orators in Kansas and Nebraska had a familiar sound. The message had been heard before south of the Mason and Dixon line from South Carolina to Louisiana. Of course, any attempt to obtain outside capital on a vast scale meant going hat in hand to New York banking interests. No one else had access to the sums of money necessary to determine the course of national development. Thus when Grady and others asked for investors to come South, they were in effect trying to promote New York domination. This was a historic turn of events in Dixie.

For understandable reasons, supporters of the New South creed glossed over the need for New York capital. Instead, they emhasized that southern whites were rebuilding their defeated land. An attractive investment climate had been created, Grady claimed: "We have reduced the commercial rate of interest from 24 to 6 percent, and are floating 4 percent bonds."[14] He spoke with pride of the South's recovery from the Civil War: "The South has been rebuilt by Southern brains and energy. We regret that our brothers from the North have not taken larger part with us in this work."[15] This statement underlined the fact that, despite the propaganda, the South held little appeal to outsiders. It was not viewed as a land of opportunity.

Spokesmen for the New South creed wanted what Grady called the "better class of immigrants."[16] Grady placed wealthy Anglo-Saxon farmers from the North and prosperous immigrants from western Europe in the same category. Most of the people attracted to America's shores brought hardly any money, however, for they had been peasants in the old country. As for northern farmers, even those who failed on the Great Plains showed no desire to migrate to the South to become sharecroppers. Rather, if forced to move, they went farther west. New South advocates did not welcome everyone. Richard Edmonds of the *Manufacturers' Record* said that he opposed "all schemes looking toward the colonization of large numbers of ignorant foreigners." He wrote that the South had room "for thousands, even millions of industrious people," but not for "socialists and anarchists."[17] Given prevailing migration and immigration patterns, southerners were going to have to continue building their section with very little outside help, and they found this prospect discouraging.

In 1879 Walter Hines Page wrote an article that appeared in the *Atlantic Monthly* in which he used satire to vent his frustration over his fellow southerners' failure to adjust to a changing America. His unflattering portrait of "An Old Southern Borough," the piedmont village of Hillsboro, North Carolina, contained none of the optimism of Edward King. Page found no difference between the Old South and the New South. Old-fashioned southern gentlemen continued to dominate the ruling class and to maintain the correctness of secession and the values of antebellum times. A general atmosphere of indolence prevailed. The white villagers relied on the "darkeys" to do the menial and hard work. All whites considered blacks members of an inferior race. Paternalism characterized race relations. The value structure of the white society emphasized faith in old religious forms, loyalty to family, and veneration of women. A major focus of community thought was hatred of northerners. A hopelessly unprogressive spirit characterized village

life; common sights were whittling loafers at the railroad station, dilapidated houses, and antiquated methods of agriculture. Page concluded
his sketch by stating that there were so few new ideas and so little
enterprise that even the dogs looked old-fashioned.[18]

Page saw very little future for such a sorry place. If Hillsboro was
representative of the hundreds of hamlets throughout the South, the
land was becoming one that time had passed by. Page believed in the
New South creed, and if his analysis was right, the future of the South
was bleak indeed. The decadent villages of Dixie had been of little
consequence since antebellum times and were no different from the
thousands of urban failures in the Midwest. Once a place lost out in the
struggle for urban supremacy, it declined and was lucky to survive,
even as a crossroads hamlet. Speculators moved on, and business
gravitated to more favored towns. People with ambition drifted away,
leaving only a few discouraged people, the old and the unsuccessful.
Page could just as well have been writing about a village in Ohio as in
North Carolina. The future of the nation, North and South, did not lie
in unsuccessful backwaters. Rather, it lay in the growing cities of the
emerging national urban network.

The extent to which southern communities integrated into a nation
of cities was of vital significance for the section's future. As an urban
society cut sharply across old sectional barriers, economic integration
was only one aspect of a larger whole. If southern cities were radically
different in character from those elsewhere, they might not fit into the
urban system, and the New South creed would die aborning. The
South might be reduced to permanent colonial status. Therefore, the
social statistics of southern cities took on new importance. Numbers
and percentages about a wide variety of subjects, from the incidence of
immigrants tc school attendance, mirrored the state of urban progress
in the South. The figures showed what southern cities were like and
where they stood in relationship to the rest of America.

Between 1870 and 1880 the population of the United States rose
from 38.6 million to 50.2 million people, an increase of 26 percent. High
birth rates and immigration were responsible for this growth. Great
strides were made in the settlement of the Far West, and population in
the East continued to move from farms to cities. The southern states
grew at rates above the national average. In 1880 there were 14.2 million
southerners, accounting for 28 percent of the people in the country. But
the character of this population differed sharply from that elsewhere.
Of the nation's 6.6 million blacks, 6 million or 91 percent lived in the
South. Conversely, the South contained only 306,000 of the country's
6.7 million foreign-born for a total of 5 percent. These figures alone set
the South apart. Of all southerners, 47 percent were black and 2
percent foreign-born. Three states, Louisiana, Mississippi, and South

Carolina, had more blacks than whites. No southern state had a foreign-born population of over 10 percent. In the rest of the United States, under 1 percent of the people were black and 19 percent foreign-born. A census official summed up this situation in 1880, when he wrote that with slight qualification, "where the colored are found the foreign-born are not, and *vice versa.*"[19] Southern orators liked to boast that the section's population was homogeneous, but such claims ignored the blacks. The population statistics showed that the rest of the nation was far more homogeneous racially.

The population profiles of the thirty southern cities with more than 10,000 people in 1880 did not fit into any neat category. A total of 1.4 million people, 10 percent of the southern population, lived in such cities. These cities differed from the South as a whole in that blacks accounted for 31 percent and foreign-born for 13 percent of the urban population. Indeed, 61 percent of all immigrants in the South lived in the cities, compared with only 8 percent of the blacks. Oppressive legislation made it hard for black sharecroppers to leave the land. Cities had attracted most of the foreigners who settled in the South since before the Civil War. Yet the South's cities were unlike their counterparts throughout the rest of the United States. Most of the 198 cities of over 10,000 population in the Northeast, Midwest, and West had insignificant numbers of blacks, and roughly 30 percent of their population was foreign-born. Southern cities could be said to represent potential bridges from the South to the rest of the nation. Naturally, being white supremacists, none of the New South supporters emphasized the racial mix in southern cities. Yet the figures illustrated that change was under way in the urban South. The cities were far from being declining places with languid populations of society's losers. For better or worse, they represented the South's best hopes for a relatively quick recovery. As in the antebellum period, they were the most progressive components of the section.

The social statistics of the southern cities provided a microscopic view of southern urban society. The figures supplied basic data for helping to answer a wide variety of questions. Were there major differences in the composition of the inhabitants of individual cities? What were the percentage disparities between blacks and whites? What were the numbers and nationalities of the foreign-born? Were there significant differences in the numbers of men and women? Were many southern city dwellers born outside the section? What groups made up the work forces? Was religion a strong factor in holding together the fabric of the communities? What influence did educational institutions have? As Benjamin H. Hill, a senator from Georgia, whom Grady quoted in his Delmonico's speech, had said in 1871, "The pressing question, therefore, with every people is, not what they have been, but whether and what they shall determine to be; not what their fathers were, but whether and what their children shall be."[20] If Hill was right, the future of southern civilization rested on the shoulders of city people.

The distribution of blacks and foreign-born in the thirty southern cities of more than 10,000 people is shown in Table 3.1.[21] The six cities with the largest percentages of immigrants had the lowest percentages of blacks; all six were less than 30 percent black and 13 percent or more foreign-born. The totals for Newport (2 percent black and 25 percent foreign-born) and Covington (6 percent black and 22 percent foreign-born) reflected their status as suburbs of Cincinnati. Cincinnati was 29 percent foreign-born and .03 percent black, so it would have been wrong to say simply that Newport and Covington had the same racial components as their much larger neighbor. It would also have been incorrect to say that all cities in the southern border states had similar characteristics. For example, Cumberland was 9 percent black and 13 percent foreign-born; Lexington was 46 percent black and 6 percent foreign-born. Cumberland was a railroad town; Lexington was an agricultural marketing center with some light industry. The distinguishing factor was that American railroad section hands were predominantly white. Because of such differences in their economics, it is difficult to generalize about southern towns in the border states.

No other cities in the South were less than 30 percent black. They had correspondingly small foreign-born populations. Washington's sectional antecedents were reflected in its population, which was 33 percent black and 10 percent foreign-born. The layering that had characterized the building of the southern urban network made little difference in these cities' racial components outside the border states. Wilmington was 60 percent black and 3 percent foreign-born, Petersburg 54 percent black and 2 percent foreign-born, and Montgomery 59 percent black and 4 percent foreign-born. Eight southen cities were more than 50 percent black, and nineteen were less than 10 percent foreign-born. Atlanta, billed as a showcase of the New South, was 44 percent black and 4 percent foreign-born. Grady did not mention those figures when he talked about how the people of Atlanta had rebuilt their community after the Civil War.

Absolute numbers provide another way of looking at the populations of the southern cities. Fifteen of the thirty cities had more than 10,000 blacks. The most, 57,700, were in New Orleans. Baltimore had 53,700 and Washington, 48,400. Only forty cities in the United States had in excess of 48,300 inhabitants of all races. Indeed, only three northern cities had more than 10,000 blacks. They were Philadelphia (31,700), St. Louis (22,300), and New York (20,000). The greatest number of black urban dwellers were in the South. Foreign-born were

Table 3.1.   Foreign-Born and Blacks in Southern Cities, 1880

City	Total Population	Number of Blacks	Percentage of Blacks	Number of Foreign-born	Percentage of Foreign-born
Alabama					
Mobile	29,132	12,240	42	2,937	10
Montgomery	16,713	9,931	59	651	4
Arkansas					
Little Rock	13,138	4,507	35	1,446	11
Dist. of Columbia					
Georgetown	12,578	3,758	30	815	7
Washington	147,293	48,377	33	14,242	10
Georgia					
Atlanta	37,409	16,330	44	1,416	4
Augusta	21,891	10,120	46	1,198	5
Columbus	10,123	4,476	44	294	3
Macon	12,749	6,584	52	486	4
Savannah	30,709	15,654	51	2,994	10
Kentucky					
Covington	29,720	1,790	6	6,487	22
Lexington	16,656	7,583	46	1,081	6
Louisville	123,758	20,905	17	23,156	19
Newport	20,433	315	2	5,011	25
Louisiana					
New Orleans	216,090	57,723	27	41,157	19
Maryland					
Baltimore	332,313	53,716	16	56,136	17
Cumberland	10,693	931	9	1,422	13
Mississippi					
Vicksburg	11,814	5,836	49	939	8
North Carolina					
Wilmington	17,350	10,462	60	528	3
South Carolina					
Charleston	49,984	27,276	55	3,950	8
Columbia	10,036	5,698	57	338	3
Tennessee					
Chattanooga	12,892	5,082	39	719	6
Memphis	33,592	14,896	44	3,971	12
Nashville	43,350	16,337	38	3,025	7
Virginia					
Alexandria	13,569	5,380	39	599	4
Lynchburg	15,959	8,474	53	398	3
Norfolk	21,966	10,068	46	835	4
Petersburg	21,656	11,701	54	356	2
Portsmouth	11,390	3,829	34	526	5
Richmond	63,600	27,832	44	3,340	5

another matter. Thirty-nine places in the nation had in excess of 10,000 foreign-born. The South had but four of these communities: Baltimore (56,100), New Orleans (41,200), Louisville (23,200), and Washington (14,200). These numbers represented large concentrations of people. Nevertheless, they were not comparable to the numbers in the seven cities with over 100,000 immigrants, which included the 593,500 in the New York–Brooklyn area. The fewest immigrants in the southern cities were the 294 in Columbus and the 338 in Columbia; the lowest black totals were the 315 in Newport and the 931 in Cumberland. Obviously, in these respects southern cities were different from the rest of urban America.

The large numbers of blacks in southern cities had long been a source of concern and embarrassment to whites. Many would have agreed with the editor of the *Montgomery Daily Ledger*, who in 1865, claimed that cities were "intended for white people." He asserted, "Our advice to them [blacks] is to go into the country and cultivate the soil, the employment God designed them for and which they must do or starve."[22] Antebellum slavocrats had contended that urban life undermined the peculiar institution because slaves could not be so easily controlled as on remote plantations and clandestine associations with free blacks sparked slaves' desires for freedom. Alarmists frequently raised the specter of Denmark Vesey's alleged plot in Charleston to foment a slave rebellion in 1822. There were charges that urban owners routinely reported fewer slaves than they actually had so as to avoid paying municipal head taxes. Some whites feared that large numbers of runaway slaves lurked inside town limits in secret hiding places. Official statistics did indicate a sharp increase in urban black populations between 1830 and 1850, but this was a natural result of increased urban activity throughout the section. There was no danger that cities would become predominantly black. Large increases in the numbers of whites more than counterbalanced the black growth. But the concentration of several thousand slaves in small areas caused concern in many quarters. The very presence of many blacks was in itself a problem that some authorities thought needed a remedy.[23]

In the 1850s several cities attempted to reduce their black populations through propaganda campaigns that encouraged owners to ship their chattels back to the country. The results varied. Savannah cut its black population virtually in half from 14,700 to 7,700. The number of slaves in Charleston declined from 19,500 to 14,000, but the Free Negro population of slightly over 3,000 remained unchanged, and the city's total population decreased slightly during the decade. Savannah was a growing town, and its white population increased by more than 14,000. Because a few of the new interior cities were unable to attract enough white laborers, their black populations grew correspondingly.

The number of blacks in Montgomery rose from 2,200 to 4,500 and in Atlanta from 500 to 1,900. New Orleans, a major port of arrival for immigrants, was a different matter. Thousands of the foreign-born stayed in the city, displacing black workers, taking over most of the day labor and service jobs. The number of Free Negroes in New Orleans grew only slightly, from 9,900 to 10,700; that of slaves fell from 17,300 to 14,000. The lesson was clear; where there was competition, foreign labor drove out black labor. But New Orleans had been exceptional even before the Civil War. It had been a cosmopolitan city since before the Louisiana Purchase. For most growing southern cities, slaves were the only available source of skilled and unskilled labor, so in the 1850s there was no major reversal of black population trends in southern communities.[24]

During the immediate aftermath of the Civil War the movement of newly freed blacks into cities greatly outran that of whites. Nashville and Richmond are cases in point. In the 1860s, and primarily after 1865, the black population of Nashville increased from 23 to 38 percent and of Richmond from 38 to 45 percent. Blacks flocked to the cities because of dislocations in the countryside caused by the end of slavery and for other reasons. Just as elsewhere, the lure of the city attracted black southerners. More opportunities existed and services were better than in rural sections. One white editor noted that the influx resulted from "the inherent love of the negro for a crowd, for shows, for amusements, and for opportunities of making a precarious living by occasional jobs when they may be idle at other times."[25] The other factors more than outweighed such judgments.

The large numbers of blacks attracted to even the most provincial of southern cities frightened whites.[26] The odious "Black Codes," aimed at reinstituting slavery under a different guise, were their reaction to the problem of controlling these people. Southern legislatures enacted the codes despite the advice of President Andrew Johnson, who argued correctly that they would inflame northern opinion. A symbolic illustration that accompanied Edward King's "Great South" series showed several blacks with whips yelling at a white man. "As at Lynchburg," King wrote about Petersburg, "the Northerner is at first amazed by the mass of black and yellow faces. The hackmen who shriek in your ear as you arrive at the depot, the brakeman on the train, the waiter in the hotel, all are African. In the tobacco factories hundreds of dusty forms are toiling, and an equal number are slouching in the sunshine. On the day of my visit a colored Masonic excursion had arrived from Richmond, and the streets were filled with stout negromen, decently clothed, and their wives and sweethearts, attired in even louder colors than those affected by Northern servant girls. Each was talking vociferously; officials, in flaunting regalia and sweating at every pore, rushed to and fro; bands thundered and urchins screamed."[27] Blacks never had direct control of any southern city. By the 1880s whites held all the leadership posts. Talented blacks had a choice of either remaining in inferior positions or seeking opportunities elsewhere.

In antebellum times the South attracted few of the hundreds of thousands of foreign-born who came to America's shores. Most were from western Europe, and the southern climate was too unlike that in their homelands to appeal to them. The existence of the peculiar institution also worked against immigration, for many foreign-born opposed slavery. And except for a few southern cities, there was no demand for white labor. A great many more immigrants passed through the South than stayed. Between 1820 and 1860, before through railroad connections were built from New York to Chicago, more than 550,000 foreign-born entered the United States at New Orleans. After New York, the Crescent City was the nation's second biggest immigrant port. It was easier to travel to the nation's heartland via the Mississippi River than to take the Erie Canal and Great Lakes route.[28] Most of the foreigners who never got beyond New Orleans stayed out of necessity—they ran out of money. A large number of the immigrants who entered at New Orleans were famine victims or paupers. The port had such lax admission regulations that no one was ever turned away. Most of the immigrants who went upriver, usually as deck passengers on steamboats, settled in the Midwest.[29] Only a small number stayed in the South, augmenting the numbers of those who came down from the North. Most of the foreign-born settled in the border states. Many worked in the fast-growing cities at the portals between North and South, especially in the 1850s, when Germans and Irish settled in appreciable numbers in Baltimore and Louisville.[30]

There was a white blacklash against immigrants in the urban South.[31] As early as 1839 the Louisiana Native American Association warned of the dangers posed at New Orleans by "hordes and hecatombs of beings in human form, but destitute of any intellectual aspiration,—the outcast and offal of society—the pauper, the vagrant . . . reeking with the accumulated crimes of the whole civilized and savage world."[32] The nativists sought successfully to promote changes in the federal naturalization laws. During the next decade, two incidents in New Orleans inflamed nativists. First, a state judge illegally naturalized 1,800 immigrants. Then, in the so-called Plaquemines Fraud, immigrants denied the right to vote in New Orleans were transported to another point to cast Democratic ballots in the presidential election of 1844. Throughout the 1850s the nativist American party was a potent political force in New Orleans, outliving the national organization by more than half a decade. Know-Nothingism was a political force in the other southern cities with immigrant elements. The American party had a powerful organization in Baltimore. On 6 August 1855—"Bloody Monday"—foreigners and nativists battled in the streets of Louisville.[33] Protestant opposition to Roman Catholicism, the religion of many immigrants, exacerbated emotions. Clearly, the attitudes toward foreign-born urbanites in the Old South created difficulties for advocates of programs to promote immigration in the postwar era.

Some halfhearted efforts to encourage immigration had more substance than the rhetoric about the need for desirable immigrants promoted by New South propagandists. All the southern states established immigration boards, copying those already operating in the North. As standard procedure, state boards produced foreign-language tracts extolling opportunities and resources, stationed agents at dockside to meet immigrant ships, and sent representatives abroad to give promotional speeches. Throughout the South, the efforts of private land companies and local societies supplemented the public activities. At one point Louisiana boasted more than a hundred immigration societies. Most had little money and lasted but a short time.[34] There was some talk a about attracting Oriental laborers as a substitute for slave labor. In 1880 the most Orientals in any southern city were the 80 in New Orleans. Baltimore had 8 and Atlanta none. Despite all efforts, only a small portion of the millions of immigrants who arrived in America in the decades after the Civil War went to the South. It was not until near the turn of the century that railroad companies started in a major way to encourage immigration into the South. Even then, the vast numbers of foreign-born continued to avoid Dixie.

In 1880 a total of 146,000 of the 182,000 foreign-born in the South lived in the eight largest cities in the section. They accounted for 80 percent of the immigrants in the thirty largest southern cities. The most foreign-born in the eight cities were from Germany, Ireland, and Great Britain, as illustrated by Table 3.2.[35] These groups constituted the chief components of the foreign-born population of the country.

Most immigrants from Britain in the nation were in New England or Michigan, places easily reached from British Canada. Few had come to the South since colonial times. Baltimore had the largest number in 1880, around 3,000. The only other cities with more than a thousand British-born residents were New Orleans, Washington, and Louisville. Despite the claim that the South personified the best of Anglo-Saxon civilization, the region's cities had attracted few Englishmen. Like the majority of other immigrants, they found the North better suited to their needs.[36]

A floodtide of Hibernians came to America in the wake of the potato famine. Most of these people stayed in the North, as did later

Table 3.2.   Germans, Irish, and British in Eight Southern Cities, 1880

City	Germans		Irish		British	
	Number	Percent	Number	Percent	Number	Percent
Baltimore	34,051	10	14,238	4	2,973	1
New Orleans	13,944	6	11,708	5	2,262	1
Washington	4,154	3	6,448	4	1,892	1
Louisville	13,463	11	6,474	5	1,173	1
Richmond	1,274	2	1,037	2	529	1
Charleston	1,537	3	1,611	3	352	1
Nashville	664	2	1,349	3	425	1
Atlanta	471	1	465	1	190	0.5

Irish immigrants. In 1880 between 15 and 20 percent of the inhabitants of New York, Boston, and Chicago were from Ireland. Seventeen places outside the South had more than 10,000 Irish immigrants. Even so, there were considerable congregations in Dixie: 14,200 in Baltimore and 11,700 in New Orleans. Two-thirds of the Irish in the country lived east of Pittsburgh.

Two-thirds of the German-born population in the United States resided west of Pittsburgh, the largest numbers in the Midwest.[37] The great German aggregates that came after the revolution of 1848 in Europe spilled over into the South. Their coming coincided with rapid urban growth in the border cities and in New Orleans. At the same time, there was rising concern over the number of urban slaves, and some observers saw Germans as good substitute laborers. A resumption of German immigration after the Civil War continued trends already under way. In 1880 the seventh largest concentration of Germans in the South was in Baltimore, where they numbered 34,100, accounting for 10 percent of all the people in the Monumental City. In addition, the 13,900 Germans in New Orleans and 13,500 in Louisville represented large totals when compared with many other places in the nation. Adding in the children of immigrants—what the census office referred to as the "so-called 'German family' "[38]—roughly doubled the concentrations of immigrant stock. If success in city building in the America of the Gilded Age meant attracting immigrants, a few southern cities had done just that. The increased immigrant population had the subtle effect of gradually changing these cities' character and making them more like cities outside the section.

New Orleans had a reputation as the most cosmopolitan city in the South. It had 6,900 French-born residents, the most in the United States after New York with 9,900. New Orleans had an extensive French heritage, which attracted the immigrants. Edward King tried to pture the meaning of the French experience in New Orleans. Like other visitors, he was captivated by the Creole women of French descent, whom he described as having "an indefinable grace, a *savoir* in dress, and a piquant and alluring charm in person and conversation, which makes them universal favorites in society." King's opinion of the French Quarter was that its populace was provincial. "The majority of the people in the whole quarter seem to have a total disregard of the outside world," he claimed, "and when one hears them discussing the distracted condition of local politics, one can almost fancy them gossiping on matters entirely foreign to them. . . . They live very much among themselves. French by nature and training, they get but a faint reflection of the excitements in these United States."[39] Many New Orleans natives thought the growing Italian element was even more insular. In 1880, with 2,000 Italians, New Orleans had proportionally the most people of that nationality in the country.[40] Almost all the Italians were young men, who had come as contract laborers. Few showed an inclination to adopt American ways. Native resentment of them was indicated in official Louisiana state documents, which derogatorily called them "Dagos." They were classic examples of the immigrants white southerners considered undesirable. Their presence posed questions skirted by advocates of the New South concept. If the South should boom, where would the main components of the additional population needed to build up the section come from? Indeed, as more and more Italians moved into New Orleans, riots directed against them followed almost as a matter of course. Would the poor of other southern or eastern European nations receive a more cordial welcome?

In 1880 both the black and white populations of the eight largest southern cities had been born close to home.[41] A total of 90 percent of the people in Richmond were born in Virginia. Eighty-eight percent of all Charlestonians were from South Carolina. Their immediate states had contributed between 70 and 80 percent of the populations of Atlanta, Nashville, Baltimore, and New Orleans. Some 74 percent of all Washingtonians were from the District of Columbia or from neighboring Virginia and Maryland. Louisville, even though right across the Ohio River from Indiana, still counted 67 percent of its inhabitants as Kentucky natives. None of the other fifty largest cities in the country had such provincial population characteristics. In Boston, one of the nation's oldest cities, 54 percent of the populace was from Massachusetts. Roughly 51 percent of Chicago's residents were Illinois natives. The continual influx of people into the Windy City changed the figures daily. Denver, founded in 1854, had a population profile in keeping with that of a booming town in a new state. Only 11 percent of its inhabitants were from Colorado. The 1880 census noted the "astonishing readiness" with which Americans moved "under the smallest economical or social impulse."[42]

The simple truth was that the major southern cities had failed to attract many outsiders. Only two cities had more than a thousand persons who had been born more than a southern state away. New Orleans had 4,300 Virginians, 1,700 Kentuckians, and 1,300 Marylanders. Atlanta had 1,000 Virginians. More startling were the statistics for migrants from outside the South. Only the four metropolises had more than a thousand northerners. Baltimore boasted 7,000 Pennsylvanians and 3,000 New Yorkers. In Louisville there were 4,800 Indianans, 2,600 Ohioans, 1,500 Pennsylvanians, and 1,300 New Yorkers. Washington had 5,300 people from New York, 5,000 from Pennsylvania, 1,700 from Ohio, and 1,500 from Massachusetts. New Orleans claimed 2,100 residents born in New York. More typical figures were the 24 Wisconsinites in Atlanta, the 86 Rhode Islanders in Atlanta, and the 3 Nebraskans in Nashville. The figures further reinforced the insular nature of southern life. The South remained very different, despite the contentions that without blacks it was much like the Midwest. In population, as in other areas, there was a direct connection between the Old South and the New South.

Some observers expressed fear that the population mix would create a state of bucolic individualism based upon a limited world view in southern urban life. Under this theory, rural migrants, intimidated by blind and hostile forces beyond their understanding, would lash out violently at society. This idea ignored the role of the city as a crucible of change. By their nature, the transforming trends of urbanization muted agrarian values. The same forces that shaped city life elsewhere in the United States were at work in the South, and the birthplace of the white native population had very little practical meaning. The presence of blacks, on the other hand, added the problem of race. The outcome of their presence obviously depended upon the attitudes of the dominant white groups. If integration was promoted, a period of racial harmony lay ahead, with black and white urban dwellers working together to promote a common destiny. Unfortunately, a policy of white supremacy negated that happy vision, promising a great waste of talent, efforts, and resources. For instance, blacks from Washington to New Orleans were forced to construct their own "hidden communities." In addition, the denial of social mobility placed serious strains on black family life. Immigrants, on the other hand, because they were so few, had a good chance of assimilating, despite some local hostility. Although neither origins nor race in themselves constituted problems to city building, the reaction to them did.

In 1880, 26 of the 28 southern cities with populations over 10,000

Table 3.3.   Male and Female Populations in Southern Cities, 1880

City	Males	Females	% Females
Alabama			
Mobile	13,189	15,943	55
Montgomery	7,591	9,122	55
Arkansas			
Little Rock	6,966	6,172	47
Dist. of Columbia			
Georgetown	5,847	6,731	55
Washington	68,310	78,983	54
Georgia			
Atlanta	17,677	19,732	53
Augusta	9,827	12,064	55
Columbus	–	–	–
Macon	5,709	7,040	55
Savannah	13,936	16,773	55
Kentucky			
Covington	14,192	15,528	52
Lexington	7,721	8,935	54
Louisville	58,982	64,776	52
Newport	9,925	10,508	51
Louisiana			
New Orleans	100,892	115,198	53
Maryland			
Baltimore	157,393	174,920	53
Cumberland	–	–	–
Mississippi			
Vicksburg	5,575	6,239	53
North Carolina			
Wilmington	7,910	9,440	54
South Carolina			
Charleston	22,585	27,399	55
Columbia	4,639	5,397	54
Tennessee			
Chattanooga	6,512	6,380	49
Memphis	16,302	17,290	51
Nashville	20,912	22,438	52
Virginia			
Alexandria	6,438	7,221	53
Lynchburg	7,483	8,476	53
Norfolk	10,069	11,897	54
Petersburg	9,779	11,877	55
Portsmouth	5,489	5,901	52
Richmond	29,483	34,117	54

Table 3.4. Working Men and Women in Eight Southern Cities, 1880

City	Total	Males	Females	% Females
Baltimore	130,364	97,561	32,803	25
New Orleans	78,336	59,173	19,163	24
Washington	57,262	39,703	17,559	31
Louisville	45,244	34,987	10,257	23
Richmond	24,550	17,007	7,543	31
Charleston	20,325	13,280	7,045	35
Nashville	16,738	11,591	5,147	31
Atlanta	17,078	11,118	5,960	35

had more females than males (see Table 3.3).[43] The United States had 900,000 more females than males. The differences were most apparent in the cities over 10,000. In the Northeast, 108 out of 133 cities had more women than men. Forty-three of 62 Midwest communities had an excess of females. Demographers have attributed this situation to migratory patterns. East of the Mississippi River the number of women migrants into cities exceeded men, particularly black women domestics in the South. Only in the West did a majority of the urban centers—18 out of 23—have more males. In the course of the American frontier experience, men were traditionally in the vanguard of settlement. In fact, the only two southern cities with more males—Little Rock and Chattanooga—were only recently removed from the frontier. The former was 53 percent male and the latter 51 percent. Fourteen of the southern cities were 54 to 55 percent female. These percentages were similar to those for many of the older northeastern centers. If anything, the southern statistics indicated that the South was not gaining heavy industry as fast as advocates of manufacturing might have liked. Moreover, the South was not keeping or attracting ambitious young men. Instead, they went West. Of course, these facts were realized by Grady and other advocates of the New South creed, who tried to emphasize that better opportunities existed within the section. Yet even the most realistic of evaluations did not stop the westward movement.

The work forces of the eight largest southern cities in 1880 contained appreciable female minorities, as shown in Table 3.4.[44] The aggregates of working women varied from 35 percent in Charleston and Atlanta to 23 percent in Louisville. The figures for the southern centers were much higher than those for the fifteen largest cities in the Midwest and the West, where totals ranged from a high of 22 percent in Cincinnati to a low of 11 percent in Denver. Generally, the figures for the Northeast were higher than for either the West or Midwest. The lowest were the 14 percent in both the steel center of Pittsburgh and the coal town of Scranton. The highest were the 40 percent in the textile manufacturing towns of Lowell and Fall River. Furthermore, women made up 24 percent of the gainfully employed in New York, Philadelphia, and Boston, the three largest metropolises in the section. The vast majority of the working women of the Northeast toiled in low-paying and unskilled positions. If they were not domestic servants, they more than likely worked in the garment or textile industries. Baltimore's employment pattern for women was close to that of the northeastern centers, with 13,900 domestic servants, 8,000 garment workers, and 4,300 laundresses.[45] These three classifications accounted for 79 percent of all employed women in the city. In general, the other southern centers had lower percentages of garment workers than did Baltimore, but that figure was bound to change as industrialization increased.

If the South developed a significant manufacturing base, jobs in the textile and tobacco industries would open up for many southern women. Given the low pay schedules and long hours in northeastern mills, it was an unhappy prospect. Of course, southern industrial evangelists did not dwell on such mundane concerns as working conditions. They took a higher ground, equating industry with civic piety. Francis W. Dawson set the tone when he campaigned for cotton mills in the South Carolina piedmont. The illustrious Charleston editor wrote in 1880 that mills would have an elevating social influence upon employees, encouraging them to seek education and improve their way of living in "every conceivable respect."[46] He suggested that investors could expect annual profits of 25 percent but said nothing about opportunities for advancement for women mill workers. If the experience of Northeast was an indication, job advancement was unlikely, especially for black and white unskilled women workers.

Southern employers did not adjust quickly to the use of former slaves as employed laborers. Some former slaveowners could not understand why freedmen quit after watching whippings of fellow workers. Other employers thought blacks shiftless because they did not work hard for the very low wages offered. The odious Black Codes reflected the lack of understanding about the differences between slave and free labor. The Mississippi law contained heavy penalties for anyone who persuaded a black to change jobs. Provisions of the Louisiana code called for the punishment of blacks who feigned sickness or swore at their bosses. All the southern codes were repealed at the time of the establishment of military governments in 1867, despite southern assertions that the laws copied standard northern apprenticeship and vagrancy statutes.[47] Gradually, blacks learned the importance of fulfilling labor contracts and whites came to the realization that slavery was over. Looking back on the changes wrought, Henry Watterson wrote in 1903, "Under the old system we paid our debts and walloped our niggers. Under the new we pay our niggers and wallop our debts."[48]

The gospel of industry extolled in the postwar era by enthusiastic advocates of the New South creed gave greater urgency to experiments in the use of blacks in industry. In 1874, King visited a Lynchburg tobacco factory that employed black men, women, and children. He wrote, "These negroes earn good wages, work faithfully, and turn out vast quantities of the black, ugly compound known as 'plug.' . . . In the manufactories the negro is the same cheery, capricious being that one finds him in the cotton or sugar-cane fields; he sings quaintly over his toil, and seems entirely devoid of the sullen ambition which many of our Northern factory laborers exhibit. The men and women working around the tables in the basements of the Lynchburg tobacco establishments croon eccentric hymns in concert all day long; and their little children, laboring before they are hardly large enough to go along, join in the refrains."[49] The employment of blacks was a logical outgrowth of their use in Richmond iron mills before the Civil War. There were not enough native white laborers—either males or females—to build an industrial society. And in the South, immigrants, the backbone of the unskilled labor force in the factories of the North, were unavailable in large enough numbers to fuel an industrial machine.

In 1880 the work force in the eight largest southern cities was overwhelmingly American in origin (see Table 3.5).[50] The low numbers of foreign-born immigrants provided further proof that the South was different. Atlanta, Richmond, Nashville, and Charleston had smaller percentages of immigrant workers than any other of the fifty largest cities in the country. Only 4 percent of the 16,300 employed persons in Atlanta had been born overseas. Few immigrants had accepted Grady's invitation to come to Atlanta. In all eight cities, Germans and Irish accounted for more than half the foreign-born workers. Germans made up 14 percent of all the employed persons in both Louisville and Baltimore. The largest totals for Irish workers were the 7 percent in both Louisville and New Orleans. These percentages appear low when compared with those in some northern towns. Milwaukee's work force was 39 percent German and Jersey City's 25 percent Irish. As throughout the nation, the percentages of foreign-born workers in seven of the southern cities were greater than the percentages of foreign-born. Thus Baltimore, which was 19 percent foreign-born, had a work force that was 22 percent foreign-born. Washington's ratio was seven to twelve and Nashville's seven to eight. Atlanta was the only exception. It had the same proportion of foreign-born residents and workers. Just as in the North, most immigrants in the South held unskilled jobs that required heavy labor. For example, there were many German stevedores in New Orleans. Of course, immigrant workers faced much

Table 3.5. Nativity of Workers in Eight Southern Cities, 1880

City	United States		Ireland		Germany	
	Number	Percent	Number	Percent	Number	Percent
Baltimore	101,484	78	7,306	6	17,769	14
New Orleans	58,771	75	5,543	7	6,968	9
Washington	50,309	88	3,146	5	2,100	4
Louisville	34,012	75	3,099	7	6,412	14
Richmond	23,013	94	454	2	620	3
Charleston	18,379	90	758	4	796	4
Nashville	15,232	91	643	4	356	2
Atlanta	16,339	96	237	1	280	2

City	Great Britain		Sweden/Norway		British America		Other	
	Number	Percent	Number	Percent	Number	Percent	Number	Percent
Baltimore	1,442	1	169	0.1	258	0.2	1,936	1
New Orleans	1,218	2	137	0.2	210	0.3	5,489	7
Washington	865	2	42	0.07	141	0.2	659	1
Louisville	578	1	21	0.05	205	0.5	917	2
Richmond	220	0.9	9	0.04	31	0.1	203	0.8
Charleston	138	0.7	14	0.07	12	0.06	228	1
Nashville	206	1	35	0.2	18	0.1	248	1
Atlanta	108	0.6	16	0.09	26	0.2	72	0.4

greater challenges in the South than in the North. They not only had to compete against each other and native Americans for jobs but against blacks as well. This competition meant that wages were low and immigrants were discouraged from coming to the southern interior cities that had large black populations. Southern leaders were right when they told northern industrialists that labor costs were lower in the South than elsewhere. But for workers this bleak situation showed little sign of changing.

In an effort to make the South appear attractive for industry, the spokesmen for the New South creed embraced their own version of Social Darwinism. This concept, expounded by the English economist Herbert Spencer, applied naturalist Charles Darwin's theory of evolution by natural selection to human affairs. In his more extreme moments, Spencer even opposed extending sewer lines into poor districts on the grounds that improved sanitation would affect the selection process. The southern Social Darwinists rejected a straight survival-of-the-fittest approach. Rather, they held that successful businessmen would end poverty by sponsoring programs that would bring material progress. Richard Edmonds wrote in his *Manufacturers' Record* that he found it difficult to understand why people were "prone to sermonize against the spirit of 'commercialism.' " He insisted, "We are all cogs in the great machine." Another New South proponent, newspaper publisher and industrialist Daniel Augustus Tompkins, expressed the belief that "the survival of the fittest is, has been, and will always be the law of progress." Grady did his part by consistently praising bankers, industrialists, and railroad owners. Another New South supporter, the Reverend John C. Calhoun Newton, felt that the future of the South lay with "wealthy capitalists, and prince merchants, and lordly bankers," who acted as "stewards of God." Material progress was to be stressed above all else. A thoroughly modern South was not only in step with the rest of the nation but out in front in industrial philosophy. Capitalists were community benefactors beloved by lesser citizens, who accepted the gospel of work as the formula for success. Only a few social degenerates opposed the inevitable capitalistic thrust of Anglo-Saxon civilization. Above all, southern religious institutions stood as bulwarks in the defense of the new industrial order. Edmonds said that carriers of the New South aspects of Social Darwinism were more than mere men. "Yea," he announced, "they are really messengers preparing the way for religious advancement itself."[51]

The New South advocates used religion to buttress their creed. Grady claimed "The South is American and religious"; "God-fearing people" supported the "old fashion" by according equal honor to God and the United States Constitution. They practiced "the straight and simple faith of our fathers, untainted by heresy and unweakened by speculation." It was as if the Civil War had never happened. "The spirit of Americanism—of popular liberty, of love for democratic principles and institutions—burns steadily and unobstructedly here." Grady intoned, "Anarchy, socialism—that leveling spirit that defies government and denies God—has no hold in the South. Here the old churches are the best churches, and the old creeds still living and saving. Here law and order reign. Here government is supreme, and if we love well that government which touches us most closely, we love none the less that government which, above all, blesses all."[52] Mythmaking always was an integral part of the New South creed. Grady and his colleagues were not dogmatists; they were promoters trying to sell proposals that would quickly change the course of southern life.

In 1890 the United States census office took what officials claimed was the nation's first scientifically conducted religious census. It indicated that the 17 southern out of the nation's 124 cities over 25,000 population had many religious organizations, numerous houses of worship, much valuable property, and substantial membership counts (see Table 3.6).[53] Of special significance were the percentages of church members. There was a marked difference between rural and urban areas. The national average for urban communicants was 38 percent;[54] the national percentage was 45 percent. Membership statistics, of

Table 3.6. Religious Statistics for Seventeen Southern Cities of More than 25,000 Inhabitants, 1890

City	Population	Organa-izations	Church Edifices	Value of Property	Number of Members	% of Population
Baltimore	434,439	371	371	$9,528,838	175,995	41
New Orleans	242,039	165	154	2,553,107	95,716	40
Washington	230,392	195	186	6,370,575	94,572	41
Louisville	161,129	129	144	3,332,750	73,355	46
Richmond	81,388	79	83	1,476,150	38,114	47
Nashville	76,168	101	105	1,292,796	30,195	40
Atlanta	65,533	92	81	1,073,050	27,237	42
Memphis	64,495	51	51	1,011,200	17,333	27
Charleston	54,955	73	90	1,502,592	24,117	44
Savannah	43,189	73	71	705,300	18,905	44
Covington	37,371	28	28	574,600	15,575	42
Norfolk	34,871	42	43	623,443	13,611	39
Augusta	33,300	65	71	711,775	16,936	51
Mobile	31,076	54	54	806,119	21,729	70
Chattanooga	29,100	51	46	713,830	9,830	34
Birmingham	26,178	55	45	664,525	12,214	47
Little Rock	25,874	40	39	497,600	8,298	32

course, are not exact measurements. Some organizations counted babies as members. Others did not admit children to full membership status until they were in their early teens. Moreover, the federal government obtained the data by asking clergymen to fill out reports. Still, taking the faults into consideration, the membership totals indicated the strong strain of religiosity in the late-nineteenth-century urban South. Only three of the southern cities had lower percentages of communicants than the nation as a whole. There appeared little doubt that religion played an important role in the lives of many southern urban dwellers. Less than half of the city people belonged to religious bodies, however, countering the extravagant claims of southern leaders about the importance of religion. The number of urban church members was not appreciably higher than in urban areas outside the South.

The 1890 totals for the major religous bodies in the seventeen largest southern cities reflected the diversity of religion in America (see Table 3.7).[55] The most surprising figures were those showing the numerical strength of the Roman Catholic church. In eight cities, Roman Catholics accounted for 10 percent or more of the total population. Three cities were more than 20 percent Roman Catholic: New Orleans (28 percent), Covington (27 percent), and Louisville (21 percent). The totals for Protestant groups followed sectional trends. Regular Baptists accounted for more than 10 percent of the urban dwellers in six cities. Six places were between 5 and 10 percent Southern Methodist. Colored Methodists made up 30 percent of Mobile and 12 percent of Charleston residents. The largest percentages of Methodist Episcopals were the 6 percent in Charleston, of Episcopalians the 5 percent in Mobile, and of Southern Presbyterians the 3 percent in Mobile. One to 4 percent of the people in nine of the towns had a Jewish affiliation. In these localities, the fewest Jews were the 258 in Atlanta; the most were the 3,500 in Baltimore.[56] In addition to the main line denominations, a variety of Pentecostal and other groups contributed to the richness of southern urban religion. Such variety does little to suggest that the primary goals of religion were to support either the Lost Cause or the building of an industrial and urban New South. The reality was far different from the propaganda used to promote secular causes.

Education was another source of contention in the postwar South. Many northern educational leaders thought the Old South had a dismal record. Few of the changes pioneered by Horace Mann and other reformers, such as formal teacher training and standardized curricula, found favor in the section. Several states rejected the concept of public education. The children of the wealthy classes studied under private tutors or attended northern schools. Poor whites, if they attended at all, matriculated in church schools open only a few months of the year. The teachers were usually untrained. Many white adults could write little more than their name. Authorities estimated that in 1840 one-fourth of the population of Tennessee was illiterate.[57] Only a minimal number of slaves could read. Statutes prohibited teaching them even the bare rudiments of education. Southern spokesmen did not apologize for any educational deficiencies. Instead, they claimed that the South had no need for universal education. The southern way of life did not require the vast number of people to have book learning; rather, practical skills learned in the "school of hard knocks" suited their needs. There was a gradual reversal of this viewpoint, and in the 1850s a few states passed public education acts. Unfortunately, the Civil War negated any progress that had been made.

During Reconstruction officials struggled to rekindle interest in education.[58] Jabez Lamar Monroe Curry, an ordained Baptist minister and former president of the University of Alabama, spoke widely on the "universal right" of all citizens to state-supported education. He argued on practical grounds that educated citizens would further the interests of the state. "Poverty is the inevitable result of ignorance," he preached. "Capital follows the school house. Thrift accompanies government action in behalf of schools."[59] A basic problem was that hardly any money was available. In the 1870s Georgia, Alabama, and South Carolina all temporarily closed their public school systems. On the

Table 3.7. Membership of Eight Religious Bodies for Seventeen Southern Cities of More Than 25,000 Inhabitants, 1890

City	Regular Baptists	Roman Catholics	Jewish	Methodist Episcopal	Southern Methodist	Colored Methodist	Southern Presbyterian	Episcopalian
Baltimore	18,759 (4%)	77,047 (16%)	3,500 (0.8%)	5,963 (1%)	790 (0.2%)	5,610 (1%)	1,028 (0.2%)	12,193 (3%)
New Orleans	2,681 (1%)	67,156 (28%)	2,750 (1%)	3,938 (2%)	2,301 (1%)	2,375 (1%)	2,953 (1%)	2,910 (1%)
Washington	21,781 (19%)	36,488 (16%)	976 (0.4%)	9,144 (4%)	872 (0.4%)	4,781 (2%)	246 (0.1%)	7,315 (3%)
Louisville	13,753 (9%)	33,740 (21%)	515 (0.3%)	1,613 (1%)	3,154 (2%)	3,117 (2%)	2,001 (1%)	3,654 (2%)
Richmond	24,003 (29%)	3,570 (4%)	493 (0.6%)	201 (0.2%)	1,871 (2%)	300 (0.4%)	2,017 (2%)	3,045 (3%)
Nashville	5,722 (8%)	6,000 (8%)	290 (0.4%)	1,143 (2%)	7,094 (9%)	1,926 (3%)	2,496 (3%)	953 (1%)
Atlanta	9,999 (15%)	2,050 (3%)	258 (0.3%)	1,493 (2%)	4,886 (7%)	4,411 (7%)	1,880 (3%)	863 (1%)
Memphis	2,018 (3%)	6,400 (10%)	905 (1%)	575 (0.9%)	4,559 (7%)	4,984 (8%)	1,320 (2%)	1,245 (2%)
Charleston	1,758 (3%)	3,756 (7%)	890 (2%)	3,301 (6%)	1,593 (3%)	6,359 (12%)	1,008 (2%)	2,156 (4%)
Savannah	8,226 (19%)	3,585 (8%)	505 (1%)	265 (0.6%)	1,570 (4%)	2,096 (5%)	325 (0.8%)	1,397 (3%)
Covington	943 (2%)	10,192 (27%)	– (–%)	1,424 (4%)	563 (2%)	188 (0.5%)	426 (1%)	550 (1%)
Norfolk	4,091 (12%)	1,400 (4%)	150 (0.4%)	40 (0.1%)	2,412 (7%)	2,784 (8%)	809 (2%)	1,692 (5%)
Augusta	6,228 (19%)	2,725 (8%)	393 (1%)	100 (0.3%)	2,739 (8%)	2,236 (7%)	665 (2%)	729 (2%)
Mobile	2,540 (8%)	5,400 (17%)	375 (1%)	319 (1%)	1,160 (4%)	9,219 (30%)	787 (3%)	1,576 (5%)
Chattanooga	1,854 (6%)	1,700 (6%)	300 (1%)	1,529 (5%)	1,145 (4%)	504 (2%)	500 (2%)	900 (3%)
Birmingham	2,429 (9%)	2,500 (10%)	1,075 (4%)	1,017 (4%)	1,575 (6%)	1,543 (6%)	827 (3%)	698 (3%)
Little Rock	1,644 (6%)	1,000 (4%)	400 (2%)	579 (2%)	955 (4%)	1,447 (6%)	451 (2%)	760 (3%)

Note: Figures within parentheses are percentages of population.

local level, religious and political disputes interfered with the building of public schools. It was frequently difficult even in the best of times to persuade wealthy citizens to support increases in school levies. After the end of Reconstruction, financial retrenchment at all levels of government further handicapped educational progress. The establishment of separate systems for black and white children caused further fiscal problems. No federal money was forthcoming. Most northern white reformers chose to help other concerns than black education. Some influential reformers actually opposed desegregating schools on the practical grounds that it would give legislatures an excuse to abolish public schools. The efforts of northern philanthropists John F. Slater and George Peabody to improve southern schools, particularly for blacks, only touched the surface.[60] In the end, both white and black children paid an educational price for the application of accepted racial norms, and all students suffered from the South's slow acceptance of general education. This is not to minimize the progress that had been made, particularly in a time of dislocation and financial instability. Surveys of southern public education seldom mentioned that conditions were little better elsewhere in the country. Few school districts anywhere had the funds or the inclination to fulfill the dreams of the educational reformers.

The southern urban school systems suffered from many of the same wants as those in rural areas. The 1880 school statistics for the thirty largest southern towns told a depressing story, as indicated in Table 3.8.[61] Only the four largest cities spent in excess of $100,000 during the year. Thirteen towns spent less than $30,000. Generally, student-teacher ratios in the city schools were sixty to one. For blacks the rates frequently went as high as one hundred to one.[62] Inadequate facilities added to a depressing situation. Many schoolhouses were poorly maintained converted sheds or private homes. Overcrowding was a frequent problem. Atlanta authorities tried to alleviate matters by giving white students priority over blacks. Savannah officials instituted an automatic promotion policy. The course of instruction in the urban schools minimized so-called "frills." Mobile students, for instance, studied basics: orthography, reading, writing, grammar, geography, and arithmetic.[63] Few places had foreign language, music, or physical education courses. The educational system challenged only a small number of students. Daily attendance was poor everywhere, usually under 50 percent. Edward Alderman, an advocate of public education in the New South, summed up the situation in 1889 when he stated, "Improvement in schools generally comes last."[64]

Developments in higher education appeared much more promising. Considerable attention had been devoted to college education in the antebellum period. Supposedly, the various institutions, most

Table 3.8. School Statistics for Southern Cities of More than 10,000 Inhabitants, 1880

City	School Age Youth	Estimated Private Enrollment	Public Enrollment	Average Daily Public Attendance	Public Teachers	Public Expenditures
Alabama						
Mobile	–	–	4,659	4,014	125	$40,607
Montgomery	3,793	–	849	645	14	–
Arkansas						
Little Rock	6,169	400	2,503	1,655	33	28,264
Dist. of Columbia[a]						
Georgetown & Washington	27,142	5,481	15,728	12,508	259	391,294
Georgia						
Atlanta	10,500	1,000	4,100	2,609	68	51,073
Augusta	9,366	1,236	4,027	–	32	24,977
Columbus	2,863	200	1,359	1,086	23	11,704
Macon	7,909	300	3,349	2,001	59	20,136
Savannah	10,917	–	2,110	2,290	56	–
Kentucky						
Covington	10,094	3,000	3,286	2,485	60	56,317
Lexington	5,299	600	2,262	1,615	31	18,319
Louisville	46,587	–	19,990	13,498	325	197,699
Newport	6,780	–	2,692	2,032	44	27,898
Louisiana						
New Orleans	56,947	12,000	17,886	15,190	407	250,444
Maryland						
Baltimore	86,961	14,000	48,066	29,961	822	617,152
Cumberland	–	–	–	–	–	–
Mississippi						
Vicksburg	3,000	–	1,196	–	21	9,845
North Carolina						
Wilmington	4,921	936	866	–	–	11,486
South Carolina						
Charleston	12,727	–	7,284	–	91	62,840
Columbia	–	–	–	–	–	–
Tennessee						
Chattanooga	3,061	350	2,185	1,382	30	25,621
Memphis	9,011	–	4,105	2,389	63	49,000
Nashville	12,460	400	6,098	4,299	96	89,343
Virginia						
Alexandria	4,582	1,094	1,048	804	17	11,131
Lynchburg	4,907	590	1,815	1,070	31	19,525
Norfolk	6,695	550	1,613	1,117	26	16,214
Petersburg	7,417	1,000	1,985	1,494	28	14,568
Portsmouth	3,210	819	1,010	611	14	9,640
Richmond	21,536	3,500	5,821	4,778	129	83,802

[a]The District of Columbia had a single school system.

Table 3.9. Major Colleges and Universities in Southern Cities of More than 10,000 Inhabitants, 1880

Institution	Location	Faculty	Students	Books in Library
Arkansas				
St. Johns College of Arkansas	Little Rock	8	108	200
District of Columbia				
Georgetown University	Georgetown	23	62	30,000
Columbian University	Washington	10	47	7,000
Howard University	Washington	4	15	7,000
National Deaf-Mute College	Washington	7	30	1,411
Georgia				
Atlanta University	Atlanta	12	26	5,000
Mercer University	Macon	6	96	6,000
Pio Nono College	Macon	4	45	1,100
Kentucky				
Kentucky University	Lexington	3	66	12,221
Louisiana				
New Orleans University	New Orleans	4	23	500
Straight University	New Orleans	7	16	300
Maryland				
Baltimore City College	Baltimore	13	524	–
Johns Hopkins University	Baltimore	33	159	9,000
Loyola College	Baltimore	14	70	11,000
South Carolina				
College of Charleston	Charleston	7	30	7,000
Tennessee				
Christian Brothers' College	Memphis	12	60	2,600
Central Tennessee College	Nashville	5	18	1,525
Fisk University	Nashville	6	24	2,037
Vanderbilt University	Nashville	15	191	8,000
Virginia				
Richmond College	Richmond	8	121	6,000

founded by church organizations, prepared scholars for southern living. In 1860 statistics indicated that some 25,000 students attended southern universities. This was more than in the rest of the nation combined. The Civil War disarranged southern schools, and many closed during the hostilities. When Louisiana State University reopened after the war it initially had four students. Other schools from Virginia to South Carolina had only limited student populations. Recovery was fairly rapid.[65] A new development was the establishment of several small black universities by northern philanthropic and benevolent organizations. These schools were not innovative. Their courses of study and aims were the same as those of the older white universities. By the end of Reconstruction, southern higher education was on almost as firm a ground as before the Civil War.

In 1880 many of the leading southern colleges were in cities. These institutions had few students, faculty members, and books (see Table 3.9).[66] Yet this did not diminish their intellectual importance. Enrollments varied from 524 at Baltimore City College to 15 at Howard University. Baltimore City had a large normal school that concentrated on teacher training. Howard University was typical of the emerging black schools. An observer claimed that its professors taught students a "different kind of religion from mere shouting and confusion."[67] All the schools, black and white, had preparatory departments. Teacher-student ratios, roughly one to ten, were very good. Library holdings left much room for improvement. The libraries of several institutions contained less than 2,000 books. The Johns Hopkins University in Baltimore was the most prestigious school in the South. It had 159 students and a faculty of 33. The library contained 9,000 volumes. Many of the teachers had ties with the university's pioneer graduate school, which boasted 59 students. Overall, the urban colleges of the South compared favorably with institutions of higher learning outside the section. Boston College had 186 students and 12,600 books. Purdue University had 76 students and 2,000 books. The University of Kansas had 114 students and 3,800 books.[68] Southern urban higher education represented an important sectional asset. But the question remained as to how much influence a few small elitist institutions had in changing the course of community policy in the South. There was no evidence that colleges, with their predominantly classical curricula, would lead the way in building an urban and industrial society. They appeared to be bastions of conservative thought, rather than harbingers of change.

The advocates of the New South creed had to overcome the reality that their section did not appear ready or capable of a great shift in policy. Moreover, there was no reason to believe that interests outside the South wanted the section to change. Indeed, the evidence seemed the opposite. Otherwise, northerners would not have acquiesced to the end of Reconstruction. The argument that the carpetbaggers pulled out only after finding "scalawags" to do their bidding made little sense within the larger framework of national progress. State governments had always been probusiness. The Bourbon regimes were in step with the traditions of the country. Indeed, none of the state governments under the Confederate States of America were antibusiness. Grady wrote, "The new South is simply the old South under new conditions."[69] He was right, but unlike the Old South governments, those of the New South professed to welcome Yankee capital. The problem was that the South, as before the Civil War, remained a sideshow for northern money men. If profits could be made, so much the better, but the main thrust of financial and material development was in other directions.

There were population differences that appeared to set most southern cities apart from those in the rest of the land. The southern cities tended to have more blacks and fewer foreign-born than their counterparts in the North. Most of the native-born in the southern cities were from the South. The work forces in the cities of the South contained high proportions of native Americans. There were no other major differences. Like many other places, almost all the southern cities had more females than males. In the urban South, as throughout the land, organized religion was an important institution. And, as elsewhere, the educational systems were generally neglected and of questionable quality. In short, except as interpreted by rabid racists, the social statistics suggested that southern cities were not much different from their counterparts above the Mason and Dixon line. This did not mean that all the southern cities were ready to compete on a national level. The problems involved resources and attitudes. Money was in short supply. Lingering animosities spawned by the Civil War and Reconstruction continued to divide the sections. The race question was a further barrier to understanding. Despite the fine talk about progress by Grady and other New South spokesmen, the urban South did not appear poised for a great forward movement. An urban ethos was several decades away. It was not enough simply to have the material from which cities are made.

4

Railroads Are
Talismanic Winds

In the first half of the nineteenth century, students of an emerging American empire envisioned the South as part of a smoothly operating national transportation network. A favorite postulate was that unalterable "natural laws of commerce" shaped the character and level of commercial activity. Experts concluded that the United States had two distinct economic systems, each dictated by geography, with the consequence that commerce tended to move along North and South lines. The Allegheny Mountains served as a natural barrier between the two divisions. On the eastern side of the mountains, one system embraced the entire Atlantic coast and adjoining commercial waters. On and beyond the western slope, the second system spanned the Mississippi River Valley. The Mississippi River, which divided the valley into two parts, functioned as what one observer called a "great natural highway." Although the two systems were separate, they could be linked by "tributaries." Externally, coastal shipping would operate between the Atlantic and Gulf ports. Internal links would take the form of roads, canals, or railways. Natural laws of exchange would govern the commercial relations between the two parts. The end result would be a great interdependent commercial emporium.[1]

The planners of this great commercial empire did not anticipate the rise of southern nationalism. Neither King Cotton nor the peculiar institution fitted into the scheme. The American System called for a division of the nation along agricultural and industrial, rather than geographic lines. No one predicted the Northeast's dramatic penetration and dominance of the Midwest though the building of canals, lake shipping, and railroads. The conflicting philosophies and crosscurrents that characterized the nation before the disruption of the Union did not envision the South as being outside the broader contours of the American economic system. True, southern propagandists, in excoriating New York, urged people to "buy southern." "New York with her rotten bankruptcies permeating and injuring almost every solvent community in the Union," were the words used in a routine denunciation in the *New Orleans Crescent* in 1857. "New York, the centre of reckless speculation, unflinching fraud and downright robbery. New York, the prime cause of four-fifths of the insolvencies of the country; New York, carrying on an enormous trade with capital mostly furnished by other communities." All but the most fanatical fire-eaters, however, assumed that southern independence would terminate economic ties. The best most southerners hoped for was relationships on what they considered more equitable grounds. As a governor of Virginia said in 1856, "It is absurd to think of deposing New York from her position. New York is irresistibly made, by the law of the trade winds, by the law of icebergs, by her position, the first seat of commercial trade for the country."[2]

Before the war, southern rivers, east and west of the Allegheny Mountains, served as natural thoroughfares that governed the movement of cotton bales from river to ocean ports. After that, coastal schooners and ocean vessels carried cotton to northern ports or directly overseas. The method also worked in reverse for distributing imported items and northern products throughout Dixie. This system, however, furthered the dependency on the North deplored by many southerners. The imbalances cut across the "natural lines" as defined by the experts. The role of the Mississippi Valley created further and larger problems on a geopolitical level, not the least of which was the struggle for midwestern commercial supremacy. The Erie Canal was never simply a "tributary" line through the mountains serving as a connecting link between systems. Rather, it created an "artificial" east-west link that cut across the Atlantic coastal and Mississippi Valley lines. The Erie Canal was a great trunk that altered commercial patterns beyond the dreams of its original proponents. In some ways, the canal was too successful. It so disturbed emerging business patterns that it promoted sectionalism rather than acting as a unifying element. An alliance of southern forces on both sides of the Alleghenies emerged in direct response to northeastern dominance of the Midwest.

The advent of railroads introduced a new factor into the national transportation scene. In the 1830s and 1840s railroads had supplemented natural lines. Only a few bold projects, such as the Baltimore and Ohio Railroad, had large objectives. Most roads, among them the cotton lines in the southern states, had limited purposes. As railroad technology was perfected in the 1850s, long lines became feasible. Many innovations came together at almost the same time. Telegraphy linked division points. Air brakes made it possible to stop heavy trains. Engineering advances led to more powerful and reliable locomotives. Stronger iron rails did not shatter under continual heavy traffic. A gradual evolution of a policy of aid to railroads by all levels of government served as growing evidence of their importance. In November of 1852 the editor of the *Western Journal and Civilian* provided a thoughtful analysis of the import of railroads. "Railroads are talismanic winds," he told his readers. "They have a charming power. They do wonders, they work miracles. They are better than laws, they are better than schools, they are essentially political and religious. They announce to the world as the Angel announced on the plains of Judea: 'On earth peace, good will toward men.' " He concluded, "The centrifugal force of secession is lost, the centripetal force of union is won."[3] Railroads had little to do with causing the Civil War, but they overwhelmed existing transportation lines and provided the basis for a transcontinental network. Unfortunately for the South, the iron rails that were pushed into the West in the years immediately after the Civil War accrued to the advantage of other parts of the nation. It was small if any consolation to southerners that many of the workers who built the Union Pacific Railroad west out of Omaha, Nebraska, were Confederate veterans.

Southern railroading had gotten off to a promising start in the 1850s.[4] The decade saw the completion of the basic outlines of the American railroad system east of the Mississippi. National mileage increased from 8,500 miles to 30,500 miles. The South shared in this growth; it had roughly 2,000 miles of track at the start of the decade and 9,000 miles at the end. More than one hundred railroad companies, many owned by local interests, operated in the South. The average length of southern lines was 85 miles. Most had cost less to build than lines in the Midwest or Northeast. The use of slave labor, lighter rails, and level coastal terrain held costs to around $28,000 a mile, compared to $37,000 in the Midwest. The southern roads generally had less equipment, however, and it was inferior to that of their northern counterparts. The four largest northern lines in 1860 had as much locomotive and rolling stock as all the southern states put together. Passenger trains in the South were slow. Only a few fast express trains on main lines ran at average speeds of twenty-five miles per hour. Many cities did not allow trains to run through them, causing aggravating gaps and necessitating the location of stations in the outskirts.[5] Only one railroad was more than 300 miles long, meaning that passengers frequently had to change trains. Seven different lines operated between Atlanta and Memphis. It took forty-two hours at best to travel from Charleston to Memphis. A further vexation for travelers was that few of the short lines ran more than one rickety passenger train a day each way over their tracks. The railroads, designed to carry cotton, moved only small amounts of other freight. Until shortly before the Civil War, most roads took in more revenue from passenger than from noncotton commercial business. Freight volume did not rise markedly until open sections were filled in to make long-distance service feasible.

Throughout the 1850s, the thrust of southern railroad construction was to fill in the missing links in the emerging system. Jefferson Davis was a leading southern railroad strategist. One of his objectives, an east-west line through the South's midsection, was achieved with the opening in 1857 of a trunk route from Charleston to Memphis, via several railroads. Davis hoped to persuade Congress to subsidize a Pacific railroad from Memphis to California, but the fires of sectional conflict dashed his plans. By 1861 there were four other main railroad routes that served the southern interior. One ran from just outside Washington—there was no railway bridge over the Potomac River—to Mobile. This cumbersome route, 1,215 miles in length, embraced several roads. It looked better on a map than it functioned. The route zigzagged through such points as Charlottesville, Lynchburg, Bristol, Knoxville, Atlanta, and Montgomery. Theoretically, it was also possible to go indirectly from the Potomac to Cedar Keys, Florida. There were several gaps, and few people ever attempted the trip. A more important railroad thoroughfare ran from Louisville to Atlanta and from there to Charleston. The Mobile and Ohio Railroad, 472 miles in length, was the South's longest line, running from the Gulf of Mexico to the obscure hamlet of Columbus, Kentucky, on the Ohio River. Links between the North and South were unsatisfactory. It took over two hours by steamboat to travel from Columbus to the Illinois Central Railroad's terminal in Cairo, Illinois. No railroad bridge spanned the Ohio River at Louisville until 1870.[6] At the beginning of the Civil War the Baltimore and Ohio Railroad was the only southern railway with direct connections outside the South.[7] The war revealed many imperfections in the southern railroad system, but the railroads of the South were never designed to serve the needs of military forces fighting a basically north-south war. For prewar commercial relations, the southern railroad network worked well and served sectional needs.

During the Civil War many southern railroads went through a cycle of prosperity, inflation, deterioration, and destruction.[8] The free enterprise system continued to operate. The Mobile and Ohio Railroad made large amounts of money carrying freight between the sections before Union soldiers occupied northern Kentucky. The Louisville and Nashville Railroad profited in much the same way and later handled military traffic for both sides. The Baltimore and Ohio Railroad, which tried to stay neutral, moved goods for Confederates one week and Unionists the next, depending on the fortunes of war. A short line, the Wilmington and Weldon Railroad, had a large enough income to declare a 31 percent dividend in 1863. For most roads, higher prices soon ate up most of the profits. From 1861 to 1864 the price of lubricating oil rose from $1 to $50 a gallon and car wheels from $15 to $500. Late in hostilities, the president of the Georgia Railroad complained about his road, "The more business it does, the more money it loses, and the greatest favor that could be conferred upon it—if the public permitted—would be the privilege of quitting business until the end of the war!"[9] The Confederate government turned the South's few railroad machine shops and iron rail manufactories to ordnance production. Equipment wore out and roadbed repair became very difficult. The railroad companies blamed everything from missing seats to broken water coolers upon the war. The government seized and tore up the tracks on some branch lines to obtain badly needed iron. Confederate troops destroyed tracks to prevent their use by Union forces. General William T. Sherman's policy of conducting the war led to the destruction of thousands of miles of track in Georgia, the Carolinas, and Virginia. Sherman boasted at a council of war attended by Abraham Lincoln, "Why my 'bummers' don't do things by halves. Every rail, after having been placed over a hot fire, has been twisted as crooked as a ram's horn, and they can never be used again."[10] In April of 1865 much of the southern railroad network lay in shattered ruins.

Most of the railroads of the South were in southern hands at the close of hostilities, but more than half the section's track had been destroyed.[11] Conservative estimates placed damage as high as $28 million. Some short lines had vanished, and all the lines still in operation were in bad shape. Their roadbeds were rough, burned bridges impeded traffic, and station houses had been destroyed. Passenger tickets cost much more than a few years earlier. All during the 1870s southern roads charged twice as much or more per mile to carry freight than did railroads in many other parts of the country. Officials attributed the high differentials to financial problems and a paucity of traffic. Restoration of the lines was aided by the return of 3,000 miles of track to private owners and the sale on liberal terms of $11 million in equipment by the federal government. Despite pleas, little northern money was put into southern railroads, largely because of fear about financial security in the South. State aid, tinged by the corruption of carpetbag regimes, benefited a few lines. In South Carolina a ring composed of seven state officials plundered the state treasury in the course of railroad machinations. The Georgia legislature gave millions of dollars to corrupt railroad interests. State railroad policies in North Carolina were marked by bribery, blackmail, and stealing.[12] The corruption, most of which had either ended or been brought under control by the early 1870s, was part of general looting by the victors and the moral laxity associated with the Gilded Age. The majority of southern lines rebuilt as best they could without much outside help.

They sold twisted tracks for scrap at about two-thirds the original cost. Much less money was required to put a road back into operation than to build it initially. Within five years after the Civil War all but a few unimportant railroads were back in operation.

The railroads entered the first postwar decade in precarious financial condition. Only 4,000 of the 35,000 miles of railroads built during that decade in the United States were in the South, and more than half of this new construction was in three states. Railroad trackage increased by 700 miles in Kentucky, where the existing railroads had suffered very little from the war. Indeed, the Louisville and Nashville Railroad turned large profits. In Georgia and Alabama, generous and corrupt legislatures liberally financed railroad programs. In other states, building activities aimed at filling in gaps. Mississippi added 120 miles of track, none of which appreciably changed the contours of the existing network.[13] Every state, of course, wanted more mileage. Tennessee's efforts were typical. Lavish subsidies provided by the legislature resulted in little construction. The Volunteer State's credit rating was so poor that it proved difficult to float the necessary bond issues. The aftermath of the Panic of 1873 forced close to half the railroads in the South into either receivership or default. Most of the carpetbaggers lost control of lines they had acquired,[14] which had been weak and in bad financial shape to begin with. Private interests inside the South did not have the means to run railroads on a large scale because they lacked capital. It was an era of railroad consolidation, and northern interests gradually moved in to start the process that would lead to large southern systems patterned after those elsewhere in the nation.

The movement of northern railroad interests into the South added a new and important dimension to the southern economic experience. One of the largest and strongest northern lines, the Pennsylvania Railroad, led the way.[15] After the war it gained a connection from Philadelphia to Washington. In 1871 the Pennsylvania management group organized a holding company, the Southern Railway Security Company, which gained control of the Richmond and Danville Railroad and soon had a direct route from Richmond to Atlanta. Other acquisitions followed until soon Southern Railway Security dominated eleven major and many more minor southern roads. Its holdings cut across the middle of the South from Richmond to Memphis. Then, in 1875, the holding company abruptly folded, a victim of the depression and the unhealthy state of the southern economy. Despite its failures, Southern Railway Security had made some gains. Reorganizations and mergers had created two important railroads. One was the Atlantic Coast Line. The other, started as the powerful Richmond and West Point Terminal Railway and Warehouse Company, ultimately became the Southern Railway System.[16]

Other northern railroad interests also ventured south. Collis P. Huntington headed a group that gained control of the Chesapeake and Ohio Railroad. He extended its tracks from Richmond across the mountains of West Virginia to the Ohio River, discovering great coal deposits along the way. In 1882, the Illinois Central Railroad acquired a New Orleans trunk connection.[17] Even the Louisville and Nashville, the most profitable of southern roads throughout the early postwar era, fell under the domination of northern stockholders,[18] as did the Baltimore and Ohio, the only southern line with major trackage outside the section.[19] By the 1890s northern interests controlled southern railroads. This trend was bitterly resented in the South. Even lines that remained under nominal southern management were poor relatives of northern banking houses. There was little solace in knowing that railroads all across the land suffered the same fate. New South spokesmen played little part in determining what happened to southern lines. The northern railroad barons moved south within the framework of a national policy. Their interest was not in southern restoration, except when to do so would make them more money. It was only incidental if they left the region with better rail service.

By 1880 all the important towns in the South had access to through rail service. Local leaders considered such connections of great import to their urban plans. Portsmouth authorities reported, "The Seaboard and Roanoke railroad, termini Portsmouth, and Weldon, North Carolina, connects the city with lines of railroads offering almost direct communication with the important cities of the south Atlantic seaboard." A proud Richmond official claimed that his city had railroad ties "with the leading places in the whole country." Six railroads ran into Chattanooga. "These lines," a booster said, "give to the city the most ample connections with all points in the country." An Atlanta spokesman commented, "The city has long had much importance as a railroad center."[20] These claims only stated the obvious. Almost every city in the nation—even the mining town of Leadville, Colorado, high and remote in the Rocky Mountains—had railroads. The most minor of lines all led somewhere, usually via obscure junctions and division points to trunk roads. It was virtually impossible for a town to succeed without a railroad. Yet the iron horse did not automatically assure success. It was one thing to have railroads and another to take advantage of them.

The southern cities that benefited most from railroad were Louisville, Baltimore, and Atlanta. The success of Louisville in no small measure grew out of its defeat by Cincinnati for domination of Ohio and Indiana trade. The Louisville and Nashville leaders did not plan to control the economy of much of the middle South. Their first goal was to work out a mutually beneficial connection with Nashville.

During and after the Civil War, the road's directors achieved success by taking advantage of opportunities as they arose.[21] As Henry Watterson wrote in 1880, the Louisville and Nashville made a " 'United Germany' of the Southern railways lying about loose . . . instead of leading to Louisville as they should."[22] Unlike Louisville, Baltimore had a strategy from the earliest days of railroading, although the builders of the Baltimore and Ohio did not expect that it would take forty years to reach primary midwestern markets.[23] Nonetheless, the railroad ultimately gave Baltimore an established intersectional connection and a prosperous western Maryland hinterland. Atlanta was a railroad town from the beginning. The calculations of outside interests, such as Augusta cotton factors, helped make it the railroad center for the Southeast. Thus in promoting Atlanta, Henry Grady rode an obvious tide. Originally, several Atlantic coastal cities had better railroad plans than Atlanta.[24] Savannah, Charleston, and Norfolk, for example, could not succeed without the full cooperation of junction points in the piedmont. Denied that—Norfolk and Richmond's mutual animosity over railroad matters hurt both places—their efforts were unsuccessful and in retrospect appeared flawed. Other places, notably New Orleans and Mobile, formulated promising railroad strategies in the 1850s. The Civil War and the resulting changed economic climate cost both cities the chance to build railroad empires. Despite the building of 15,000 miles of tracks in the South in the 1880s, few if any towns improved their positions through railroad connections. There was no change until the next decade, when railroad building led to the rise of Miami and other Florida towns.

The magnificent harbors of the South were far more visible assets than single railroad tracks leading to shipping platforms in Millstone, Horse Cave, Gulf Crest, and thousands of other points. Baltimore had one of the South's best anchorages. Ships passed through a narrow entrance at the mouth of the Patapasco River that dramatically widened to form a broad estuary. Coastal traffic docked in the inner harbor called the Basin. Deepwater ships dropped anchor at Fell's Point and Canton. These roads were among the most important on the eastern seaboard. Other Chesapeake Bay harbors varied considerably in quality. The Potomac River at Alexandria was a mile wide and had a thirty-foot-deep channel. Although its harbor was adequate for most ocean traffic, the city had few port facilities and was a poor distribution point. Washington, where the Potomac River was deep enough to carry large ships, was never a major port. The depth over the bar at Georgetown was ten feet, and no attempt was ever made to dredge the river or build a harbor at the city. Norfolk and Portsmouth remained Virginia's primary ocean portals. The approaches to some other significant southern harbors varied in quality. Shifting sand at the mouth of the Cape Fear

River impaired entry into Wilmington. Charleston continued to rely on its magnificent harbor, easily reached from the Atlantic Ocean. Savannah had drawbacks because large vessels had to anchor 18 miles away, and smaller ones had to battle heavy tides to reach the city's wharves. Mobile had even more complicated problems. The Mobile River was so shallow opposite the town that all except the smallest of ocean vessels had to stop 25 miles away on Mobile Bay. New Orleans was a special case. At the mouth of the Mississippi River, ships passed a series of jetties intended to keep the channel clear of silt.[25] They then had to negotiate 107 miles of winding water before reaching harbor. Despite their drawbacks, New Orleans and other southern ports had some of the best harbors in North America. Good harbors had been a strength of the South since the early days of settlement.

In 1880 there was great variance in the overseas trade of the principal southern ports. Baltimore and New Orleans handled the most shipping. Baltimore had exports of $76.2 million and imports of $20 million. Exports from New Orleans were valued at $90.2 million and imports at $10.8 million. Other principal ports showed wide disparities between exports and imports: $24 million against $484,000 in Savannah; $19.6 million against $203,000 in Charleston; $14.1 million against $47,100 in Norfolk; $7.2 million against $426,000 in Mobile; and $4 million against $101,000 in Wilmington.[26] Except for Baltimore, all the southern ports exported large quantities of cotton. Naval stores and lumber products remained other export staples. Only Baltimore and New Orleans exported many products from outside the South. In 1880 New Orleans ranked second nationally in exports, and Baltimore followed in third place. Even though New York was way ahead of these ports, with $400.6 million in exports, the showing of the two largest southern cities was impressive. Imports were another matter. By southern measurements the totals for New Orleans and Baltimore were imposing. No other ports received as much as $1 million in imports, although four cities outside the South had more imports than all the southern ports combined. Imports into New York amounted to $543.6 million. The Empire City's gigantic totals were way ahead of those for the other three largest importing cities. Imports into Boston amounted to $68.7 million, into San Francisco $41.3 million, and into Philadelphia $36 million.[27] The southern ports were so far behind that it was hard to see how they could ever challenge northern cities as importing centers. Only an unforseen surge of prosperity would create enough business opportunities to encourage foreign importers to abandon traditional channels and ship goods directly to the South. If that happened, a long-cherished southern dream would be realized.

In the days after the Louisiana Purchase, New Orleans had seemed destined to serve as the commercial emporium for what boosters enthusiastically called the "Great Interior Basin of North America." In 1817 an estimated 1,500 flatboats and 500 barges floated downstream to the Crescent City. Four years later, steam power had markedly changed the traffic's character (the first steamboat descended the Mississippi River in 1812, but it took a decade to develop the boiler power necessary to make ascents against the strong current). In 1821 287 steamboats, 174 barges, and 441 flatboats were recorded as arriving at the levee. Members of American, French, and Creole business combinations looked with pleasure upon an expanding commerce that choked streets and landings. Imports and exports reached $40 million in 1834, rising sharply to $53.6 million the next year. Cotton, sugar, and tobacco planters borrowed money in the city. Consequently, the Panic of 1837 severely affected the banks of New Orleans. At one point, $72 million in uncollectible mortages caused a temporary suspension of specie payments.[28] Although the situation discouraged promoters, it was far from fatal. Every other aspiring city underwent an economic illness, and the great river continued to run to the sea.

Unfortunately for the aspirations of New Orleans, the river trade failed to develop as fast as expected. Even though it was profitable, it was somewhat sluggish—it did not generate enough money to make New Orleans the number one city on the continent. In the last half of the 1840s annual receipts for all grain products numbered in hundreds of thousands of barrels and sacks. The peak years came during the Mexican War, when New Orleans served as a major logistics center. But with the coming of peace, arrivals seldom approached prewar levels. Sharp ups and downs continued to plague trade along the route. More disturbing was that a large share of the grain brought down the Mississippi was transshipped to the Northeast—the very section with which New Orleans competed for the commerce of the emerging Midwest. The export trade was too small to sustain a rapid expansion There was little domestic market in Louisiana and Mississippi because of the plantation economy and lagging urbanization. Shippers and outside receivers could be counted upon to take advantage of any shorter or cheaper connections.[29]

Given the massive additional acreage annually placed under cultivation in newly opened regions of the Midwest in such states as Wisconsin, Illinois, and Iowa, the Mississippi River statistics made grim and depressing reading. Although shipments of pork and lard augmented profits in the downriver trade, and steamboats carried large quantities of goods upriver, computations showed that midwestern shippers were not using the Mississippi River to the extent expected. From the mid-1840s onward, more grain flowed northeast through the Great Lakes and the Erie Canal than to New Orleans.[30] Some southerners failed to understand what was happening. Until the

Civil War they predicted an alliance between the Midwest and the South based upon economic necessity. As late as February of 1861, Virginia economist William M. Burwell, discoursing on the "commercial magnetism" designed to bind American localities in the Mississippi Valley with European "Market Cities," continued to promote outmoded theories. "We anticipate," he wrote, "a series of trade zones— so to speak—which shall lie parallel with each other, along, and within which, the commerce between reciprocal interests will be conducted. . . . Upon this theory, Chicago, Cincinnati, Louisville, Memphis, and New Orleans, would become principal depots for the collection and exportation of the trade along the Ohio and Mississippi valley, as well as for the importation and distribution of merchandise."[31]

The New Orleans route always had enough drawbacks to make it surprising that the myth that the route would make the city great prevailed for as long as it did. It cost six times as much to operate a steamboat on the Mississippi than on the northern lakes, and the accident rate was much higher. The Mississippi River system closed in the winter. Certain tributary streams opened for traffic only during short periods of high water in the spring. Frequent shifts in the channel and variations in river stages impaired navigation. So did sandbars in South Pass at the gateway to the Gulf of Mexico. The South Pass problem became more serious as vessels increased in size. Money appropriated by Congress in the 1830s hardly paid for the initial survey work. Near the mouth of the Mississippi, Northeast Pass never provided more than a twelve-foot channel. When silt closed it in 1851, a shift to Southeast Pass caused serious navigation problems. In a short time in 1852 forty ships ran aground on bars and mud lumps for periods ranging from two days to eight weeks. Cargo either had to be transshipped or thrown overboard. As if these problems were not enough, humid southern temperatures caused extensive damage to grain in general and corn in particular.[32] Lack of adequate storage facilities, a serious concern from the first, became especially pronounced by the 1850s because of increased production of cotton, sugar, and tobacco in the South Central states. In fiscal 1851-52 those commodities accounted for roughly 80 percent of the value of all domestic commerce reaching New Orleans. These regionally grown products were much more immediately important than the upper river trade and competed with it for storage space.[33]

Throughout the antebellum period, New Orleans had virtually no port facilities. The levee, where most ships docked, was a long, narrow dike, which the city tried to improve by building a series of wharves set on huge wooden piles. As long as the flow of commerce brought profits, calls for better facilities never went beyond the talking stage. Vessels, sometimes as many as six deep, moored with their bows facing the current. Portable bridge works and wooden stagings connected the ships with the shore. There were no cranes, so longshoremen had to unload each boat by hand. The levee and wharves had no roofs. Tarpaulins were the primary means of protecting shipments from the elements. The lack of a belt line railroad caused unnecessarily high drayage expenses. On top of all these problems, the port authorities took a casual attitude toward their work. They were content to collect duties and fees and to see goods and produce move across the levee.[34]

The means of distributing goods from New Orleans compared unfavorably with those of the larger northeastern ports, making it a poor importing center and causing shipping rates on outbound items to be comparatively high. Nor could New Orleans compete for overseas trade with South Atlantic ports. Detailed computations in 1858 showed that a seven-hundred-ton vessel sailing between Charleston and Liverpool could expect a profit of $2,054.01. The profit for the same ship sailing between New Orleans and Liverpool would have only $552.90.[35] More serious for New Orleans' future as a port was that the construction of several midwestern feeder canals helped the Erie Canal and the perfection of the railroad threatened to deal a death blow to all natural lines of communication.[36]

The impact of the railroads was crucial in hurting New Orleans. In 1853 a perceptive federal bureaucrat, Israel Andrews, in a lengthy report on North American trade prepared for the United States Senate, stressed the extent to which railroads had diverted New Orleans' Mississippi Valley trade to eastern ports. According to Andrews, *"natural* channels" were "insufficiently matched against those of an *artificial* character." He concluded that New Orleans officials had ignored this reality, avoiding action "till the danger to be averted became imminent." He attributed the city's problems to more than blind faith in the false security afforded by fifty thousand miles of inland navigation, noting that three municipalities with separate political jurisdictions inside the city had accumulated heavy debts before their consolidation. Consequently, Andrews decided that it took an obvious threat to convince Louisianians that large internal improvement projects such as railroads could not be "executed by private enterprise."[37]

The leaders of New Orleans did not need a federal report to inform them about the economic facts of life. They had only to read the financial compendiums in their commercial publications, *DeBow's Review* and the *Price Current*. Better yet, they could check the commodity price indexes and their own bills of lading.[38] In 1853 and for the remainder of the antebellum period American manufacturing products generally cost more in Louisiana than in other parts of the country. The main reason was use of the river route rather than price levels. The quantities of products shipped to the city on the river from the upper

Mississippi Valley remained more or less constant. But regional trade grew rapidly as new land opened in western Louisiana and eastern Texas, resulting in an increased demand for northeastern goods. Such considerations had an obvious impact on New Orleans, causing a reexamination of the city's goals.[39] The river no longer lulled the city's leaders into a sense of self-confidence. They desperately wanted railroads, although not to corner the flow of grain from the Midwest. They reconciled themselves to the realization that the bulk of the upper river trade was permanently lost, despite southern propaganda to the contrary. As a result, New Orleans interests began to think regionally rather than nationally. They concentrated on projects designed to help secure their immediate hinterlands and on obtaining connecting lines to the Pacific Coast via either Texas or the Republic of Mexico.

Although this policy seemed to mark a sudden departure from past practices, it had evolved gradually. Even in the great days of the river trade, in the 1830s, several promoters had advocated the construction of a railroad to Nashville.[40] A combination of inexperienced management, insufficient money, and inflated faith in the river by planter-aristocrats doomed the railroad. New Orleans' railroad activities languished throughout most of the 1840s, although a few short lines were constructed, but revived in the early 1850s when a railroad convention sparked renewed interest.

Three men were prominently associated with the new movement. J.D.B. DeBow helped shape a railroad program. He used statistics to contrast New Orleans' development with that of other large cities. Politician, lawyer, and plantation owner Judah P. Benjamin lent his prestige to railroad projects, incorporating them into a broader vision of southern greatness. James Robb, a controversial figure whom critics claimed engaged in unsavory business practices, called for northern connections, handled many of the practical aspects of New Orleans' railroad building, and stressed the need for a diversified economy. "We should look to something more than sugar and cotton planting," he wrote in a prorailroad pamphlet. "We should invite and foster every species of industry that tends to make a commonwealth permanently great and prosperous."[41]

The New Orleans railroad builders of the 1850s adhered to a rational strategy, but problems of geography and money precluded success. It was very difficult to lay tracks through swamps, marshes, and bayous. Great amounts of the city's private capital continued to flow into plantation properties.[42] Changes in Louisiana law, pushed by DeBow, Benjamin, and Robb, which made it easier for the state and local units of government to aid railroads, helped some but not enough. Outside funds were unavailable in the amounts needed, because foreign investors and northeastern financiers poured their surplus assets into the Chicago roads. Federal land grants, a crucial element in helping New Orleans interests, ran through uninviting territory. A mile of swampland in Louisiana was far different from a mile of prarie in Illinois; comparative figures meant nothing, for here the general rule that it cost less to build railroads in the South than the North did not hold. Slightly over $16 million went into antebellum Louisiana railroad enterprises, a very large sum for the day and more money than was spent in the pre–Civil War period in any state west of the Appalachians except Illinois. The New Orleans leaders deserved credit for having raised the money through various public and private means. But incredibly high construction costs, such as for the twenty-six miles in Louisiana between Paceland and Tigerville, used it up in short order.

During the 1850s New Orleans railroad promoters struggled to overcome obvious vicissitudes, complicated by the 1853 yellow fever epidemic in which more than ten thousand people died. Newspaper reporters wrote that the unburied dead were "piled on the ground, swollen and bursting their coffins, and enveloped in swarms of flies." Several bad epidemic years followed, accentuating the city's health difficulties and discouraging outside investors. The hopes of DeBow and Benjamin for a great transcontinental system were not to be realized.[43] A grandiosely conceived road, the Southern Pacific Railroad—not to be confused with the later railroad of the same name—went bankrupt after the building of approximately two miles of track. Controlled by New Yorkers, it was underfinanced and never had any hope of success. Another project, in which Judah Benjamin was involved, called for a railroad in Mexico across the Isthmus of Techuantepec. This scheme was tied in with plans for a combined sea and land link between New Orleans and the West Coast, but it never proceeded past the initial surveying. Dissension within the company, unstable political conditions in Mexico, opposition from a rural Louisiana firm controlled by New York interests, and covert opposition from Cornelius Vanderbilt, who owned a railroad across Nicaragua, all combined to doom the plan. It became nothing more than empty resolutions passed by the New Orleans city council.

Two other railroads were to secure hinterlands. Robb's 206-mile-long New Orleans, Jackson and Great Northern Railway ran to Canton, Mississippi. There it joined other lines, consolidated the Black Belt cotton trade, and helped open up new fields for cultivation. Of the two, it was the more successful.[44] DeBow had championed the other, the New Orleans, Opelousas and Great Northern Railway. Projected to terminate in the Red River Valley of Texas, it fell short of its goal because of high construction costs. The road, extending eighty miles from the New Orleans suburb of Algiers to Brashear on Berwick Bay, where it made connections with the Morgan Line of steamers, passed through snake- and alligator-infested swamps and bayous. It brought little additional trade to New Orleans, and places in the sugar regions along the main track, such as Des Allemands, Lafourche, and Chacahoula, remained miserable backwaters.[45]

Because the New Orleans' railroad program worked out imperfectly, critics depicted the organizers as a "bungling generation" of promoters and dwelt on the ethnic factionalization within the business community. On a broader level the New Orleans leaders seemed to prove a favored myth—that southerns by temperament and training did poorly in the crass world of business. The field was supposedly better suited to a northerner such as Robb, who did not worry about behaving like a gentleman. But although mistakes abounded and goals overreached realities, the men involved made their decisions within an objective framework that recognized the declining importance of the Mississippi River. On the basis of hard economic statistical evidence they scaled down their hopes and aspirations. They realized that regardless of what New Orleans accomplished in improving its transportation net, the bulk of the mounting Midwest trade was not going to flow in a southerly direction, either by rail or water. Goods and produce would move through the portals at Pittsburgh, Buffalo, and Oswego on the way to the northeastern seaboard.

The continual increase in the amount of grain shipped eastward from the Great Lakes cities was destined to grow into such a torrent that it would result in a fundamental shift in the relationship of the Midwest with the other sections.[46] It started in a small way. The first shipment—a mere thirty-eight bags of wheat in 1837—went to Grand Haven, Michigan, but much of the trade fell to the emerging city of Chicago. Implicit in the railroad strategy of the Windy City's leaders was the assumption that natural lines had had their day because railroads could operate successfully over long distances. Their counterparts in New Orleans, who reached a similar conclusion at about the same time, did not have the geographical luxury of flat praries on which to lay track. After an early Chicago line, the Galena and Chicago Union Railroad, garnered an impressive amount of upper Mississippi River trade, the Chicagoans never had trouble, as they had earlier, obtaining northeastern capital to build extensive systems. In the 1850s several new railroads helped the rapidly growing city obtain grain that otherwise would have gone to the river cities of St. Louis and Cincinnati and from those points down to New Orleans. In the last full year of peace before the Civil War, Chicago elevators moved more than 30 million bushels of grain and flour. Chicago handled six times more grain and flour than St. Louis and eleven times more than Cincinnati.

The failure of the two river towns to compete with Chicago for the grain and flour trade doomed New Orleans' chances of winning the Midwest. As Crescent City businessmen recognized, they had no way of charting their own course on the Mississippi. They were dependent on what happened upriver, and in fulfilling their hopes, what happened was not good. Errors, complacency, and miscalculations spelled disaster for Cincinnati and St. Louis.[47] Cincinnati leaders, who had the first opportunity to control the Midwest, concentrated on the Ohio River trade. They failed to realize the extent to which the Erie Canal would shift the course of western migration from the river to the Great Lakes, and in the end, the Queen City won only a portion of the Ohio River Valley trade. First overconfidence and then a recognition that it had no way of countering Chicago's railroad strategy ended the hopes of St. Louis. To add insult to injury, the two cities did so badly that Milwaukee became a grain flow center of greater importance than New Orleans.[48] Milwaukee had to build a harbor from virtually nothing, and it had far fewer railroad connections than Chicago. Receipts at the eastern Great Lakes ports indicated the scope of the massive shift in the direction of midwestern trade. Grain and flour shipped east in 1860 topped 17.3 million bushels at Oswego and 37.1 million bushels at Buffalo, in stark contrast to less than 3 million bushels at New Orleans.[49]

At the close of the Civil War, numerous experts predicted that the Mississippi River would regain its former importance.[50] Using dubious logic, they assumed that there would be a new relationship between foreign and domestic markets. Because cotton prices in the immediate postwar era were more than 200 percent above those of antebellum times, they foresaw a tremendous increase in cotton production throughout the lower South, which would convert the section to a one-crop economy. Massive grain shipments would have to go down to New Orleans simply to fulfill southern regional needs. There was a great fallacy in this assumption. The high prices were a direct result of the Lancashire cotton famine in the United Kingdom caused by artificial wartime conditions. Only a tremendous expansion of the textile industry, coupled with a sudden drying up of recently opened sources of supply in India and Egypt, would have brought about permanently high prices. Curiously, what should have been seen immediately as sophistry caused renewed optimism in the river cities and some anxious moments in Chicago.

The Midwest trade of New Orleans did rise above pre–Civil War levels. Receipts for 1872 totaled more than 20 million bushels of flour and grain, but in the same twelve months more than 178 million bushels moved east by rail and boat.[51] By then the fight for the trade had entered another phase, with trunk railroads between the Midwest and Northeast competing against lake shipping. Even though it was carrying more freight than ever before, the Mississippi River had declined in relative importance as a trade route. The prospect of massive new southern markets proved an empty hope; they never materialized. New Orleans fell further and further behind in the national grain trade.

At the same time, Baltimore reclaimed a role as a major grain-shipping center that it had not held since colonial times. As one southern town lost out, another advanced. This was unusual because in antebellum times intersectional losses by one southern city had hardly ever been countered by compensating gains by a rival town. When Louisville lost out in competition for Ohio and Indiana trade, no other Kentucky city moved in to take its place. Neither Wilmington nor Savannah had been able to reclaim for the South markets taken away from Charleston by New York. After Memphis failed to obtain the eastern terminus of a transcontinental railroad, the possibility of a federally subsidized line to the Pacific from a southern point ended. A harsh reality of the southern urbanization process was the inability of city builders to operate within a wider framework. A logically built system that adequately served the needs of a plantation economy did not have the strength to respond to outside challenges. The result throughout antebellum times was greater and greater outside domination. Baltimore's efforts to compete directly with New York for western trade connections had fared badly initially, but the city gained through railroad connections into the heart of the Midwest at precisely the time when a great change was going on in the nature of the grain-transporting business. As a consequence, Baltimore was in a position to take advantage of and further the economic predicament of New Orleans. Again, the oft-repeated charges that Baltimore had embraced Yankee values and was no longer a true southern metropolis were heard.

The Baltimore and Ohio's entry into Chicago in 1874 came at just the right time. Grain production throughout the Midwest was on the rise. The consolidation of short lines into great rail systems facilitated the establishment of fast through freight service between Chicago and the eastern seaboard. The erection at Chicago of gigantic elevators for railroad use following the fire of 1871 encouraged eastern lines to enter the grain-shipping business. For the first time, the eastern railroads with Chicago connections could compete favorably with Great Lakes grain shippers. By 1872 over 67 percent of all grain and flour that moved east went by train. The railroads carried 99 percent of all flour, 58 percent of all corn, and 41 percent of all wheat. Most of the grain and flour moved through Chicago. Freight differentials made it cheaper to ship flour by rail through Chicago than to send it east by the Great Lakes route or directly from another midwestern railroad junction. In addition, the midwestern railroad network was built in such a way that numerous regional lines terminated in Chicago. The Windy City was the hub in the center of a great wheel.

Railroad rate practices, especially that of charging by the mile, benefited Baltimore. By rail from Chicago it was 912 miles to New York, 822 miles to Philadelphia, and 802 miles to Baltimore. Baltimore thus had an advantage of 110 miles over New York and 20 miles over Philadelphia. This advantage was significant because the lines used a system of freight differentials. The lack of federal rate regulations was a burning question. State attempts to fix rates through the Granger Laws became bogged down in the courts. Monopolistic arrangements such as this ultimately led to the establishment of the Interstate Commerce Commission in 1887. The railroads claimed that they engaged in self-regulation through an equitable system of freight differentials. Theoretically, the freight differentials were intended to counterbalance disadvantages and equalize conditions. In actuality, the railroads determined the differential in relation to the amount of traffic that natural and artificial advantages awarded each terminal. The capacity of elevators, for example, affected the rate structure.

The differentials for carrying grain and flour from Chicago to New York, Philadelphia, and Baltimore grew out of the settlement of railroad rate wars. The owners or their representatives met privately and made deals. At first, the differentials covered short time periods. There were frequent violations and withdrawals until an agreement was negotiated in the spring of 1877. The rates favored Baltimore, awarding the city between 20 and 25 percent of the grain and flour trade. Between 1873 and 1880 wheat receipts alone rose from 2.8 to 35.4 million bushels. During the same period, New York's share of the flour, wheat, and corn trade dropped from 61 to 52 percent. Much of this loss was a direct result of the diversion of Chicago shipments to Baltimore. In 1880 the mighty New York Central Railroad and other Empire City lines rejected the 1877 accord. There was no noticeable impact on the market, so the New York railroad interests accepted Baltimore's dominance.[52] Baltimore's economic victory over New York demonstrated that when given the means, southern gentlemen could compete on an equal basis with northern capitalists. The problem was that such competition was seldom possible.

No other southern city was in a position to duplicate Baltimore's success. The rebuilding of transportation links restored the commercial relationships that had existed before the war. For many places the movement of cotton remained the primary activity. Again, the interior communities became staging areas. Cotton from Macon went through Augusta and on to Charleston. Bales assembled at Montgomery passed through Mobile. More than ever, Atlanta acted as a junction for cotton shipped north through Louisville to New England mills. Memphis remained a great gathering area. The thousands of bales that piled up in the streets during the fall and winter shipping seasons eventually went down the river to New Orleans. The Crescent City remained the world's greatest cotton port.

When journalist Edward King visited New Orleans in 1873 he learned what cotton exporting meant in human terms. Noting the size of cotton receipts, he wrote, "Knowing these statistics, one can hardly wonder at the vast masses of bales on the levée at the landings of the steamers, nor at the numbers of the boats which daily arrive, their sides piled high with cotton. About these boats, closely ranged in long rows by the levée, and seeming like river monsters which have crawled from the ooze to make a little sun, the negroes swarm in crowds, chatting in the broken, colored English characteristic of the river-hand. They are clad in garments which hang in rags from their tawny and coal black limbs. Their huge, naked chests rival in perfection of form the works of Praxiteles and his fellows. Their arms are almost constantly bent on the task of removing cotton bales, and carrying boxes, barrels, bundles of every conceivable shape and size; but whenever there is a lull in the work they sink down on the cotton bales, clinging to them like lizards to a sunny wall, and croon to themselves, or crack rough and good-natured jokes with one another."[53] Many outsiders continued to think of the South as a land of black labor gangs and cotton. Unfortunately, the image was all too true. The New South seemed incapable of escaping from a King Cotton economy.

A basic tenet of the New South creed called for diversified agriculture. Its spokesmen denounced what Richard Edmonds called "the all-cotton curse."[54] Henry Grady wrote about the wonders of coming agricultural change in the South. He discussed Tennessee berries, Georgia peaches, Mississippi cream, and South Carolina vegetables. Believing that urbanization was the key to a new agrarian order, he claimed, "With increase in urban population—with shops and factories and artisans—with great systems of railroads and consequent reduction of time and freights—with canning factories and evaporators—came farm husbandry in its true sense to the South."[55] But although farmers grew vegetables in South Carolina and workers canned peaches in Georgia, there were not enough of such activities to change the face of southern agriculture.

The section remained weighted down by an increasingly backward system based on cotton. Of course, this problem had been recognized for a long time. As early as 1852 DeBow had written, "No mind can look back upon the history of this region for the last twenty years, and not feel convinced that the labor bestowed in cotton growing during that period has been a total loss to this part of the country."[56] There seemed no way out of the trap as long as cotton remained an easily cultivated cash crop with a marketing system tailored to suit its needs. Some of the same frustrating conditions prevailed with tobacco and rice, the South's other two staple crops. They were regional crops mostly grown on or near the coast and moved to market within the confines of a broader system created to handle cotton.

In the post–Civil War era southern agriculture was controlled by sharecrop land barons and crop-lien country store merchants. Frequently, these people were members of the former slaveowning aristocracy. The big land barons sometimes had as many as two to three hundred sharecroppers. Some merchants charged interest as high as 300 percent on stock items. Lien agreements stipulated that farmers had to grow primarily cotton. "For years a class of merchants encouraged their credit customers to raise cotton exclusively, or very largely," critic Charles Otken wrote in 1894. "They reasoned very naturally and very logically, that, the more goods sold to farmers, the greater their sales and the greater their aggregate profits . . . . The debts of the farmer bound him to cotton. He was powerless."[57] The land barons and merchants needed ready cash to pay their annual debts. They had credit lines in rural banks. The corresponding banks for those institutions were in the southern cities. Few of these financial houses had the resources to fund vast undertakings. In turn, they dealt through northern banks, many of which were in New York, the only place in the country with gigantic amounts of surplus capital. Just as in antebellum times, New York financiers continued to make major decisions that affected the South's agricultural economy.

There was no New South in agriculture. The southern interior cities, upon which so much depended in building an urban civilization, were little commercial capitals located in the middle of depressed areas. Southern urban leaders could only look with envy on midwestern cities surrounded by wealthy farming regions. The cotton economy did not generate enough money to promote rapid urban progress. In the Old South, some economists had unsuccessfully called for the joint marketing of cotton through "planters' union depots."[58] Agrarian reformers in the New South placed hope in cooperative marketing arrangements. In Populist times, and without much success, the Southern Alliance tried cooperative marketing. Only part of the failure stemmed from business opposition. Cotton was what economists called a renewable resource. The new sources of supply in Egypt and India made it impossible for American producers to influence prices. Attempts to break the sharecropping and crop-lien systems failed. Medium-sized southern cities that wanted to advance had to look for alternatives to reliance on farmers trapped in the morass of debt peonage. Under the circumstances, it was not surprising that

Table 4.1. Manufacturing in Sixteen Southern Cities, 1880

City	National Rank in Population	National Rank in Value of Products	Number of Establishments	Capital Invested	Average Hands	Wages Paid	Value of Materials	Value of Products
Alabama								
Mobile	68	97	91	$ 525,708	704	$ 261,643	$ 830,961	$ 1,335,579
District of Columbia								
Washington	14	44	971	5,552,526	7,146	3,924,612	5,365,400	11,882,316
Georgia								
Atlanta	49	79	196	2,468,456	3,680	889,282	3,159,267	4,861,727
Augusta	86	92	60	2,069,275	1,680	448,825	2,247,665	3,139,020
Savannah	62	90	120	1,102,970	1,130	447,640	2,457,606	3,396,297
Kentucky								
Covington	65	71	181	3,182,141	2,925	1,033,463	3,935,727	5,864,530
Louisville	16	17	1,108	21,767,013	17,448	5,835,545	21,207,110	35,423,203
Newport	98	88	94	1,700,745	1,748	711,019	2,526,936	3,996,995
Louisiana								
New Orleans	10	33	915	8,565,303	9,504	3,717,557	10,771,892	18,808,096
Maryland								
Baltimore	7	8	3,683	38,586,773	56,338	15,117,489	47,974,297	78,417,304
South Carolina								
Charleston	36	93	194	1,718,300	2,146	639,030	1,468,375	2,732,590
Tennessee								
Memphis	54	82	138	2,313,975	2,268	845,672	2,419,341	4,413,422
Nashville	40	57	268	3,892,380	4,791	1,312,765	5,312,527	8,597,278
Virginia								
Norfolk	83	96	105	570,276	752	317,528	861,026	1,455,987
Petersburg	89	80	115	1,755,415	4,196	602,749	3,290,116	4,643,015
Richmond	25	31	598	6,884,386	14,047	3,006,456	12,141,512	20,790,106

many places tried to embrace manufacturing as a panacea. But to do so was easier said than done.

The great currents of industrialism that transformed the United States missed the South. Sometime between 1850 and 1880 the American economy "took off"—a term used to describe the time at which a nation reaches the point of rapid industrial growth. The Civil War may or may not have speeded the process in the United States. The economy was flat at best throughout the 1870s. Nevertheless, between 1850 and 1880 the gross value of products advanced from $1 billion to $5.4 billion, a gain of 427 percent. Industrial capitalization increased by 423 percent from $533 million in 1850, to $1 billion in 1860, $2.1 billion in 1870, and $2.8 billion in 1880. The South's contribution to this tremendous advance was relatively slight. In 1860, Mobile, the largest city in Alabama, had factories valued at $1 million that employed 764 persons.[59] During the Civil War decade, with the ravages of military operations and a slow recovery, five states experienced declines in industrial capitalization. In 1880 there were thirty-eight states in the Union. Only three states in the entire South were among the top twenty in manufacturing rank. Maryland was fourteenth, Kentucky seventeenth, and Virginia twentieth.

With industry concentrated in a few northeastern and midwestern states, the southern states were comparatively very far behind in manufacturing. Rapid industrialization was possible. Indeed, in the 1880s new iron furnaces built Birmingham, Alabama, into an imposing industrial city. Near the end of the decade, Grady wrote, "The industrial growth of the South in the past ten years has been without precedent or parallel. . . . In 1889 the Birmingham district alone will produce more iron than the entire South produced in 1887."[60] Unfortunately, it would have taken a whole series of Birminghams to build an industrial empire in the South. The manufacturing base remained weak. Little outside capital was forthcoming. The South had neither the industrial know-how nor access to the capital needed to compete with the industrial parts of the United States.

In 1880 the backbone of manufacturing in the South lay in the sixteen cities that ranked among the hundred largest in the United States. Table 4.1 shows the state of manufacturing in the southern centers.[61] The only places in the top twenty in value of products were Baltimore and Louisville. New Orleans, Washington, and Richmond were the only other cities in the section that ranked forty-fourth or higher. The total value of products for the sixteen cities amounted to around $200 million. Over half were in Baltimore ($78.4 million) and Louisville ($35.4 million). By comparison, the value of products for the three largest American industrial centers exceeded $1 billion. The value of products for New York was $473 million, for Philadelphia $324 million, and for Chicago $249 million. Southern industry had a long way to go to reach those production outputs. Of considerable significance were the capitalization figures. Of the $130 million invested in southern manufacturing, $100 million was in the sixteen largest cities. The only southern cities with an industrial capitalization of more than $9 million were Baltimore and Louisville. The figures for the former were $38.6 million and for the latter $21.8 million. New Orleans had 915 manufacturing establishments valued at $8.6 million. The 598 plants in Richmond were capitalized at $6.9 million. Statistics for other towns indicated a pattern of many small and undercapitalized firms. For instance, Atlanta had 196 factories capitalized at $2.5 million and Petersburg 115 establishments with an estimated worth of $1.8 million. Although most cities had registered advances since the Civil War, Mobile had regressed. It had fewer workers and half the industrial capital in 1880 than twenty years earlier. Without a dramatic broadening of the South's industrial capitalization, there seemed no way that the section could ever gain parity on a national level.

In 1880 southern urban manufacturing mirrored the traditions and needs of the section.[62] Agribusiness was the major pursuit. In Baltimore more than $8 million was invested in flour milling, fertilizer processing, tobacco manufacturing, and meat packing. Capitalization figures for Louisville showed $1.6 million in liquor distilling, $2.1 million in meat packing, and $460,000 in tobacco production. The refining of cottonseeds, rice, and sugar was important in New Orleans. The capitalization of seventeen establishments totaled $1.5 million. Richmond had five flour mills valued at $1.2 million. Petersburg's fourteen tobacco plants represented capital investments of $1.7 million. Covington had $580,000 in tobacco manufactories. The capital in Augusta's six cotton mills amounted to $1.4 million. The South's primary lack was heavy industry. The only large shipyards were in Baltimore. The only concentrations of machine shops and foundries, basic to the operation of an industrial economy, were in New Orleans, Richmond, Baltimore, and Louisville. The net capitalization of the machine shops and foundries in those cities was $6 million. Six steel mills in Covington and Newport had a capitalization of $1.4 million. The only other large iron and steel mills were ten in Baltimore capitalized at $1.6 million. The cities of Atlanta, Charleston, Memphis, Mobile, Norfolk, and Savannah had no specified industries with a capitalization or value of products over $1 million. Factories in all sixteen major cities combined employed an annual average of fewer than 150,000 workers. Obviously, opportunities existed for an expansion of manufacturing in the South. The question was not simply whether industry was desirable but where the money would come from to create it.[63]

A popular theme in the aftermath of the Civil War was that northern capitalists dominated southern manufacturing. Acquiescent native whites acted as managers and received a free hand on the race issue. Though true in part, this thesis ignored the South's failure to offer investors many real opportunities during Reconstruction. The hostile attitude toward carpetbaggers was only one of the reasons. Ambitious northern capitalists went where the action was—to Chicago and San Francisco rather than Nashville or Atlanta—although some northern speculators put money into southern transportation and industry. A number of schemes prospered, others failed. But a prostrate South was not flooded with outside money. Large-scale projects, such as the development of Birmingham or the formation of Southern Railway Security, were few in number. The reality was that the region's future rested more in modest offices in Memphis and Mobile than in paneled board rooms in the North. By the end of Reconstruction the South's economy remained in virtual isolation. A way still had to be found to integrate the urban South into the emerging national economy.

5

Joy Brightens Her Face

In 1887 M. B. Hillyard wrote a promotional book intended to impress potential northern investors with the opportunities available in the South. Through the selective use of economic and statistical data, he delineated what he considered the region's distinctive and salient characteristics. Central to his analysis was the contention that the New South philosophy had gained such widespread acceptance that it had fundamentally changed the way white southerners thought about themselves and their section. "To the writer, no aspect of Southern progress is so marked and cheering as the hopeful, erect, self-assertive industrial spirit of the South," he explained. "No longer is she supine, inert, self-mistrustful, with head bowed down. Hope elevates and joy brightens her face, and on her brow sits courage plumed."[1] He contended that a new wave of energy had swept over Dixie. Old cities such as New Orleans and new ones like Anniston would take the lead in providing unparalleled chances for wealth and progress.

Urban conditions in the post-Reconstruction South were a source of pride to advocates of city building. A spirit of optimism prevailed, buoyed by developments deplored by critics in and outside the South. Supporters of the New South movement, however, saw nothing wrong with either northern entrepreneurial values or traditional southern concepts of racial relations. Most urban whites were pleased that the old dominant groups were firmly in control. Far from being "new men"—either carpetbaggers who remained behind or scalawags who made quick fortunes—they were representative of the same commercial interests responsible for building cities in antebellum times. During the 1870s the civic leaders had added to their local prestige by directly supporting or acquiescing in the persecution and intimidation of black voters. White supremacists controlled all the elected municipal governments. Operating under stringent fiscal restraints, officials in many places had made considerable efforts to improve the already pleasing urban environment through beautification schemes. A variety of architectural styles, notably Greek and Georgian forms, further enhanced the quality of the landscape. A significant number of theaters and lecture halls attested to the South's cultural traditions. Although a great deal remained to be done, the cities seemingly had the potential of emerging as showcases for a new southern way of life. With some reason, boosters claimed that towns constituted Dixie's best hope for the future.

The plantation leadership of the Old South never recovered from the ravages of Civil War and Reconstruction. In the aftermath of defeat, southern agrarians attempted to salvage what they could from the Confederate debacle, fighting particularly against social change and racial equality. They tried to reimpose slavery in effect through the Black Codes. They attacked "bayonet rule" and damned "Black Reconstruction." They denounced carpetbaggers and scalawags, supported the Ku Klux Klan and the Knights of the White Camellia, and embraced the Lost Cause. At this point the agrarians who looked backward to the Old South parted company with their urban New South contemporaries.

The plantation interests were a negative and anachronistic force. Their support of Bourbon rule was a reactionary cry. It was probably only natural that they related the writings of Sir Walter Scott about the plight of Scotland conquered by England to their own situation and thus spawned a southern literary school patterned after eighteenth-century European romanticism. This important strain of intellectual thought was a reaction to the perceived trend toward an increasingly materialistic and technological civilization. The movement asserted the validity of subjectivism as an intellectual means of reemphasizing classical values. The southern version romanticized a classical civilization that had fallen victim to a brutal military machine. The idealized South that never existed was one of contented "darkies" playing banjos and singing spirituals, of stately plantations along the banks of the Copper and Chattahoochee rivers, of gentlemen and beautiful women with aristocratic bloodlines, of enlightened statesmen practicing Greek democracy, of duels, of horse races, and of lavish hospitality. Every lamp shattered by a Yankee bullet, every wall demolished by a Yankee cannonball, and every building blackened by Yankee flames epitomized the anguish of defeat. According to the myth, an ideal world had been destroyed by cruel barbarians who looted for pleasure, wrecked for fun, and killed for lust. The cult of chivalry, the legend of Pickett's charge, and the burning of Atlanta provided other symbols for southern romanticism.[2]

Unfortunately, a body of thought that dwelled on the virtues of a civilization that never existed had little relationship to the South of the Gilded Age. The defenders of the "old order" had retreated into the past, underscoring the calamity that befell southern agrarianism. By necessity, leadership had to come from other directions, and the vacuum created an opportunity for urban interests. But did the leaders of the New South crusade want to change the direction of the South, to use cities as a means of making the region more like the rest of the nation? After all, the centers of romanticism in the South were in Charleston, New Orleans, and Norfolk. Actually, the goals of the New South were compatible with those of the Old South. A general program had been spelled out at a series of prewar commercial conventions.

Commercial conventions held between 1837 and 1859 attempted to establish economic policies for Dixie. The widely promoted meetings attracted as many as a thousand delegates, including John C. Calhoun. The conventions first recognized problems, then established goals, and finally expressed a general sense of frustration with the course of national events. Calhoun hoped that the conventions would transcend parochial political prejudices, but unfortunately, even he was unable to create unity from the spirited rivalries among cities in the South. All the conventions stressed the need for a great commercial city that could compete with New York.[3] The reasons why such a center could not be built went deeper than nationalistic theory; southern urban leaders were reluctant to sacrifice their own ambition for sectional nationalism.

In the postwar period Robert E. Lee tried to convince southerners that they should take the lead in furthering a national spirit of reunion to surmount narrow materialistic concerns. Through example and moral philosophy, the great Confederate general sought to show his countrymen how they should react in the aftermath of the fall of the Confederacy. Although he refused to abandon the concept of a separate South, he said, "I prefer to struggle for its restoration and share its fate, rather than give up all as lost." As president of Washington College in Virginia, he believed it incumbent to teach the young to submit to authority. He expressed a determination "to educate Southern youth into a spirit of loyalty to the new conditions and the transformation of the social fabric which had resulted from the war, and only through a peaceful obedience to which could the future peace and harmony of the country be restored."[4] Lee dreaded the thought of any youth leaving college as anything less than a sincere Christian. The new South he envisioned would be characterized by cooperation, accommodation, and humanitarianism. These ideas harked back to the pristine visions of southern nationalism advocated by Calhoun and other statesmen of the Old South in the heyday of the commercial conventions. Just as their plans fell prey to economic consequences, so did Lee's. Human greed proved a stronger force than dignified appeals to old values.

The leaders of the New South movement were careful to speak in broad terms. Rather than appearing divisive, they wanted to establish themselves as southern nationalists, the direct inheritors of the southern convention tradition. "What a pull it has been!" Henry Grady proclaimed, "Through the ashes and desolation of war—up the hill, a step at a time, nothing certain—not even the way! Hindered, misled, and yet always moving up a little better until—shall we say it?—the top has been reached, and the rest is easy! . . . The ground has been prepared—the seed put in—the tiny shoots tended past the danger-point—and the day of the mighty harvest is here!" Henry Watterson told the American Bankers' Association that the South was a land of one people who guaranteed "peace and order" and were eager to accommodate northern investors. More emphatically, Richard H. Edmonds said, "Well may the people of the South rejoice that it is in their power to make this section hold a dominating position in this, the dominant power of the world."[5] Taken by themselves, these statements appeared to have the purest of motives. Yet they had another side.

The New South creed also contained the destructive spirit of urban rivalry that was inherent to national development in the nineteenth century. The pleasing generalities cloaked restrictive objectives. When Grady extolled southern progress in the face of adversity, he only thinly veiled his paramount plan, which was to boost Atlanta. Indeed, to Grady the New South meant Atlanta. He saw the two as interchangeable. Almost all of his speeches and writings referred favorably to Atlanta. Under the sub-title "The Creators of the New South," he claimed, "The South has been rebuilt by the Southern people. I shall also use Atlanta as an example, for it is a typical Southern city." He stressed that Atlanta had been built by southern capital and enterprise. "This will," he noted, "astound those Northern men who, amazed at Atlanta's simple and comprehensive growth, have declared the South never had built and never could build such a city, but that it was a 'Yankee city' in the South."[6] Grady cleverly conveyed the idea that Atlanta was a bustling and wealthy city, rapidly emerging as the center of the New South. Clearly, then, it was a good place to invest money. Watterson sought to impart similar impressions about Louisville and its marketing region. He informed northerners, "We need the money. You can make a profit off the development."[7] Although Edmonds used the pages of his *Manufacturers Record* to convey the idea that a prosperous South was good for the nation, he hoped that any influx of outside money into Dixie would help Baltimore. Another apostle of the New South creed, Francis Dawson, editor of the *Charleston News and Courier*, was more direct. At the same time that he violently attacked carpetbag rule, he suggested that Charleston residents would welcome Yankee promoters. On 13 June 1885 the editor of the *New Orleans Times-Democrat* referred to the chief newspapers in the New South movement as "metropolitan and unprejudiced."[8] He was wrong; although they had metropolitan aspirations, their aims were local and promotional.

No sectional commercial convention was held in the South of the Gilded Age to set an urban direction for Dixie. Nor was a serious effort made to form a regional economic organization patterned after the Knights of the Golden Circle of the 1850s. DeBow had hoped to use the Golden Circle, which had chapters throughout the Mississippi Valley, as a vehicle to take the lead in creating an inland empire with New Orleans as the center of power. New South propagandists contented themselves with fatuous statements about the wonders of the South's business climate and the riches that awaited in their own cities. Beneath the fine words, they were as blatant promoters as their contemporaries in Chicago, Kansas City, and Los Angeles. Boosterism was more than simply shrilling for a project. It provided an ideology that sustained city builders in both good and bad times. Their own statements gave them hope in the inevitability of success. Sometimes boosters did bring in outside capital. Grady's contribution to Atlanta's economy, for example, was clear. The mythmakers of the New South creed spun tales of urban greatness that played an important part in rekindling a flame of optimism that sustained hope and uplifted the spirits of a defeated society.

The actual task of driving Dixie ahead fell to urban business leaders all across the South.[9] In antebellum days they seldom had the power to translate their ideas into action. Freed from the restraints imposed by the peculiar institution, they intended to dominate affairs and shape sectional progress. But with perhaps only one exception, no southern businessman of the Gilded Age had the talent of John D. Rockefeller, the technological genius of Andrew Carnegie, or the financial ability of J. P. Morgan. Some of the most masterful capitalists in the South were from the North. Henry Morrison Flagler of Cleveland, Ohio, a former Rockefeller partner, played a major role in the settlement of Florida through a mix of promotional projects. William D. ("Pig Iron") Kelley of Pennsylvania was instrumental in building up the Alabama iron industry. The greatest native southern industrialist was James Buchanan Duke of Durham, North Carolina, who turned a small tobacco company founded by his father into one of the largest trusts of his times, the American Tobacco Company. He achieved success through a combination of ability, taking advantage of technological breakthroughs in cigarette production, lack of government regulations, and ruthless methods. Critics called him a North Carolina version of Rockefeller. Duke agreed. Looking back on his career, he recalled, "I had confidence in myself. I said to myself, 'If John D. Rockefeller can do what he is doing for oil, why should I not do it in tobacco.' "[10] By the dawn of the twentieth century Duke's empire was estimated to be worth half a billion dollars. Despite his numerous philanthropic activities, he earned a place among those President Theodore Roosevelt called "malefactors of great wealth."

In considering the quality of urban business leadership in the South it is easy to fall into the trap of concluding that there were too few men like James Buchanan Duke and too many like Basil Wilson Duke. The latter was a slightly built, cheerful man, best described as a southern gentleman of the old school. Born in 1836 in Scott County, Kentucky, he held a law degree from Transylvania College. Before the Civil War he practiced before the bar for several years in St. Louis. He took an active part in the unsuccessful Missouri secessionist movement. After that failure, he became an officer in the Lexington Rifles of the Second Kentucky Cavalry, soon distinguishing himself in the field. His book, *Reminiscences of Basil W. Duke, C.S.A.*, described many exploits. Wounded in action at Shiloh, he recovered only to fall captive during an aborted Confederate raid into Ohio. Exchanged, he participated in Jefferson Davis's last council of war. After the surrender, Duke settled in Louisville, where he resumed the practice of law. Following a short public career—he served a term in the Kentucky House of Representatives—he became the legal counsel of the Louisville and Nashville Railroad, holding that job for more than twenty years. Widely known and respected throughout the South, he had a minor business reputation and few if any entrepreneurial instincts. Rather, he succeeded by playing the role of a "Kentucky colonel," complete with mustache, goatee, string tie, cane, and white suit. Accustomed to a leisurely life, he spent his happiest days in a retirement position. From 1895 until his death in 1916 he held the ceremonial post of a commissiner of Shiloh National Park. His attractive personality, dignified demeanor, and good war record made him a perfect front man for northern railroad interests.[11] In many ways Duke played a role throughout his life. He was typical of the men who contributed to the widely held impression in the North that only a few southerners had the skill to run vast enterprises.

Actually, there were many businessmen of ability in the South, ready to take the risks necessary to achieve a measure of economic success. The leaders of the Wilmington, North Carolina, firm of Alexander Sprunt and Son, for example, used innovative methods to transform the overseas cotton-exporting business, undertaking considerable experimentation and enduring hardships that would have deterred lesser risk takers. Until near the end of the 1870s the shipping of the cotton crops in North Carolina, South Carolina, and Georgia depended upon factors. The middlemen stored the planters' consignments of cotton and found buyers in port cities. The buyers then shipped the cotton north, where receivers either sold it to New England mills or exported it overseas. The arrangement was expensive for the producers. Alexander Sprunt and Son took the lead in modifying the system. In 1908, James Sprunt, one of the firm's partners, explained to a congressional committee, "In 1879, after a thorough study of the problem of better facilities for the direct cotton trade, we became the pioneers of the present system which has brought the producer and consumer together without an excessive number of intermediaries! We chartered the first steamer that ever sailed from the port of Wilmington for a port abroad. The result of this experiment was . . . disastrous. We repeated the effort again and again and ultimately established upon its present foundation, the system which has saved our farmers millions of dollars since 1875, and which has been accepted at all cotton ports from Norfolk to New Orleans."[12] Central to the change wrought by Alexander Sprunt and Son was the installation in Wilmington of efficient cotton presses, warehouses, and wharves. By 1900 a subsidiary firm, the Champion Press Company, had six presses and a thousand workers. Wilmington gradually evolved into a major cotton port, with the Sprunt interests controlling most of the trade. It made little difference that the partners had to go through a New York banking house, Laird and Gray, for financing. Most of the profits remained in North Carolina. The Wilmington partners served as a shining example of how native southerners could build a large business in the New South.

There were numerous similar accomplishments. E. H. Summers built the New Orleans cotton firm of Hilliard, Summers and Company into a major enterprise. In Columbus, a locally owned cotton mill, the Columbus Manufacturing Company, employed hundreds of women and children. More than two thousand operatives worked in eight cotton manufactories in Petersburg.[13] The credit reports collected systematically by the Mercantile Agency, the predecessor of Dun and Bradstreet, gave evidence of the success of a wide variety of businesses. But more than the efforts of some able businessmen was needed to change the economic outlook for the South. The activities of Alexander Sprunt and Son did not significantly improve Wilmington's position in relation to the other Atlantic coastal ports. New Orleans had lost any chance of becoming the great city of the Mississippi Valley. Depressed agricultural conditions in surrounding areas tended to cancel out the manufacturing advances in Columbus and Petersburg. The sorry state of southern farming and the continued dependence on outside capital precluded the spectacular gains envisioned by the proponents of the New South creed.

The resourcefulness of urban business combinations made only a limited difference in controlling the course of events. Carnegie and Rockefeller combined would have been hard-pressed to find ways to improve the fortunes of an Alexandria or a Newport. Baltimore and

Louisville had prospered as a consequence of carefully conceived railroad plans. As economic relationships engendered by the railroads solidified, it appeared more and more doubtful that any of the cities in the southern interior could find quick formulas for rapid gowth and prosperity. Industrial developments generated some ready capital and raised morale by providing a sense of growth rather than decline. Unfortunately for boosters, the creation of a few new mill towns could not transform the South into an urban giant able to compete on equal terms with the Northeast. In addition, the long-held hopes for a great inland commercial center were far from realization. The yellow fever epidemics of the 1870s hurt the development of Memphis. Recurring epidemics raised another obstacle to southern urban progress. It was simply not enough for Dixie's entrepreneurs to master what Grady called "the great commercial chessboard."[14]

A comparison of Atlanta with a new western community, Kansas City, Missouri, illustrates the sectional economic burdens faced by southern city builders. In many towns, the local businessmen attended chamber of commerce meetings, gave lip service to community cooperation, and then went their own ways. Atlanta, however, was different. The city's leaders determined during the postwar rebuilding process that they could not afford the luxury of competing against each other, so they banded together to form plans to advance their town's fortunes. The same formula well served Kansas City. A unified business community working through the Kansas City Chamber of Commerce played a major role in making the western Missouri city a national railroad center and regional metropolis. Atlanta's businessmen did not succeed on the same scale. Their greatest obstacle was that they were in the South. Kansas City, which had many southern-born civic leaders, benefited from the opening of Kansas and the construction of railroads from the city into the Southwest. Millions of cattle roamed the southern plains, and the introduction of Turkey Red wheat made the central plains a new breadbasket. By 1880 Kansas City was well on the way to becoming a great livestock, packing, and grain center.[15] Atlanta was burdened by sharecropper agriculture, which limited the city's chances and prevented the progress and prosperity enjoyed by Kansas City. The continuing backward status of the South made a mockery of the bright predictions of the mythmakers of the New South creed.

Urban interests had important roles on state levels in the Redemption movement.[16] Railroad builder John C. Brown was governor of Tennessee at the end of Reconstruction. Leaders from Norfolk and Richmond strongly supported Gilbert C. Walker's successful bid for governor. Walker, who claimed to have moved to the Old Dominion from the Northeast for his health in 1865, was a Norfolk banker whom his admirers called the "savior of the state." The Redeemer governor of

Alabama, George Houston, called the "Bald Eagle of the Mountains," favored the promotion of railroads and industries. In Louisiana, the powerful and corrupt Louisiana Lottery Company of New Orleans reputedly spent $250,000, a huge sum at the time for a political contest, to help Francis T. Nicholls obtain the governorship in 1877. Throughout much of the Gilded Age, Atlanta businessmen acquiesced in control of the statehouse by the unsavory "Bourbon Triumvirate," because of its prorailroad policies. Grady, who denounced the "political filthiness" of the organization's leaders, willingly associated with them socially to discuss business matters informally. In South Carolina, Governor Wade Hampton adroitly linked his political fortunes with those of both the New South and the Lost Cause. Most of the Redeemer politicians practiced the philosophy of Joseph E. Brown, the war governor of Georgia, who survived Reconstruction to become a United States senator in 1883. He said, "The Statesman like the business man should take a practical view of questions as they arise."[17]

Astute observers noted that the southern Democrats who engineered the redemption had mixed political antecedents. "A few years after the war all lovers of good government in the South concluded to celebrate a marriage," the editor of the *Jackson Clarion* wrote on 19 September 1883. "The high contracting parties were Whiggism and Democracy and the ceremony took place in 1875, though the betrothal may antedate that time. . . . As is usual in such cases the parties have now one and the same name, but the Whig party is no more dead than is one of our fair damsels, because she has concluded to cast her lot with the man of her choice for weal or for woe." In 1875 a writer in the *Memphis Appeal* had noted, "We do not know what a Bourbon Democrat means . . . unless it implies there is a class of politicians who, . . . forgetting nothing and learning nothing, do not recognize any issues as settled by the war and are ready to inaugurate another rebellion. We know of no such Democrats."[18] The twin problems of race and outside rule overrode partisanism, bringing about political realignments.

Along with the vast majority of southern whites the leaders of the New South movement had opposed the Reconstruction governments. In 1887 M. B. Hillyard scathingly denounced what he claimed had occurred. He said, "A troop of gibbering apes tricked in the paraphernalia of power, and playing at Kings, would be a mild mockery of state, compared to the grotesque and groveling saturnalia of that wild and hideous rabble in those dark and direful days."[19] Actually, Hillyard and others of like mind supported programs similar to those advocated by the Radical Republican governments. It could be argued that the Radical Republicans were in the forefront of the New South movement. The new state constitutions lessened the power of the planters, creating broader opportunities for city people. They also promoted railroads and manufacturing. The investment climate was favorable, and carpetbaggers brought in money that otherwise would have flowed into other channels. Birmingham, invariably cited as an example of an industrial project that benefited both northerners and southerners, was a direct outgrowth of the policies of a Radical government. But the frequently wasteful and corrupt Radical administrations were products of bayonet rule. They epitomized northern determination to change the nature of southern life. Widespread white opposition to that goal superseded support for the economic policies that southern urban interests had favored since before the Civil War.

The Gilded Age state administrations in the South continued to follow probusiness policies. Northerners who found southern leaders eager to accommodate and to embrace "Yankee values" should not have been surprised. The Old South, after all, was commercial in character. Linkage existed between the prewar administrations, those of the Confederate and Reconstruction eras, and the ones that emerged following the redemption. Although support of plans to encourage commercial development varied greatly in the Old South, the conception that the South needed the means to compete on equal terms with the rest of the nation was just as clear to the planter aristocrats of antebellum times as it was to their counterparts of the Gilded Age. Unfortunately, all the old questions remained unanswered. Where would the capital come from? What strings would be attached? How would the changes affect agricultural interests? The biggest change in the 1880s was that alternatives considered unacceptable in antebellum times suddenly became more palatable. Overnight, New York money became a blessing rather than a curse. It became acceptable for southern whites to manage Yankee-owned properties. In exchange for very limited progress when compared with the rest of the country and for the right to control racial policies, the Redeemers accepted a status that was for all practical purposes colonial. As part of the ongoing tragedy of the South, the best southern urban leaders could offer their fellow citizens was the economic subordination that agrarian secessionists had sought to avoid with blood and treasure.

A historic connection between urban business interests and municipal government made the transfer of control easier.[20] From colonial times onward, city administrations in the South had responded to the needs of businessmen. The owners of the proprietary colonies saw the creation of a favorable climate for economic activity as one of their primary functions, and accordingly, their administrators formulated plans designed to give the vast majority of city residents as little say as possible in their own affairs. There were no elections. The chief municipal officers and other high-ranking officials, all appointed by the governor, were members of closed corporations. Individuals frequently served for life, which made it difficult for new blood and ideas to come to the fore. This impediment was not as serious as might have been expected because of the nature of the system. In keeping with a very limited conception of urban government that had roots dating back to medieval England, the municipal leaders had few non-ceremonial functions beyond the control of trade. Of special concern was the regulation of weights and measures. If local merchants cheated customers, especially visitors, a city could acquire a bad name, so a chief function of colonial southern city governments was to protect business reputations.

Local governments in the northern colonies generally supported business and were far less restrictive in their formation and functions. In New England, the Puritan tradition of collective covenants led to the adoption of the town meeting form of government. This had a lasting impact. Boston had a town meeting at the end of the colonial period, when it was the third largest city in North America. It was no accident that following the Revolution the New England states took the lead in passing legislation that led to a shift throughout the nation toward greater voter participation in municipal affairs. The change toward more democratic civic structures came slower in the South. Southern state governments were slow to grant home rule; Charleston and Baltimore did not receive charters that granted a measure of self-government until the 1790s. Gradually, just as elsewhere, an elected mayor and council became the standard practice in the South. Critics claimed that the system was a backward step because it was inefficient, led to assorted "rings" and "gangs" that catered to special interests, and created a climate of corruption. Even though there was plenty of evidence to support these assertions, city governments helped promote the fortunes of local business communities. In the South political support for bond issues and franchises was very important in furthering the railroad strategies pursued by many cities, including Baltimore, Louisville, and New Orleans. Moreover, politicians in their roles as civic spokesmen were important in giving credence and official sanction to the antebellum commercial conventions. No matter what the outward trappings of power, if they wanted to advance community economic fortunes and stay in power, elected city officials had little choice except to go along with the plans of their business communities.

Civil War and Reconstruction brought trying times for the southern urban governments. President Abraham Lincoln suspended habeas corpus in designated war zones. Throughout most of hostilities, Baltimore was under martial law even though Maryland remained in the Union. Louisville officials had to contend with severe trade restrictions. Congress ran the District of Columbia as an armed camp. All the Confederate cities experienced occupation governments.

Early in the Civil War, Union officials seemed unsure about how to govern towns taken by federal troops. Memphis, the first major Confederate city that fell, was allowed to retain its elected government for several months before the establishment of military rule. At the time of the capture of New Orleans, Union forces established military rule as a matter of course. Benjamin "Spoon" Butler's reign in the Crescent City remained a source of controversy until well after the restoration of the Union.[21] New Orleans was a special case among cities that experienced long-term occupations; most of the other occupation governments were relatively mild. Ultimate control rested with the military, but in practice elected officials, bureaucrats, and service employees continued to do their jobs. The Union had neither the capacity nor the inclination to overturn the machinery of city government. As long as conditions remained peaceful, the occupied towns operated much as they had before the war and in many instances under Confederates in all but name. After the return to urban civilian government all across the South in the months that followed Appomattox, the politics of Reconstruction became a central concern. One theme remained consistent: no matter what the political situation at any given time, the city governments as throughout their corporate lives remained steadfastly on the side of free enterprise.

The Gilded Age was generally an unhappy period for American city governments. The excesses of the political machine run by William Marcy Tweed in New York became a symbol of urban corruption. The scandals of the Ulysses S. Grant administration lingered on long after their resolution. The urban graft that occurred in the District of Columbia became standard fare in denunciations of Grantism. But what happened in Washington demonstrated that an urban government, if given the means, had the capacity to transform a city and to improve the quality of its life. Significantly, the experiment happened in the South.

The Washington example belied the claims of northerners who charged that southerners were incapable of progress. In 1880 Albion Winegard Tourgée wrote a popular semiautobiographical novel, *A Fool's Errand*. Tourgée, a native Ohioan and Civil War veteran, was a carpetbagger in North Carolina. The central character in his book was a man named Fool. Like Tourgée, Fool went south to seek his fortune. He did well in politics until forced out of office at the end of Reconstruction and returned to the North empty-handed. Tourgée, analyzing Fool's experience, wrote, "He represented another civilization, another development, of which they were naturally suspicious, and especially so on account of the peculiar restrictions which slavery had put around them, and which had acted as an embargo on immigration for so many years before the war."[22] Those assertions may have accurately applied to certain parts of the Tar Heel State during Reconstruction, but they did not apply to Washington.

In 1871 Congress significantly modified the government of the District of Columbia.[23] The mayor and council forms of government were abolished in both Washington and Georgetown, and a district administration patterned after those in the territories was created. Under the new legislation, the voters elected a lower house and the president appointed a governor, upper chamber, and board of public works. The five-person board, which became the center of controversy, was given the power to plan and construct all public improvement projects within the District of Columbia. For such purposes, the board had an important say over matters of taxation and the issuing of general obligation bonds. It could also assess a third of the cost for public improvements upon adjoining property holders. Opponents charged that creation of the Territory of the District of Columbia was a means of cutting the power of Washington's newly enfranchised blacks. One result of the change, however, was boss rule sanctioned by the federal government.

Alexander Shepherd, first as a member of the board of public works and then as governor, initiated a massive construction and beautification program. The thirty-seven-year-old Shepherd was a boy wonder of the Washington construction industry. As a residential developer he had used methods considered reckless in his day. Unlike most builders, who constructed and sold one house at a time, Shepherd went deeply in debt building a large number of homes and then hoped for volume sales to turn a profit. His reputation as a plunger bothered his more conservative business colleagues, especially when he followed similar policies as a public official. His aim was to turn Washington into a model seat of government. He later told an investigating committee that he wanted to make improvements "as rapidly as possible . . . in order that in this respect the capital of the nation might not remain a quarter of a century behind the times."[24]

With the approval of President Grant, Shepherd highhandedly distributed lavish patronage and construction contracts through the board of public works. With reason, the press called him "Boss" Shepherd. He began massive projects, ignoring debt ceilings. Apparently he assumed that Congress would make up the deficits. He once reported to a congressional committee that the board of public works had spent $6.6 million when the actual total was $18.9 million. Such lies were too much even in an age of free and easy public morality. In 1874, after the size of the debts became known, Congress abolished the Territory of the District of Columbia, set up a temporary government, and started to untangle the financial mess. Shepherd, his public career in shambles and his private real estate business ruined in the Panic of

1873, moved to Mexico. He left behind a significant legacy. Upon the completion of the physical renovations, Washington emerged as one of the country's most beautiful and livable cities. For the first time, it was a true national capital. Shepherd's unsavory tactics repelled honest citizens, but he demonstrated that a city government could take positive steps to improve the lives of its citizens by changing the physical environment. Despite excesses and mistakes, the Territory of the District of Columbia experiment stood out as an innovative bright spot in the general morass of urban government in the Gilded Age. Unfortunately, few other cities had the resources to follow the standards for beautification set in Washington.

Statistics for 1880 indicated that almost all of the South's largest towns were in poor financial shape (see Table 5.1).[25] The high costs associated with Reconstruction and a concurrent reluctance on the part of municipal authorities to assess property at its true valuation and to establish adequate tax bases were partly responsible. Methods of determining total valuation differed considerably from one place to another, although most cities kept rates as low as possible. The highest tax per $100 in total valuation was Vicksburg's $4.45. The lowest was Baltimore's $1.22. Nationally, Des Moines's tax rate of $5.18 per $100 was the highest among all American cities of over 10,000 people in 1880. At the bottom was the 89-cent rate per $100 in Quincy, Illinois.[26] The vast number of cities in the nation had rates in the range of $1 to $2 per $100. Many southern cities fell within the national norms, which was small consolation to taxpayers. Per capita debts varied greatly among American cities. There was no pattern, North or South. Epidemic-ravaged Memphis had a per capita debt of $135.58, the highest in the United States. The Memphis government had collapsed, and the state legislature had made the municipality part of a county taxation district. Washington, as might have been expected, was second with a debt of $127.66 per capita. Certainly, residents of both Washington and Memphis must have envied Baltimore's per capita debt of only $2.57. Average net indebtedness—not to be confused with bonded indebtedness—was slightly higher in southern cities than in those elsewhere. The state of Dixie's economy made the taxes far harder to bear than in the more prosperous portions of urban America.

Outstanding bonded debts added to the tax burdens in the cities of the South.[27] The District of Columbia's debt, the nation's largest, amounted to $21.7 million. Baltimore's $20.2 million debt and those of New Orleans and Louisville, $15.3 million and $8.1 million, respectively, were also discouraging. Twelve other southern towns had bonded debts of more than $1 million. Funding floating debts and refunding old debts were the main reasons for outstanding bonded debts. The cities had floated bonds for a wide variety of purposes. At least nine-

Table 5.1.   Public Indebtedness in Southern Cities of More Than
10,000 Inhabitants, 1880

| City | Valuation | | Indebtedness | | Tax Rate |
	Total	Per Capita	Net	Per Capita	Per $100
Alabama					
Mobile	$ 12,991,795	$466	$2,609,250	$89.57	$2.60
Montgomery	5,506,994	330	567,900	33.98	2.41
Arkansas					
Little Rock	4,465,205	340	335,243	25.52	3.85
Dist. of Columbia					
Georgetown &					
Washington	99,401,787	560	22,675,459	127.66	1.48
Georgia					
Atlanta	18,000,000	481	2,180,000	58.27	2.20
Augusta	13,730,681	627	1,959,519	89.51	1.93
Columbus	–	–	–	–	–
Macon	6,222,000	488	743,000	55.28	2.05
Savannah	15,060,445	490	3,425,000	111.53	2.93
Kentucky					
Covington	14,521,725	489	1,030,000	34.66	2.17
Lexington	4,964,005	298	112,000	6.72	1.63
Louisville	65,809,000	532	4,849,935	39.19	2.28
Newport	6,588,653	322	966,618	47.31	2.36
Louisiana					
New Orleans	91,794,350	425	17,736,509	82.08	2.63
Maryland					
Baltimore	244,043,181	734	854,466	2.57	1.22
Cumberland	–	–	–	–	–
Mississippi					
Vicksburg	3,582,000	303	373,218	31.59	4.45
North Carolina					
Wilmington	4,759,890	274	539,845	31.11	3.13
South Carolina					
Charleston	22,543,423	451	4,129,102	82.61	3.10
Columbia	2,600,000	259	854,850	85.18	2.42
Tennessee					
Chattanooga	3,600,925	279	116,264	9.02	2.75
Memphis	16,784,314	500	4,554,355	135.58	1.79
Nashville	13,336,760	308	1,606,200	37.05	3.00
Virginia					
Alexandria	3,673,674	269	1,037,088	75.93	2.73
Lynchburg	8,405,610	527	794,837	49.80	1.97
Norfolk	11,057,249	503	2,187,371	99.58	3.35
Petersburg	9,132,330	422	1,136,100	52.46	1.95
Portsmouth	2,906,324	255	283,014	24.85	2.01
Richmond	39,522,356	621	4,399,021	69.17	1.85

teen cities had yet to pay off bonds issued for railroads or other transportation projects. Louisville owed $3.5 million and Baltimore $3.3 million for those purposes. As towns grew they had no choice but to fund necessary urban services. Baltimore had incurred $7.2 million in outstanding waterworks bonds; Louisville's debt was $1.4 million. Surely, there were some frivolous expenditures and in more than a few instances suspicions of corruption. Yet as cities broadened their functions to cope with the challenge of modern life, urban leaders had to resort to bond issues to stay afloat. They hardly needed reformers to tell them about the reasons for the rising costs in government at a time when even street light fixtures sold for as much as $75 apiece. Few southern cities could have afforded the luxury of the $1.1 million in bonds floated by San Francisco authorities for the construction of public buildings.[28] And there was no way communities in the South could finance large, necessary, and expensive projects such as sewerages and waterworks without increasing their bonded indebtedness.

In 1880 urban governments throughout the South had yet to assume the additional burden of administering rigid segregation systems.[29] That would come a decade later following the sharp drawing of racial and class lines that accompanied the Populist revolt. The impetus for codifying white supremacy came chiefly from rural people. Political demagogues skillfully played upon white emotions. The so-called rednecks had long been suspicious of cities, which they viewed as sinister places where races mingled, challenging conventional morality and defying the accepted order. Impassioned orators easily convinced them of the need for legislation designed to keep the races apart. De facto segregation had started in urban America before the Civil War. In Ohio, for instance, custom dictated that blacks sit in the back or upper balconies of theaters. Congress delayed Wisconsin's statehood for two years by refusing to accept a proposed state constitution that prevented blacks from voting. Actually, there was more mingling of the races in antebellum New Orleans and Charleston than in New York or Chicago, and it was for that reason that some slavocrats had called for the removal of as many slaves as possible from the cities.

The odious Black Codes enacted at the state level had provided for the segregation of a wide variety of facilities, including horsecars and restaurants. Because of the passage of the Civil Rights Act of 1866 and the onset of Reconstruction, the Black Codes either never went into effect or were of short duration. Urban race relations, relatively casual in the past, became strained. Whites, concerned about the prospect of black rule, placed interracial social and business relations on a much more formal basis than in the past. For their part, blacks generally acquiesced in an unwritten segregation system. David Macrae, an

English visitor who toured the South by rail in the late 1860s, observed, "There are 'nigger cars' open, of course, to white people, and often used as smoking cars, but to which all coloured passengers have to confine themselves."[30] Visiting northerners wrote glowingly about racial harmony at increasingly infrequent dinners attended by both blacks and whites, not realizing that such social gatherings had been commonplace in some southern cities before the Civil War. Reconstruction further polarized the races and only temporarily prevented the establishment of a rigid segregation system.

The conditions during Reconstruction in Baton Rouge, Louisiana, characterized white racial attitudes. In 1860 Baton Rouge was a town of 5,400 population,[31] 68 percent of which was white. Several thousand blacks swarmed into town in the last months of the Civil War. One resident thought the place on the verge of becoming a black village. He wrote in early 1865, "Take the army out and four-fifths of the town would be Negroes. They tare down Houses and build for themselves upon Confiscated Ground. The Whole flat Down in Catfish is covered With Little Negro Shantyes and the Schools are very full of Negroes." Soon after the war ended, city government established a night patrol and strengthened the police force. Although there was little violence, many whites were angered by the freedmens' bad manners. Some blacks used insulting language and pushed whites off the sidewalks. The editor of the *Baton Rouge Advocate* expressed a view held by his fellow whites when he said he longed for the days when those offenses were "settled with a dose of fifteen or twenty lashes."[32]

The reestablishment of social control over blacks became a major goal of Baton Rouge whites. City officials ordered all black places of amusement closed at 9:00 P.M., arrested black prostitutes, and carried on regular inspections of black households. White spokesmen placed a strong emphasis on the doctrines of hard work and social responsibility. "Man was not put on the earth to rove about in idleness," the *Advocate*'s editor wrote. "The abolition of slavery by no means lessens the obligations of the blacks to toil and labor for support. . . . Freedmen does not mean that one may do as he pleases."[33] Baton Rouge approved of the Louisiana Black Codes, even though they were not needed in that city. In April 1867, at the start of Radical Reconstruction in East Baton Rouge Parish, civil authorities already had race matters well in hand. The municipality acted as the key institution in reestablishing control over the "darkies."[34] Throughout Reconstruction in Louisiana the Baton Rouge city government remained steadfastly under white control. It made little difference whether Republicans or Democrats exercised power. Politicians of both parties were in agreement about the need to use intimidation, economic blackmail, and paternalistic statements to keep blacks in line. In 1880, Baton Rouge, with a population of 7,200, was 59 percent black. Even though they were in the majority, the blacks had no real economic or political power. Well in advance of a legal system of discrimination, the precedent of using the city government as a means of controlling the black population had been firmly established.

By 1880 there was a clear trend in the southern cities in the direction of residential segregation.[35] In antebellum times, urban slaves customarily lived close to their masters. Following the Civil War, although freedmen continued to reside in the major cities, they were no longer welcome in the predominantly white parts of town. Besides growing white opposition to racial mixing, there was fear of black crime and concern about property values. These factors overrode arguments that large concentrations of blacks would complicate law enforcement problems. Most of the new black districts were in suburban areas, where former slaves had gathered in makeshift shantytowns following emancipation. Hell's Half Acre and Bone Alley in Atlanta, Black Center and Black Bottom in Nashville, Baguehomma and Peacocks Tract in Montgomery were built as and remained slums. As these settlements gained semipermanence, they became a source of white concern. An official report compiled in Tennessee after an 1873 cholera epidemic noted, "Nashville, a beautiful and attractive city, is possessed of filthy and repulsive suburbs. The small streets and lanes that surround the base of Capitol Hill are occupied exclusively by the lower classes. The houses are dirty and filthy in the extreme; the streets and gutters are filled with filth." In 1881 an *Atlanta Constitution* reporter wrote about a district he claimed was populated "chiefly of niggers, bobtailed dogs and babies." He felt that whites knew little about Atlanta's black slum dwellers. "They are not employed in private homes nor in the business houses," he commented, "but drift off to themselves, and are almost as far from the White people, so far as all practicable benefits of associations are concerned, as if the two races never met."[36] Throughout Dixie, little was done to arrest the movement toward black slums or to make them more desirable places in which to live.

In 1880 average family sizes were about the same in southern cities as in those in the rest of the United States. But the average number of persons per dwelling in the South's cities was generally lower than in those of the North. Table 5.2 indicates conditions in the sixteen largest southern towns.[37] Every city except Memphis, which continued to show the effects of its epidemics of a few years earlier, had an average of at least 5 persons to a family. The city had the lowest average number of persons per dwelling (4.68) and the smallest number of persons per family (4.23) of any of the hundred largest cities in the country. Charleston contained the highest number of persons per dwelling in the South. An average of 7.63 residents lived in 6,552 structures. By

Table 5.2.   Population Ratios by Dwellings and Families for Sixteen Southern Cities, 1880

	Dwellings		Families	
City	Number	Persons Per Dwelling	Number	Persons Per Family
Alabama				
Mobile	5,276	5.52	6,133	4.75
District of Columbia				
Washington	24,107	6.11	29,603	4.98
Georgia				
Atlanta	6,494	5.76	7,799	4.80
Augusta	3,938	5.56	4,998	4.38
Savannah	5,572	5.51	6,684	4.59
Kentucky				
Covington	4,792	6.20	6,076	4.89
Louisville	18,898	6.55	24,343	5.08
Newport	3,225	6.34	4,111	4.97
Louisiana				
New Orleans	36,347	5.95	45,316	4.77
Maryland				
Baltimore	50,833	6.54	65,356	5.08
South Carolina				
Charleston	6,552	7.63	11,406	4.38
Tennessee				
Memphis	7,174	4.68	7,943	4.23
Nashville	7,072	6.13	8,525	5.09
Virginia				
Norfolk	3,277	6.70	5,098	4.31
Petersburg	3,426	6.32	4,779	4.53
Richmond	9,532	6.67	12,180	5.22

comparison, New York had an average of 16.37 persons per dwelling. The southern cities were "walking cities," meaning that people could conveniently get around town and to their places of business on foot. In contrast to the hastily built towns in the Midwest, the older southern communities showed their antecedents as old country towns.

With only a few exceptions, most of Dixie's towns had grown in an orderly fashion. The vast majority of southerners resided in single-family units, ranging from the shanties of the black districts to the comfortable brick houses in the better white residential neighborhoods. Like growing cities in other parts of the country, the southern cities displayed a vitality lacking in stagnant communities. Even Atlanta struck an English visitor in 1878 as "a new brick-built town, with no trees in the streets, but abundant mud."[38] Northern journalist Edward King agreed. Atlanta impressed him as a "new, vigorous, awkwardly alert city, very similar in character to the mammoth groupings of brick and stone in the North-west." In speaking of Savannah's affluent residential sections, however, he said, "There is nothing that reminds one of the North in the deliciously enbowered chief city of Georgia, surrounded with its romantic moss-hung oaks, its rich lowlands, and its luxuriant gardens, where the magnolia, the bay, and the palmetto vie with one another in the exquisite inexplicable charm of their voluptuous beauty."[39] Southern cities had not built the "three-decker" family dwellings of Boston and the tenements of New York, but they remained studies in contrast, from the row houses of Baltimore to the lovely homes in the garden district of New Orleans.

Praising the character of southern cities either individually or collectively was not central to the New South creed. The promoters had no desire to laud another city at the expense of their own. Crucial to the philosophy of the New South was the contention that cities throughout the section had become more and more like those elsewhere. There was no positive purpose in trying to illustrate any distinctive characteristics that could be construed in the North as showing that the South's cities were different. When Henry Grady pointed out that Atlanta was not a "Yankee city," he avoided references to geography and concentrated instead upon the pluck of the inhabitants in overcoming adversity through faith in the entrepreneurial spirit. Nonetheless, geography had an impact in shaping Dixie's cities. The section had no arid plains, treeless mountains, or monotonous prairies. One potential urban site did not look much like another. Nor were there as many available. A variety of landscapes coupled with lush vegetation, plentiful water, and mild winters contributed to a southern difference in city building.

The Tidewater contained many desirable town sites. When Captain John Smith had sailed up the James River in the spring of 1607 the forests were alive with color. The sight moved him to write, "Heaven and earth never agreed better to frame a place for man's habitation."[40] No great cities grew along the James River in colonial times, but important towns did appear at equally desirable locations. Baltimore sprawled over several low hills. The highest rose an imposing 360 feet above sea level. Despite detractors who contended that the District of Columbia was in a malarial swamp, Washington and Georgetown had pleasing locales. The gently undulating surface, with Capitol Hill as the highest point, fell away in terraces and gradual slopes to the river-banks. Adjacent Alexandria, on slightly higher ground in northern Virginia, was heavily wooded. Norfolk and Portsmouth were on low, level ground with good drainage. The river view at Wilmington impressed visitors.[41] Northern journalist Edward King commented, "The Cape Fear river, at Wilmington, is a wide and noble stream, and the scene along its banks, in the brilliant sunshine of the autumn morning when I saw it, was inspiring."[42] The neck upon which Charleston stood was such a good site that it would have been difficult to construct an ugly city. Savannah's heavy natural vegetation afforded much natural beauty. With pride, the citizens called their town the Forest City. Some observers argued that the harbors on the South Atlantic coast lacked the hilly panoramic beauty of those on the Pacific coast at Seattle, Portland, San Francisco, and San Diego. Still, without doubt the southern Atlantic cities had considerable natural beauty.

The important piedmont towns were all in rolling, heavily wooded country, enhanced by swift-moving streams and waterfalls. Richmond rested upon two undulating plateaus, divided by a creek valley. Petersburg had a picturesque location in country resembling that around Richmond. Lynchburg lay on a relatively flat surface of red clay and gravel, nestled between surrounding hills. Columbia and Augusta both had heavily wooded, rolling sites.[43] Rich foliage and shaded streets in the piedmont towns concealed blemishes such as unkept yards and dirty surroundings so evident in the new cities of the Great Plains.

The locations selected by pioneers in the New West ranged from the sublime to the bland. Cumberland, in the mountains, had a site that would have done justice to a Colorado mining town high in the Rocky Mountains. Lexington was in the heart of the bluegrass country. King tried in prose to convey the perennial beauty of the area: "These fair lands are carpeted throughout the year with a brilliant blue grass. Even in midwinter a deep green clothes the soil, and, when summer comes, the grass sends up slender shafts to the height of several feet, crowned with featherly tufts of a bright blue color."[44] It was little wonder that Lexington had a reputation as one of Kentucky's most beautiful cities. Nashville lay on a broken surface typical of mountain foothills. With reason, residents called Nashville the City of Rocks. On the south bank of the Ohio River, Louisville spread across an alluvial plain. Covington and Newport had gentle surfaces with underlays of blue limestone. Of the three Kentucky river cities, Louisville had benefited the most from builders who made the best use of relatively undistinguished sites. Most visitors were much more favorably impressed than with Newport or Covington. Indeed, given their proximity to Cincinnati, few travelers bothered mentioning either town. Possibly, the decisive factor was success. Because Louisville had attained metropolitan status, visitors usually found something good to report. King, for example, whose account of Louisville emphasized economics and railroads, alluded to "lovely" lots and "vast plains."[45]

Along the Gulf Coast, military needs had dictated the locations of Mobile and New Orleans in inhospitable spots. The first site of Mobile was so low and unhealthy that many of the original settlers died of yellow fever. The survivors moved to higher ground, which was still only slightly above sea level. According to an official report compiled in 1880, the coarse, loose, sandy soil absorbed the heaviest rain within a few hours, and the land along the Mobile River was marshy and malarious.[46] Yet Mobile was more than a windswept and unhealthy town on a desolate shore. Rich natural vegetation gave the community a semitropical appearance. New Orleans was founded in a swamp. George W. Cable, the leading Creole historian of the city in the nineteenth century, discussed the problems associated with the original site. "It was covered," he wrote, "for the most part, with a noisome and almost impenetrable cypress swamp, and was visibly subject to frequent if not annual overflow." For decades floods were a constant irritant. Only the natural loveliness overcame what Cable called "feeble attractions."[47] Despite its problems, New Orleans had a good defensive location. A chain of lakes—Maurepas, Pontchartrain, and Borgue—as well as the river and several bayous protected the approaches of the Crescent City. Mississippi Sound provided a coastal waterway to Mobile. New Orleans was never moved, but founder M. de Bienville would have done well to have considered other than military factors.

The locations of the frontier cities of the interior reflected the rugged nature of the South's heartland.[48] Columbus and Macon were on hilly and thickly wooded land. Atlanta, in the foothills of the Smoky Mountains, sat astride a ridge in the Georgia red clay country. A multitude of hills and valleys afforded numerous fine building sites. The height of Chattanooga's hills varied by more than 300 feet. Lookout Mountain and Missionary Ridge towered over the town, providing a spectacular scenic panorama. Montgomery, Memphis, Little Rock, and Vicksburg were all on river bluffs. Memphis, on the fourth Chickasaw

Bluff, was on ground higher than the surrounding countryside. The land at Montgomery sloped gradually toward the Alabama River. The rural areas around Montgomery had much higher elevations. Little Rock was built upon what its founders had considered the first good place for a city above the confluence of the Mississippi and Arkansas rivers. Arkansas Post, the first territorial capital, located on the Arkansas below Little Rock, washed away. Vicksburg, high on a neck of land above the Mississippi River, had a heritage that interested Edward King. "Vicksburg," he recorded, "the tried and troubled hill-city, her crumbling bluffs still filled with historic memorials of one of the most desperate sieges and defences of modern times, rises in quite imposing fashion from the Mississippi's banks in a loop in the river, made by a long delta, which at high water is nearly submerged."[49] The sites of the new southern interior communities pointed up an important difference between nineteenth-century urbanization patterns in Dixie and the Midwest. The cities in the South owed their locations to a careful selection process, whereas the most successful midwestern cities owed their origins to unrestrained speculation. For example, unlike the founders of Little Rock, the promoters of the dozens of "paper towns" along the Maumee River in Ohio during the land rush of the 1830s had no time or inclination for careful planning. Southern needs and economic limitations dictated a more logical and comprehensive approach. City building in the interior continued the orderly process that started at the Tidewater.

The mechanics of town planning was never a strength of the American experience. In normal fashion, the original developers determined the design of cities. Given the small chance of success, few speculators engaged in careful planning. With odds of at least a thousand to one, there was little desire to place much time or money into planning.

The high point of early American urban design came in the South at Williamsburg, Virginia, and Washington.[50] Williamsburg, founded in 1699 as the new capital for the Old Dominion, was the first colonial community in which civic design took a proper place beside city planning. The scheme featured a unique "goose feet" street pattern, a broad green mall, and a series of formal gardens. Williamsburg also successfully blended Georgian-style buildings and landscape architecture to create a pleasing planned environment. Washington's less successful plan represented the culmination of close to two hundred years of colonial urban design. Pierre L'Enfant's ideas, never entirely carried out, set high standards for future town planners. Despite its rural orientation, the South played an important role in the making of an urban planning tradition in America.

New Orleans and Savannah are two other examples of planned

southern colonial cities. Bienville's original plat of New Orleans considered New France's great inland water transportation system. The focal point of his plan was a square, the *place d'armes*, on the riverbank. Away from the river, the principal building on the square was a Roman Catholic church. Directly behind that edifice, a wide thoroughfare ran straight north. Other streets extended away from the axis in either direction as part of a conventional grid. The waterfront, square, church, and axial street gave New Orleans a central core. Although imperfectly carried out, the plan clearly demonstrated Bienville's intention to build an orderly and functional city suited to the crescent curve of the Mississippi River.[51] James Oglethorpe planned Savannah with equal care. "Mr. Oglethorpe," a writer for the *South-Carolina Gazette*, stated in 1732, "is indefatigable. . . . There are four houses already up . . . and he hopes . . . to finish two houses a week. . . . He was pallisading the town round, including some part of the common. . . . In short, he has done a vast deal of work for the time, and I think his name justly deserves to be immortalized."[52] Oglethorpe used a rectangular design. He divided the community into six parts, each of which had a five-acre tract set aside for vegetable and flower gardens. In addition, he created a number of wards, each with forty house lots that measured 60 by 90 feet. Within each ward, he set aside a 315-by-270-foot square for religious and commercial purposes. Main streets, all 75 feet wide, acted as the ward boundaries. The orderly and easily expandable plan served Savannah well as it gradually evolved from a frontier post into a successful town. Oglethorpe, as had Bienville, demonstrated the soundness of planning in building a city in the wilderness.

By 1880, whether southern towns began as forts, blockhouses, stockades, elaborately planned communities, or hastily platted promotions, a distinguishing feature was some form of rectangular street plan. The gridiron remained an enduring American legacy to urban planning. With a number of variations, the grid became more and more popular and pervasive as America moved west. Several California mining towns, for example, had square plans, cut through with grids.[53] A gridiron design was utilitarian and easy to lay out. Those factors overrode aesthetic considerations. Winding lanes may have been more pleasing to the eye than straight streets, but they were less practical. The only exception came when roads followed lines of least resistance. Hills, ravines, and rivers thwarted planners, but not very often. Usually, town builders picked a site because it was relatively flat. And even if circumstances such as a gold rush dictated an undulating spot, the builders generally ignored the topography or undertook earth-moving programs, all with the end of creating a gridiron. Indeed, building grids came close to being an obsession in the United States.

The predominance of the gridiron design tended to obscure the contribution of the South to an American urban planning tradition. The builders of Baltimore defied the town's hilly topography by following a gridiron plan. Georgetown and Alexandria had conventional rectangular blocks, in sharp contrast to the planning in Washington. Norfolk and Portsmouth featured chopped-up grids that extended inland from their waterfronts. Wilmington had a rectangular shape. The "Grand Model," replete with many squares, envisioned by the proprietors of Charleston, had long since given way to adjacent rectangular blocks. Richmond's design contained hundreds of square blocks and straight thoroughfares, as did other towns lining the piedmont: Petersburg, Lynchburg, Columbia, and Augusta. The cities of the New West started as fortifications or road junctions. After the end of the frontier, the pioneers adopted gridiron streets. Louisville's plat was almost square. Later subdivisions conformed closely to the original design. Modified grids characterized the plans of Covington, Newport, and Lexington. Cumberland had a long, narrow grid. A combination of developers' decisions and topography afforded an uneven quality to Nashville's grid. The promoters who founded the South's interior towns routinely accepted the gridiron. Chattanooga's city fathers laid out the town as if it was on flat ground rather than in the mountains. Because of land titles, Atlantans used the old street plans in rebuilding their city. Rectangular blocks predominated in Macon, Montgomery, and Columbus. The Memphis grid went up and down hills better suited for a different concept. Vicksburg had a grid, and so did Little Rock.[54] The consequence in the newer southern cities was municipal monotony that characterized planning as the frontier moved across the continent.

By 1880 the new City Beautiful movement already had strong southern roots. The idea had gained national attention with the Central Park project in New York, designed and directed by Frederick Law Olmsted in the years just before the Civil War. Olmsted, who later designed many other parks and beautification projects, popularized the concept that cities could have pleasing environments.[55] The theories behind the City Beautiful caught the national mood. On one hand it represented a reaction to the nostalgia for rural life in a nation in which many urbanites had grown up in the country. On the other hand medical authorities argued that green, tree-lined parks acted as the lungs of the city, purifying the air. Advocates of the City Beautiful wanted more than parks. They called for systematic tree-planting programs and for great boulevards patterned after those in Paris. The problem was that such projects, no matter how desirable they might have seemed, cost large sums of money and required major redevelopment. Proponents claimed that City Beautiful undertakings would automatically raise property values in their immediate vicinity.[56] Few people objected to urban beautification. The problem was to raise money, particularly in the South. No city in the section had a systematic tree-planting program. Alexandria, Norfolk, Portsmouth, Newport, and Chattanooga had no parks. Yet two other cities planned to build parks. Covington authorities expected to spend $3,500 to improve a grass plot. Officials at Montgomery had set aside two "spaces" as park lands and had changed the city code to provide for the election of a six-person board of park commissioners.[57] Moreover, a number of cities already had parks. Beautification was on old concept in Dixie.

Several of the existing park systems in the South predated the City Beautiful movement.[58] These grounds and others of more recent vintage related to the South's urban planning traditions. Efforts to create pleasing urban settings had followed the laying out of streets as a matter of course. Savannah's committee on parks spent $20,000 to improve parks, twenty-three of which were one-acre squares at intersections. Many of these had initially been part of the original plan. The city of Charleston owned 33 acres of public grounds and intended to acquire an additional 20 acres. The Battery at the harbor's edge featured tree-shaded walks and benches. In Atlanta, the 5-acre City Hall Park was the centerpiece of the city's 312-acre park system. Macon's Central City Park had a total area of 720 acres. Donated to the city by the state and designed by a former Macon mayor, it contained a large stand of trees, a race track, and a fairgrounds building. At Columbia, 117,000 persons annually visited 25-acre Sidney Park. Of New Orleans' 660 acres of public squares, the most famous was the original main square. Renamed Jackson Square, its distinguishing attribute was an imposing equestrian statue of Andrew Jackson. Throughout much of the South, there was a genuine effort to take advantage of the topography to promote community betterment. Even in a city with small park systems, private efforts sometimes resulted in pleasing vistas. A Mobile official, in a comment that could have applied to many other cities, noted, "Government street, the favorite promenade, is shaded by fine oak trees and bordered by handsome houses, surrounded by luxuriant gardens."[59]

Perhaps the finest park system in the urban South financed by local public funds was in Baltimore. The city had many park squares with statues of famous people, which was why it had the sobriquet of the Monumental City. After the Civil War, Olmsted designed one of America's greatest parks in Baltimore. Called Druid Park, it was 693 acres in size. An imposing stone gateway served as the main entrance. Visitors could savor the park's many attractions by driving over twenty miles of winding roads. Several scenic views afforded impressive vistas of the city and the harbor beyond. One of the park's attractions was a fountain in the middle of Druid Lake, actually a water reservoir. The fountain sent a jet of water a hundred feet into the air. Nearby, herds of deer and flocks of sheep ranged over the grassy hillside. A Baltimore official, attempting to sum up Druid Park's quiet beauty, wrote, "Art is not needed for embellishment, and the few structures required are generally well placed, and harmonize with the natural surroundings."[60] Judicious landscape gardening and engineering combined to make Baltimore a nationally recognized showcase.

The great improvement projects in Washington included the upgrading and extension of the park system. L'Enfant's plan had set aside numerous desirable locations for parks, public buildings, and governmental purposes. Some property was sold or given away; the rest, amounting to 513 acres, remained in federal hands. Most of the land served as the grounds for public buildings, including the Capitol and the White House. Manicured lawns, beautiful flower gardens, and winding walks in the federal districts added to the beauty of Washington. So did the numerous squares and circles that graced different parts of the city. Two of the better-known squares were Lafayette Square and Franklin Square. The former, directly north of the White House, across Pennsylvania Avenue, was a seven-acre park complete with gravel walks, benches, trees, and shrubbery. A fifteen-ton equestrian statue of Andrew Jackson, bigger than the one in New Orleans, added a dramatic touch. The latter, located several blocks west of the White House, was a four-acre tract covered by bushes and trees. A fountain and several spring-fed drinking fountains caused favorable comments. The circles and squares—Scott, McPherson, Farragut, Lincoln, Greene, and others—contained statues of famous Americans. Outlying intersections contained unimproved spaces designated as triangular reservations. Numerous opportunities existed to honor American heroes, at the same time further enhancing the beauty of Washington.[61] The redesigned city, from the Capitol grounds planned by Olmsted to the lowliest circle, represented an important manifestation of the City Beautiful movement. Parks enhanced the beauty of metropolises in Gilded Age America: Fairmont in Philadelphia, Lincoln in Chicago, Belle Isle in Detroit, and Golden Gate in San Francisco. None assumed the monumental quality or the historical character of those in the District of Columbia.

The architectural styles of Washington's public buildings, in keeping with national traditions, was eclectic. The forms combined the Georgian, Greek Revival, and Moorish vogues of antebellum times with the newer Victorian designs of the 1870s. The White House and the Capitol both displayed some of the more attractive attributes of traditional southern architecture. The White House, constructed of freestone and painted white, was three stories high, 170 feet long, and 86 feet wide. The front had a colonnade of eight simple Ionic columns. A semicircular portico was in the rear. The Capitol consisted of a central building with two great wings. Sixty-eight marble Corinthian columns set off the East Front of the massive seat of government. The building covered 3.5 acres and was 751 feet long and from 121 to 324 feet wide. Virginia freestone was used for the central section and Massachusetts marble for the each of the two wings. The huge dome was 287 feet high, with a base 136 feet in diameter. The federal government built the central building with slave labor between 1818 and 1827 and the wings and dome in the 1850s and 1860s. Total construction costs exceeded $13 million, making it the most expensive building in all of North America. The Capitol and White House fulfilled their purpose of signifying the dignity, majesty, and power of the United States government.[62]

Older forms characterized some of the best of different strains of architecture across the South.[63] One of the finest examples of Greek Revivalism was the Tennessee state capitol in Nashville. It had classical porticoes and a slim tower, all patterned after the Charagic Monument of Lysicrates in Athens. Red Georgian row houses in Baltimore demonstrated how an architectural style could give a city a special character. The Baltimore dwellings, with their well-scrubbed white steps, fronted directly on the street. Row houses in many Washington and Georgetown neighborhoods usually had small gardens before them. Alexandria, which escaped damage in the Civil War, had a treasure trove of Georgian buildings dating from colonial times. Gadsby's Tavern, erected in 1752, was a plain brick building, reflecting the general style of architecture in the older parts of town. Cities south of Alexandria had many large Greek Revival buildings such as the capitol of Virginia in Richmond, although one of the finest structures in Charleston was the Orphan House of modified English Tudor design. Built in the 1790s, its towers afforded an impressive view of the port. At New Orleans, the cathedral, built along Moorish lines, was an architectural landmark. Along the narrow lanes of the French Quarter, two- and three-story buildings with ironwork balconies and courtyards were almost all done in a Spanish style. Horrible fires that swept through New Orleans in 1788 and 1794 had destroyed most of the French architectural heritage. Mobile, as other places in the lower South, contained eclectic mansions, which showed varied Georgian and Greek Revival influences.[64] Throughout the South, the more impressive of the older homes and buildings were more than simply handsome older buildings. Rather, in many instances they served as symbols of an age of past glories.

The large plantation houses, with their characteristic wide porticoes and white columns, represented one of the Old South's greatest architectural legacies. Yet the adaptation of a culture to a particular environment was a long and complicated process. By the Civil War the South had no full-blown regional architecture. Of course, construction techniques reflected the climate. The trend from north to south called for fewer basements, more windows, higher ceilings, and thinner walls. Maryland, Virginia, the District of Columbia, and Kentucky contained a wide variety of styles, particularly an intermingling of eclectic aspects of Greek Revival and Georgian forms. In the lower South, Greek Revival was dominant in the latter stages of the antebellum period. The style gained widespread national attention during the Greek democratic revolt against Turkish rule. In the South, Greek Revival suited perfectly the idealistic democratic view of sectional institutions held by the vast majority of upper-class leaders. Even so, there was no rigid conformity. Utilitarian structures, such as the raised platform houses of the frontier and the "three Ps" (two rooms called pens and a connecting passage) of Little Rock, were as characteristic of southern architecture as Georgian row houses and Greek Revival public buildings.

Unreconstructed Confederates disapproved of the trend toward Victorian and Gothic style buildings, which they considered grotesque and ostentatious Yankee products. By earlier standards, some of the larger southern projects seemed far from handsome, trimmed with much gingerbread and lacking clean lines. The Victorian railroad station in Chattanooga repelled many people. It had a huge overhanging shed resting on arches of brick masonry and protecting six lines of tracks. The structure seemed out of place in a southern city. In Atlanta, a carpetbag member of the Bourbon Triumvirate constructed the multi-storied gingerbread and turreted Kimball House, described as Georgia Gothic. The block-square white marble Baltimore City Hall was another large Victorian structure that detractors considered a monstrosity. Constructed in the 1870s for $2.3 million, the four-story edifice had a French mansard roof topped by a large iron dome.[65]

Few of the critics of what they considered imported northern forms stopped to consider that two of America's most influential architects of the era were from the South. Henry Hobson Richardson was born on a Louisiana plantation in 1838 and John Welborn Root in Lumpkin, Georgia, in 1850. Richardson, the greatest American architect of the day, had a strong interest in Romanesque styles. His famous student, Louis Sullivan, pioneered steel frame construction. Root made important contributions in Chicago and Kansas City. Both Root and Richardson believed that their buildings were suitable for all parts of the land.[66] That idea ran counter to prevailing opinions in the South, which ignored why men such as Root and Richardson made their greatest contributions in the North. Money was unavailable for innovative projects in the depressed southern society.

All southern cities of 10,000 people or more in 1880 had theaters and lecture halls. The four largest cities had facilities comparable to the best anywhere except for New York, the nation's entertainment center. At a time when any theater that held over 1,000 patrons was considered large, there were many such in the South. Baltimore had three, two of which had more than 2,000 seats. Several Louisville houses sat between 1,200 and 2,000 spectators—the Macauley's, the Opera House, the Knickerbocker, the Metropolitan, and the Masonic Temple. New Orleans had lavishly appointed theaters. The largest, the St. Charles, held 3,000 people. Better known was the 2,000-seat French Opera House on Bourbon Street. Several other southern cities had fine playhouses in the 1,000-seat category. Memphis boasted Greenlow's Opera House and Leabrie's Theater. The principal places of amusement in Richmond were the Mozart Hall and the Richmond Theater. Observers considered the new Ford's Opera House and the National Theater the main Washington theaters. Augusta had an opera house that held 1,000 persons, plus a 1,800-seat hall. Norfolk, Lynchburg, and Atlanta all had large theaters. The Norfolk Opera House seated 1,350 and the Academy of Music 1,500. Atlanta had a 1,600-seat facility. The 650-seat Academy of Music was the chief entertainment palace in Lynchburg. Chattanooga did not have a theater, but a hall, when set up for performances, had a seating capacity of 800.[67] Throughout the urban South, even it its newer towns, places of amusement gave credence to the section's rich entertainment traditions. The heritage extended back into colonial times when Williamsburg, Annapolis, and Charleston were pioneering theatrical centers.[68] Although the legitimate theater declined in the Gilded Age, well-attended minstrel and variety shows attested to the continued strong attraction to the stage by southerners of all ranks.

In the Gilded Age there was no distinctive American urban style of social or artistic expression. In the Northeast, Puritan values found acceptance as an expression of public morality. The towns of the Midwest were workshops with a cultural heritage that mixed European and American ways. Rising new cities of the West copied eastern norms. In the South, concepts of romanticism, though in the mainstream of southern agrarianism, provided no real moorings for city dwellers. Nevertheless, southern cities strove to attain cultural identities. Although not recognized as such at the time, their residents were part of a larger American urbanization process that would create a nation of "city people," at once different and holding common values.[69]

The theater was in the vanguard of cultural activities that cut across sectional lines, breaking down older traditions associated with an agricultural republic, North as well as South. The course was far from even, and the means of urban acculturation varied as well. Horse racing was one of the threads. The first Kentucky Derby, held in 1875 at Louisville's Churchill Downs, quickly gained stature as a national event. The race gave Louisville a link to the great northeastern tracks at Belmont and Saratoga Springs and to Pimlico in Baltimore. In another way, the Washington social whirl and the winter season in Charleston provided a common ground with northeastern society in Boston and New York. Richmond was another fashionable entertainment center. Cosmopolitan New Orleans, throughout the travails of Civil War and Reconstruction, maintained its reputation for elaborate dance halls, charming Creole women, and excellent cuisine. The Crescent City was not only in the mainstream of urban culture, but it set standards that cities throughout the nation wanted to emulate.[70] Certainly, the towns of the Old Confederacy had a special southern flavor. The images brought forth from the French Quarter to Churchill Downs, clear in themselves, blurred in the context of a national urban culture. Agrarianism remained the accepted standard. Within that context, cities remained anomalies, independent from one another and from their sectional antecedents. Yet by the twentieth century it became increasingly apparent that urban refinements had the potential of drastically altering the southern way of life. This subtle process became irreversible.

Throughout the Gilded Age, northern critics continued to judge Dixie's cities with prejudiced eyes. From that vantage point, which failed to take into account the potential for change, the picture remained dark indeed. The urban leaders were products of the Old South, hardly numbering among the best and the brightest. Backward business methods and a general aversion to hard work prevented southern gentlemen from competing successfully with their Yankee counterparts. Government was stagnant. Corrupt courthouse rings and gangs dominated politics. Racial bigotry continued unabated. Black shantytowns nullified efforts at beautification. Commercial considerations thwarted the aims of planners. Architectural forms were monuments to a decadent past. So were the South's cultural pretensions.

To heap criticism on southern cities for their supposed deficiencies was to ignore the need to judge southern urbanization on its own terms. As before the Civil War, the South's cities continued to develop along traditional lines. No quick way existed to modernize urban units created to serve the needs of an agrarian society severely weakened by sectional controversy. Although an immediate realization of the goals of the more stringent advocates of the New South was impossible, the southern cities had underlying strengths that would serve them in good stead in the years ahead. To a large extent the course of future progress would depend upon the amelioration of race relations and the bringing of cities throughout the South into closer harmony with the rest of urban America.

6

Fearless in Discharge of Their Duties

Spokesmen of the New South creed ignored the housekeeping side of city building. Who, after all, could get excited about street surfaces when the paramount task was to provide the philosophical foundations for a South of cities? But someone had to fill the potholes and make decisions concerning public safety or a city could not function. In their newspapers, the New South editors urged the improvement of local services, commenting vigorously on conditions they felt needed attention and taking sides on questions of public concern. Without codifying their actions, the men of the New South used their pages to further important aspects of city building. They realized that knowledge and experience in urban problem solving and decision making were necessary for successful urbanization. The need for increasingly complex services was an important characteristic of emerging cities. No need existed for a modern sewerage in Eagle Pond or for a professional fire department in Little River.

Cities in the South as elsewhere in the nation faced common concerns regarding urban services; in this area southern urban antecedents crossed sectional barriers. Since the colonial period, frequently at times of serious intercolonial conflict, municipal offices in all the major cities had exchanged information about handling a wide variety of routine functions, thereby helping to create a cumulative North American response to urban problems.[1]

Urban authorities had to cope with many important and often vexing tasks. They needed to maintain streets, construct sewerage systems, and regulate waste removal and to solve problems arising from the erection of waterworks, gas plants, and horse railroads. They wanted to take advantage of innovations such as the telephone and the electric light. But the creation and maintenance of fire, police, and health departments required funds. The methods and priorities of the South's cities varied markedly, even within a single community. A town might expend considerable money to obtain police protection and yet do almost nothing to provide health services. There were no special regional patterns. Even some of the nation's wealthiest communities neglected important urban concerns. Services were poorest in less affluent places that lacked resources to carry on a wide range of activities and that held little attraction to private investors. Unfortunately, a majority of the cities in the Gilded Age South fit that description. Their citizens could hardly afford to pay even very low taxes, and private companies saw no profit in building expensive waterworks. It was little wonder that with few exceptions the southern cities had generally lower levels of urban services than places of similar size in other parts of the country.

Street maintenance was a constant source of frustration. No one knew what surfaces were best. Cobblestone, which reputedly lasted a minimum of fifteen years, was noisy under traffic conditions, difficult to clean, and hard to replace. The best sources were quarries in Belgium. Many of the old southern maritime cities still had some cobblestone streets dating from an earlier period. In 1880 the mayor of Baltimore reported, "Baltimore has long suffered from bad pavements; the antiquated and elsewhere almost obsolete cobblestones are here a characteristic of our reverence for the past."[2] Other surfacing materials also presented problems. Granite and sandstone blocks were noisy and expensive; wood, cheap and easily installed, wore out quickly and lacked absorbency; seashells cracked on impact, creating a surface much like broken glass; asphalt, still in the experimental stage, melted under the rays of a hot sun; and broken stone and gravel, inexpensive and readily available, proved hard to maintain. These were the most widely used substances that covered streets in late nineteenth-century America.[3] Most city governments were content to throw gravel on the main thoroughfares and simply concentrate on keeping the streets passable.

Lack of resources made it impossible to tend all the streets. Even in Washington, which had the highest level of urban services in the South, 96 miles out of 230 miles of streets remained unimproved. More startling were the figures for New Orleans, where 472 out of 566 miles of street surfaces had no pavement. Similar conditions prevailed elsewhere. Charleston had 36 miles of dirt streets out of a total of 54 miles. Only 3 of 100 miles of lanes in Atlanta were surfaced. Of Memphis's 70 miles of street, 12 miles were paved with either stone or wood. All the rest were unsurfaced. Perhaps the worst situation existed in Newport, where authorities admitted they did not even know the total mileage of the city's streets.[4]

Paving substances varied greatly in cost, quality, and availability from city to city. In 1880 the price of cobblestone by the square yard was

60 cents in Alexandria, 36 cents in Norfolk, and $2.25 in New Orleans. Broken stone sold for 70 cents per square yard in Covington and $1.50 in Memphis. Savannah paid $2.50 per square yard for stone blocks that cost $1.65 in Charleston.[5] Although the prie differences exasperated street commissioners, they were reduced to a choice of either paying the local rate or not paving their streets. Repair costs added to civic burdens. Few cities used the method employed in Macon, where the chain gang serviced the roads for an estimated $5,000 annually.[6]

Sidewalks were subject to much less wear and tear than streets. In commercial districts they were usually made of a fairly permanent substance. Louisville, Alexandria, and Augusta had brick sidewalks. Lynchburg's were of flat gneiss stone, Petersburg's of granite flagging and brick. Those in Charleston were flagstone, brick, shell, or earth. Macon's downtown had brick and granite walkways. Savannah used flagstone and bricks. New Orleans' better districts featured "banquettes" covered with German flagstone and artificial stone. Walks in the residential areas of southern cities were almost always wood planks or dirt paths running along drainage ditches.[7] High costs made other materials impractical. Most people thought sidewalks were not worth expending much money on. If none existed, pedestrians could always take their chances walking in the street.

It was virtually impossible to clean streets adequately in the horse age. In a single working day of eight hours a thousand horses deposited about five hundred gallons of urine and ten tons of dung upon the street surface. Most cities had one horse for every four persons. Theoretically, constant travel worked street dirt into the roadway of gravel and unsurfaced streets. Practice was another matter. Concrete or asphalt thoroughfares became quagmires under heavy horse traffic, unless drained adequately, which they seldom were. Street sanitation was low on priority lists for urban services. Because urban dwellers took dirt and slime for granted, officials seldom faced public pressure to undertake corrective measures. During the first half of the nineteenth century few cities employed street-cleaning crews, relying instead on street abutters, able-bodied men selected by lot from the tax rolls, and contracted scavengers. None of these arrangements worked very well. Householders shirked their duties, taxpayers showed little enthusiasm for the work, and scavenger services failed to attract a high level of personnel.[8]

Many people believed that certain animals and birds, because of their eating habits, were a cheap answer to the problem of garbage thrown into the streets. A number of large cities, including Louisville and Baltimore, relied on municipal pig herds. The hogs, protected by local ordinances, prowled the streets at will. When the herds increased too fast or aroused public indignation by attacking little children, authorities sold some of the porkers, commonly called "walking sewers," to packing plants, keeping enough to consume the garbage. Pigs were taken out of service in the Civil War era because of changing conceptions of sanitation and adverse publicity by foreign visitors. The use of pigs had long since been abandoned in Europe, except in remote parts of Bulgaria and Transylvania. Several cities in the lower South, notably Charleston, used indigenous turkey buzzards as scavengers. These unattractive vulturous birds of prey performed their duties with considerable efficiency. In Charleston, which also had drains to carry runoff, visitors wrote glowingly about the cleanliness of the roadways. They expressed uneasiness, however, about a feeling when out walking of being watched from above, and they said that the birds smelled bad.[9] One southern city abandoned the use of vultures and tried using cows to remove refuse. In the late 1850s, when Frederick Law Olmsted visited Norfolk, he said that cows wandered at will, gaining "an unhealthy subsistence from the cabbage-stalks and other substances which lie in heaps on the ground."[10] Cows never came into wide favor because the large "meadow pads" that they left behind sometimes caused more serious inconvenience than decaying garbage. Given such frustrations, city governments increasingly turned to manpower, which gave a semblance of positive action.

By 1880 street-cleaning methods reflected a low level of technology. The few firms that produced equipment for municipal cleaning did almost no research and development. Early street-sweeping machines, consisting of primitive revolving brush apparatuses drawn by horses, functioned so unreliably and cost so much that few cities considered their purchase. In lieu of machinery, sanitary engineers advocated that cities maintain a year-round regular force to clean streets by hand. Standard procedures called for a series of steps to ensure an adequate job. First, a roadway was watered to hold down the dust. Next, a crew swept leavings into neat piles in gutters or the center of the street. A following gang shoveled the unsavory piles into carts for transportation either to dumping areas or fertilizer plants. Although this system might have worked, few places had the funds or desire to establish model programs.[11]

Performances, results, and expenditures differed across the urban South. Lexington and Memphis continued to require householders to sweep in front of their dwellings before pick-ups by private crews. Alexandria, Norfolk, Covington, and Macon authorities arranged to have the streets swept only when it seemed necessary. Columbia's budget was so small that manpower was available only to scrub open surface drains. A spokesman reported, "The cleaning is efficiently done, except on certain streets which require the most attention." Charleston sanitation workers, with what an official called "medium" results, cleaned paved streets monthly, unpaved ones three times yearly, and designated "low spots" weekly. Atlanta's force did most of its cleaning in the commercial parts of town. For such per annum budgets as $810 in Alexandria, $15,000 in Savannah, and $105,800 in New Orleans, officials fought what many observers considered a losing battle to keep the streets clean.[12]

A wide variety of uses were found for the street sweepings. Street departments in Baltimore, Richmond, and Charleston sold high-grade manure for fertilizer and dumped the rest into low-lying lots. Lynchburg street crews used "inoffensive" piles for fill and threw loads considered "offensive" into the river. Wilmington laws required the disposal of sweepings at least half a mile beyond the city limits; Columbia ordinances simply called for depositing the dirt outside of town. Macon dumped street wastes south of the city. Memphis owned a special boat that carried street matter downriver for unloading. New Orleans street commissioners found it "decidedly advantageous" to dispose of "filth" in the town's "back portions." An unimpressed federal bureaucrat, remarking on the practice, said, "This opinion must of course be taken to relate to the benefit of raising the grades of the streets rather than to the effect of depositing street filth in such proximity to habitations."[13] Unhappily, perceived practical economic considerations frequently overrode the need for better health and sanitation.

The removal of dead animals constituted another exasperating urban problem. Horse carcasses left to rot in streets by owners able to get away without detection presented a major problem. Moreover, persons tossed dead cats and dogs into the streets or onto vacant lots. Most southern cities found various ways to dispose of these carcasses, acting more out of necessity than desire and usually trying to use the cheapest method possible. The quality of the work varied greatly. The city of Baltimore spent $3,500 annually to remove deceased beasts to local bone-dust factories. Washington contractors hauled away 6,415 animal remains in 1880; they were used in what an official called "various ways." An Alexandria regulation required owners to bury any creature larger than a cat beyond the city limits. Charleston attempted a cooperative arrangement whereby the municipal scavenger collected and dumped small dead beasts into a nearby swamp and local farmers carried away decayed horses, mules, and cows for grinding into fertilizer. The town contractor in Mobile charged owners 95 cents a head to ship approximately 800 animal bodies a year to a fertilizer plant downwind from town.[14] Whether by public or private means, there was a need throughout the urban South to improve methods of disposing of dead animals. It was small consolation that similar conditions existed in other parts of the country.

In 1880, when pigs and vultures were no longer used, garbage and ash disposal added to the cost of urban services in southern cities. Householders routinely mixed garbage and ashes. Every city had public garbage collectors, with exception of Covington, which hired a private contractor. Crews throughout the South removed refuse on regular schedules, from daily to twice weekly. Practices differed, depending on the city. In Baltimore the drivers of garbage wagons blew a horn at intervals to warn patrons to have their garbage ready. In some other places, citizens either had to prepare garbage for collection in cans kept in backyards and alleys, or they were responsible for placing garbage containers along the street on designated collection days. Even if people followed instructions, serious health hazards frequently resulted from haphazard disposal methods. Once the garbage wagon passed, few people cared about what happened to its contents. In Norfolk city officials had only a vague idea of how solid wastes were ultimately disposed of. "They are dumped," a bureaucrat said, "outside of the city, and are taken by farmers for agricultural purposes." Other cities did little better. Columbia garbage men spread their loads on vacant lots throughout town. Louisville sanitation workers shoveled ashes into old cesspools and hauled garbage to outlying landfills. Memphis garbage workers carted away rubbish in wagons, dumping the contents into the Mississippi River. Crews at New Orleans, working in the dead of night, took ashes and garbage to special barges for eventual pitching into the river.[15]

In some places, including Washington, large amounts of garbage went uncollected. A health officer in the District of Columbia admitted in an 1880 report that decayed matter accumulated throughout his jurisdiction in alleys, yards, vacant lots, and cellars. With the daily addition of putrefying animal waste, potato parings, egg shells, dish water, and other refuse, the resulting concoction emitted foul odors and noxious gases, especially on hot steamy days.[16] Residents of Washington and elsewhere frequently complained about poor service and piles of street garbage. To the despair of reformers, there was little interest in increasing appropriations by raising taxes. The "garbage question" remained unanswered in Gilded Age America, South and North.

Inefficient disposal of sewage caused increasing concern among southern sanitary experts and was also a national problem. Authorities, citing studies by English sanitary expert Edwin Chadwick and others, claimed that building sewers for waste products would increase the average life span of urbanites by as much as ten years. It followed that the quick disposal of dangerous forms of filth would more than compensate for the obvious long-run problem created by polluting watering grounds and river courses. Some observers, however, were not convinced by the experts' data. In addition, the technology for building massive systems of sewerage was new, and the costs were very high. The leading American sanitation engineers had no formal training.[17] These self-taught experts disagreed on such a fundamental point as what kind of sewage should be allowed to run through a given line. Officials in the urban South faced the dilemma of either building expensive, untested systems or waiting until engineers solved construction problems and possibly reduced costs. No easy solutions appeared on the immediate horizon.

In 1880 promoters of the New South ignored another problem associated with sewerage needs. At a time when there was a growing belief that a connection existed between a lack of sewers and high urban death rates, many southern cities had no formally constructed sewerage systems. Others had sanitary arrangements that were little better than nothing. At Lexington a few eighteen-inch-square limestone sewers emptied into the slow-moving Elkhorn Creek. No new lines had been constructed for several years. Augusta relied on old sewers once used exclusively for drainage. The few sewers that served Macon discharged into a swamp outside the city limits.[18] Montgomery had unventilated brick and wooden mains, none of which worked very well. "Men frequently have to be sent in to clear obstructions," a source reported. "For the past few years this kind of work has become so offensive that it is done in the night."[19] Baltimore had twelve miles of storm sewers but no system for regular sewage. Tidal waters presented such serious problems at the outlets on the river front that the city remained without sewers until the early twentieth century. Mayor F. C. Latrobe said in 1880, "The city of Baltimore requires a system of sewerage. The continuance of the plan of digging the cesspools now honeycombing the surface of the ground upon which the city is built—there being on an average about one to each of its eighty thousand houses—must be discontinued if the health of the community is to be considered. To substitute a general system of sewerage is merely a question of time and expense."[20] The recognition of needs did not automatically lead to the building of new sewers. Too many other factors clouded the picture.

Because New Orleans had a very low water table almost all sewage passed through open drainage gutters and canals. A large outlet canal ran along Canal Street, the city's main street. The state board of health claimed in an 1881 report, "The gutters . . . are in foul condition, being at various points choked up with garbage, filth and mud, and consequently may be regarded simply as receptacles for putrid matters and stagnant waters."[21] The main contribution of the drainage ditches was to facilitate the removal of surface water. Three steam "draining machines," actually paddle-wheel pumps patterned after old Dutch designs, forced water from the lower to upper levels of the drainage canals. This imperfect and antiquated system carried only a small amount of the "extremely foul" offal. The need for a sewerage system had long vexed those concerned with sanitation in the Crescent City. Financial considerations complicated the search for a solution. Politicians claimed it was impossible to raise money through public means. The granting of a franchise to the New Orleans Drainage and Sewerage Company failed to produce results. Throughout the Gilded Age, New Orleans remained without underground sewers, adding to the community's many health hazards. It remained for another southern city to be a pioneer in sewer construction.

Sewage reform came in Memphis after the devastating 1878 yellow fever epidemic that killed 5,015 people.[22] Another epidemic the following year that killed 500 people added urgency to the situation. An investigation by a new federal agency, the National Board of Health, attributed the outbreak to bad sanitary conditions. A matter of special interest to the board was the poor state of the sewerage, for the system consisted of little more than four miles of public main sewers and a few miles of private lines. For all practical purposes, Memphis was unsewered outside of the business district at the time of the yellow fever epidemics. Surface water flowed through gutters into bayous or the river. All the filth from a large black shantytown went into an adjacent bayou. The Board recommended that Memphis build a new sewerage as the cornerstone of a general effort to clean up the city. "We believe," board members wrote in their report, "that by carrying out the above recommendations, and by availing itself fully of what is now known as to the causes of the disease and the methods of destroying these causes, Memphis may soon become one of the healthiest cities in the valley of the Mississippi."[23] What remained unsaid was that any proposed solution was speculative because no one knew the cause of yellow fever.

Memphis adopted a sewerage plan formulated by George Waring, Jr., a member of the National Board of Health. Waring, a former scientific farmer, army recruiter, and author of horse stories for little girls, had acquired a national reputation as a sanitary reformer. He was a leading "noncontagionist," who rejected the germ theory of disease. Despite growing evidence to the contrary, he steadfastly argued that "sewer gas" and other noxious odors caused disease. He believed that waste from house drains and drainage ditches was a menace to the health of urban dwellers. To counter the threat of sewer gas, he promoted the concept of "separate systems" of sewerage. He opposed the use of large outlet sewers, which he claimed accumulated lethal vapors. Instead, he called for different sewers for ground runoff, household wastes, and human excreta.[24]

Construction of the Memphis system moved ahead with a sense of urgency. Laborers broke ground in January of 1880 and by June had laid nineteen miles of sewers. As the work moved forward, members of the National Board of Health confidently predicted that the new sewerage would solve Memphis's health problems. Waring was more cautious. "It is too early to determine with certainty what is to be the future of this system of sewerage, and much too early to determine its influence upon the sanitary condition of Memphis," he stressed. "In itself as it stands, it is to be regarded only as an experiment in sewerage."[25] When in operation, the system was so successful that it helped to touch off a national boom in sewer construction. At the time none of those involved realized that a "noncontagionist" approach to what was actually a problem of contagion was medically unsound and based upon false assumptions. The new system made Memphis a cleaner and hence a better city from a health standpoint. But a correct solution was based on an incorrect theory.

Large quantities of excreta in southern cities ran into porous privy vaults and cesspools rather than into sewers. In Baltimore, an investigation in 1879 of well and spring water collected by William Toury, a sanitation authority appointed by the city's board of health, produced startling results. Samples that he took contained "excrementary matter," including a mixture of free ammonia and wine.[26] Other cities courted similar serious situations. Ninety-eight percent of the dwellings in Columbia used privy vaults or outhouses. Farmers hauled off much of the night soil for use as manure for crops. Newport relied entirely on privies. When the contents reached eleven inches from the top, licensed scavengers were supposed to remove the excreta in watertight carts and dump it directly into the Ohio River. All the privies in New Orleans leaked. When they were full, workers called "vidangeurs" carried the excrement to "nuisance boats" at night. In Savannah, where city crews emptied privies, authorities sold night soil to farmers for use as fertilizer. At Augusta, city workers cleaned privies, using an odorless-excavator process. The superintendent of streets was responsible for seeing that Montgomery's privy vaults were cleaned. Richmond ordinances called for cleaning outhouses when they were "full or offensive."[27] No matter what methods were used to empty privies, serious flaws seemed unavoidable. The hundreds of thousands of urban privy vaults and cesspools inevitably befouled the earth despite regulations.

Liquid household wastes—the runoff from laundries and kitchens—were disposed of in a variety of ways. Baltimore's wastes ran into the streets, Washington's into sewers, and Lynchburg's into gutters and drains. Charleston residents let laundry and kitchen slops flow down drains directly into gutters or cesspools. Their counterparts in

Columbia were expected to dispose of all liquid wastes on the premises, pouring them into cesspools, dry wells, or onto the ground.[28] A Petersburg functionary admitted that his town had the same problems as most other places. "But a small portion of these wastes are run into the sewers," he observed, "as the city has none except on four of the principal streets; much is run into street-gutters, especially wash-water—including some surreptitious chamber-slops; in the thickly built-up portions of the city much is run into dry wells, and but comparatively little into privy-vaults."[29] As with human wastes, the problem remained unsolved until adequate systems of sewerage were constructed.

By 1880, in keeping with national trends, many southern cities had waterworks. In the previous twenty years the number of systems had increased from two hundred to five hundred. Although the general trend was for public ownership, several southern cities did not have municipal works. Indeed, neither Portsmouth nor Lexington had waterworks. Even a small system cost more than $100,000 to construct. Memphis boasted a private works valued at $650,000. The one at Montgomery cost $130,000. Both of these waterworks used machines to pump water, as did a new concern in Charleston that pumped water from thousand-foot-deep artesian wells. Chattanooga's Lookout Water Company, organized in 1866, pumped Tennessee River water through twelve miles of lines. A few places had publicly operated works. Norfolk spent $500,000 on a pumping station that moved half a million gallons of water daily through twenty-five miles of lines. At New Orleans, the waterworks had a checkered history. In 1869 the city bought an old private works, only to sell it again in 1878 to the New Orleans Water Works Company. The facility, which had an estimated worth of $1.3 million, pumped Mississippi River water through seventy-one miles of pipes.[30] No one worried much about purification.

Many systems had large machines that could move water through mains under pressure. The ability to increase pressure to help in fighting fires was of utmost importance. Because only a few waterworks used filters and almost all either pumped water directly into lines or allowed it to settle in reservoirs for less than twenty-four hours, few persons drank faucet water, which sometimes contained human excreta or dead fish. Southern urban dwellers, in common with other city people, boiled tap water before drinking, if they drank it at all. Some urbanites drank different beverages in preference to water sent through mains. Residents of New Orleans throughout the nineteenth century drank claret wine or artesian water brought from north of Lake Pontchartrain. "All the water for cooking or drinking purposes is either taken out of the Mississippi, which at this point carries such an enormous amount of detritus, that one third of the water is solid matter held in solution, or out of cisterns constructed above ground," a German settler wrote. "On examination worms 8 inches long are found in the rainwater and a multitude of smaller insects and infusoria. No amount of filtering will make such water pure. The sides of those cisterns are covered inside with a green slime and a scum of greenish filth mixed with insect life is seen on the top of the water. No wonder that hardly any water is drunk."[31]

The quality of drinking water steadily deteriorated as the Gilded Age progressed. Sewage and industrial waste polluted watering grounds so badly that in the twentieth century water needed to be chemically treated to make it reasonably safe for human use. This was the legacy of building sanitary sewers and of rapid industrialization.

In common with other places, a startling disregard for the discharges of industrial works added to pollution concerns in southern cities. Lynchburg had no regulations because authorities claimed that none of the town's factories was a potential "nuisance." Norfolk supposedly had no factory wastes that needed to be disposed of. Richmond provided only for the removal of solid wastes away from the city limits. Columbia had no regulations. Industrial by-products at Covington and Newport went directly into the Ohio and Licking rivers. Workers in Augusta plants threw liquids into the canal and disposed of solids along with garbage. A paper mill at Savannah pumped tons of polluted water daily through a sewer into the Savannah River. Atlanta officials claimed to have a program to remove industrial pollutants outside the city. Chattanooga had no manufacturing waste ordinances, but a local ironmonger sold wastes to railroads for roadbed ballast or to the city for street surfacing.[32] No municipal government followed such a sensible approach; rather, they took the attitude that their factories were not injurious to public health.

The cost of gas was of more immediate concern to southern urban dwellers than sanitary conditions. Few believed the arguments advanced by gas service companies that coal delivery costs necessitated different rate structures from place to place. Cost comparisons among cities in the same general areas showed considerable differences. The usual practice of granting a franchise to a private corporation created opportunities for fraud and automatically raised consumer suspicions about the monopolistic aspects of an essential service. Gas companies usually received lucrative city contracts to furnish illuminating gas for street lights, charging about $30 per lamp annually. Atlanta paid that sum for each of 300 street lights, Norfolk for 259 lights.[33] Critics found those costs inflated, but there appeared to be no recourse.

A modest municipally owned gas works in Alexandria, which assessed the city $30 annually for each of 150 street lights, charged private consumers $2 per unit. (A unit is a thousand cubic feet.) That

Table 6.1.   Statistics on Telephone Companies, 1880

City	Name of Company	Miles of Wire	Net Income
Arkansas			
Little Rock	Little Rock Telephone Exchange	65	$ 541
Louisiana			
New Orleans	Louisiana Telephone Company	478	16,643
Maryland			
Baltimore	Maryland Telephone Company	600	25,257
Tennessee			
Chattanooga	East Tennessee Telephone Company	185	12,724
Memphis	Memphis Telephone Exchange	120	–
Nashville	Nashville Telephone Exchange	–	–

rate was the lowest in the South and among the lowest in the nation. The cost of gas per unit was $2.40 in Norfolk, $2.50 in Portsmouth, and $2.85 in Petersburg. Similar variation occurred in other parts of the South. A Charleston company sold gas for $3.09 per unit on an average daily production of fifty thousand cubic feet. In Columbia a firm that manufactured twenty thousand cubic feet daily posted a $4.50 per unit rate. With some justification, gas company spokesmen argued that costs went down in direct relationship to a rise in the amount of gas produced. The Covington gas works, which had an average daily production of seventy-five thousand cubic feet, charged the city $1.25 and private users $2.25 per unit. The same amount of gas cost consumers $2.35 in Louisville, $2.70 in Chattanooga, and $3.50 in Augusta. Works in Lexington, Memphis, Atlanta, Macon, New Orleans, and Savannah all retailed gas for $3 per unit.[34] The suspiciously high rates brought calls for state regulatory agencies. The gas frequently failed during peak evening hours, leading to accusations that gas companies often bought cheap damp and low-grade coal. Users were just as vexed in Columbia and Atlanta as in Bay City and Stockton. But these problems were an accepted part of urban life.

The telephone, a recently developed service injected an entirely new element into the urban scene. Alexander Graham Bell unveiled his model of the device to the general public at the 1876 Philadelphia Centennial Exposition. The imperfect system—scratching sounds frequently disrupted and distorted transmissions—held great promise. Bell began manufacturing telephones in 1877 and soon formed a company to grant franchises. By 1880 six exchanges operated in the urban South (see Table 6.1).[35] Another system was under construction in Atlanta. The firms already in operation were very speculative. Largest among them was the Maryland Telephone Company in Baltimore, which had six hundred miles of wire. Early telephone exchanges were evaluated statistically by the number of miles of wire rather than number of telephones. Indeed, there were few phones. Hardly any residential subscribers could afford to have one. Some of the best customers were physicians, who had lines running from their offices to drugstores. Net annual income statistics for the phone companies reflected usage. The Maryland Telephone Company of Baltimore made $25,300, but the Little Rock Telephone Exchange generated only $541 in total revenue. Of course, the potential of the telephone was clear. By the start of the 1880s a total of 148 telephone companies operated in the United States. As with other improvements, southern interests did not have the money to risk on an untried innovation that was still in the developmental stage. But although speculators at first found more lucrative opportunities elsewhere, eventual control of southern telephone communication systems by outside interests seemed inevitable.

Public transportation was another area that underwent major changes in the Gilded Age. Privately owned horse railroads became important symbols of urban progress. Every small town wanted a line to show how up to date it was. Such desires blunted charges by reformers that bribes given to politicians in exchange for franchise rights were a source of corruption. Petersburg, Portsmouth, Columbia, Macon, Lexington, and Montgomery had no lines, but most southern cities did. Private concerns built street railroads in several cities in the years immediately after the war. Charleston's and Augusta's opened in 1866, Atlanta's in 1869, and Norfolk's in 1870. As might have been expected, the metropolitan centers had the most extensive horse railroads. Before consolidation, it was not uncommon for a city to have more than one line. Washington had five horse railroads with a total length of close to thirty-one miles. They all charged the standard national fare of five cents a ride. Baltimore boasted four horse railroads, plus several others under construction. The completed system was calculated to give the entire Baltimore metropolitan area a comprehensive transportation network. Horse lines in Louisville had a total length of fifty miles. More than 8 million passengers annually rode on the extensive system. The services of 323 men were required to operate 173 cars pulled by 726 horses and mules. One hundred and forty miles of horse railroad tracks permeated the New Orleans area. The railroads carried 24 million riders yearly. To run this large transit service there were 373 cars, 1,641 horses and mules, and 671 employees.

In smaller places, the horse railroads frequently ran for only a couple of miles down a single street. Sometimes the line ended at a pleasure ground or amusement park owned by the traction company. Lynchburg's 2-mile-long line had 6 cars pulled by 12 horses and 12 mules. Eight men operated the single-track line. The horse railroad in Norfolk had 4 miles of track. Charleston's 21-mile line hauled 1.5

million passengers yearly; it used 57 cars and 125 horses and employed 89 men. Chattanooga had 3 miles of horse railroads, employing 11 men, and 7 cars requiring 20 horses. Mobile had six lines, which was far too many for a city of its size. One ran from the city to Spring Hill, a suburb 6 miles from the city. The horse railroads of Augusta, running over 4.5 miles of track, employed 37 men. They used 7 cars and 34 horses to carry 377,300 passengers annually. In Atlanta, 10.5 miles of horse railroads, with 21 cars, 80 horses, and 45 workers, carried 800,000 riders every year.[36] The horse railroads in the southern cities afforded another indication of their increased urban dimension. Just as in the North, the cities of the South were quick to adopt a new means of transportation.

Omnibuses, large, cumbersome vehicles with a capacity of about 40 riders, augmented horse railroads in many places. Those in Washington ran between depots and hotels. In Richmond and Savannah they served hotels, railroad stations, and steamboat landings. Omnibuses in Charleston carried 75,000 paying passengers in 1880 at high fares of from 50 to 75 cents. A trip in Memphis cost 25 cents, more in line with national rates. Augusta had a large system; 5 omnibuses, with 14 horses and 7 men, carried 12,000 people annually for 25 cents a ride. The only public transportation in Montgomery was a single small omnibus line. It had 3 vehicles, 6 horses, and 4 employees. The fare was a low 5 cents. Atlanta, despite its size, had no omnibuses.[37] In many places, given the fixed routes of horse railroads and the nature of omnibus service, private conveyances, horseback, or walking remained the easiest way of getting around.

Southern municipalities took on primary responsibility for internal security. Throughout antebellum days, the fear of slave rebellions had hung over the society and was a reason for the reluctance to use slaves in industry and the argument that the peculiar institution worked best in rural settings. Factory owners feared that their slaves might listen to abolitionist dogma and sabotage operations. Rumors of clandestine black gatherings conjured up visions of machete- and cutlass-wielding blacks chopping up their masters and mistresses in an American version of Toussaint L'Ouverture's Santo Domingo. All southern cities had special night patrols responsible for checking on the activities of blacks out after dark. The emphasis on subjugating the black race led to neglect of other aspects of urban protection such as stopping crime, fighting fires, or curtailing epidemics. More money went for police protection than for other security services. The influx of blacks into cities during Reconstruction further reinforced the belief in a need for a high level of police protection. In the Gilded Age urban leaders continued to stress law and order at the expense of public health and fire fighting.

In 1880 health services were very weak in all but a few places. Medium-sized cities were especially lacking in such services. Generally, the mayor and council did little more than appoint a board of health. These boards, usually but not always including a physician, met infrequently except during epidemics and had insufficient resources to carry out programs. The boards in Lexington, Covington, and Newport did not have regular budgets. Members of Atlanta's five-man board received salaries of $100 a year to make recommendations to the city council. Columbia had a twelve-person advisory board that included only two physicians. The chief health agency in Montgomery was a branch of the state board of health. Chattanooga's board had a twelve-month budget of approximately $500. During an epidemic the board could spend up to an additional $250. It did not have authority to quarantine infected areas, but most boards could take emergency powers in a crisis. Forward progress frequently came only in the wake of catastrophe. In 1879, for instance, Memphis obtained an independent board with broad sanitation responsibilities. In its first year the board spent $35,000 on a wide variety of activities that related to the health of the city. Expenditures for street cleaning and garbage removal amounted to $20,000. Most of the rest of the money went to fill in old cesspools and privy vaults.[38] Health authorities in cities fortunate enough to have remained relatively free of epidemics were unable to convince elected officials of the need to give high priority to health services because the officials did not want to hurt their chances for reelection by implying that their city had a health problem.

Officials did realize that threats to health increased dramatically as a community grew in size. In the upper South, Baltimore had handled public health problems competently. Washington had made a good start. Louisville had a system but needed better financial backing. Baltimore's department, which had a budget of $246,300, had the makings of a true sanitary authority. Its areas of jurisdiction included the removal of garbage, the cleaning of sewers and streets, the operation of a public hospital, and the running of vaccination programs. An obvious need existed for more funds, professional employees, and comprehensive powers.[39]

The story of health in New Orleans was one of unrelenting gloom. Officials of the National Board of Health considered the Crescent City the nation's number one health hazard. Plans that were never completed called for cordoning off the New Orleans health district and requiring that trains and travelers leaving the city be fumigated. The Marine Hospital Service, a government agency, maintained a boat on the Mississippi River below Memphis to inspect upward-bound steamboats for contamination. Health officials in some northern cities requested that the federal government keep New Orleans under a permanent quarantine.[40] An enraged Louisiana medical authority countered that idea by suggesting that northerners be kept out of his state because they carried disease. Although discussions on the national level about sanitary conditions suggested a bias against the South, there was little doubt that New Orleans had serious health problems. Outbreaks of dengue, often called either "dandy-fever" or "break-bone fever," recurred with monotonous regularity. Believed to have originated in Africa, the disease was one that a person could get over and over again. The single consolation for victims of the painful and debilitating ailment was that they usually recovered. Yellow fever, however, was deadly, killing hundreds of people even in nonepidemic years.[41]

The 1878 yellow fever epidemic resulted in an official death toll of 4,046 men, women, and children. Medical experts did not know that mosquitoes carried the disease. Some attributed it to filthy Cuban sailors, but the hastily formed federal Havana Yellow Fever Commission of 1878 made a detailed study of sanitary conditions in Cuba and concluded that they were not much different than in the United States.[42] George Waring, Jr., a member of the commission, theorized that yellow fever resulted from sewer gas caused by poor sanitation in the southern United States. This "noncontagionist" filth theory of disease was widely accepted by public health authorities. The national American Public Health Association heaped abuse on New Orleans, blaming it for $175 million in costs associated with the 1878 epidemic. Threatened from within and without, the city authorities acted to improve public health conditions. Dr. Samuel Choppin, president of the Louisiana Board of Health, noted, "Undoubtedly the most impressive lesson of the great epidemic of 1878, to the people of this city, was the importance of improving its sanitary condition."[43]

The continued drain on the Crescent City's population, economy, reputation, and spirit led to concerted efforts at reform. In 1880 Dr. Choppin said, "The people who have died here of yellow fever would have built up a state."[44] This admission indicated a sharp shift in community policy. As late as the mid-nineteenth century New Orleans spokesmen had argued that the city was among the healthiest in the nation. They had often contended that most victims were newcomers who hastened their demise by consuming too much alcohol.[45] During the Union occupation, local citizens opposed General Benjamin Butler's cleanup efforts on the grounds that they were unnecessary. But by the Gilded Age the specter of the tens of thousands of dead served as a rationale to explain why New Orleans had failed to become the great city of North America. Even so, Crescent City leaders continued to feel victimized by unfair publicity. In 1882 they accused the National

Table 6.2.   Life Expectancy for Whites in Representative Cities, 1880

City	At Birth	At Age 20	At Age 30	At Age 40
South				
Baltimore	38.18	41.50	34.74	28.05
Charleston	38.34	36.24	30.08	24.60
New Orleans	38.10	35.80	29.35	23.78
Dist. of Columbia	42.36	40.42	33.64	27.36
Other Sections				
Chicago	39.70	43.20	36.02	20.05
Cincinnati	40.44	40.76	33.81	27.18
St. Louis	38.96	41.73	34.65	28.08
New York	35.02	37.64	31.11	25.08
San Francisco	41.32	37.42	30.88	24.85

National Board of Health of manufacturing a yellow fever epidemic, a charge the board vehemently denied.[46]

The chief public health organization for the city of New Orleans was the state board of health, which operated three quarantine stations on snake-infested islands in remote bayous, monitored the quality of drinking water, and tried to stop the dumping of garbage directly into the river. Annual house-by-house inspections required filing reports on more than sixty thousand premises. Many people disliked having their homes checked by bureaucrats; the practice caused what an official euphemistically called a "lack of public sentiment" toward the board.[47] Funds from the usually free-spending city council were so hard to obtain that the business community funded most of the board's $40,000 annual budget through the private Auxiliary Sanitary Association. This body, organized in 1879, was a direct response to the economic consequences of the previous year's yellow fever epidemic. Neighboring communities had blockaded the city and hurt business, using what an association leader called "barbarous shot-gun quarantines."[48] Business losses rather than human costs brought the first tentative steps in a locally supported sanitary reform program.

An unpleasant feature of living in southern cities in 1880 was that the average urbanite had a short life expectancy. The chances for a long life improved with age. After reaching twenty, an individual had a good chance of living into the late fifties or early sixties. At thirty years, age sixty seemed attainable, and at forty it was almost assured if one avoided unexpected pitfalls. Statistics from nine cities for the three years ending 30 June 1881 indicated that southern white urbanites could expect to live as long as or only slightly less long than their northern counterparts (see Table 6.2).[49] Life expectancy for whites at birth in Baltimore, Charleston, New Orleans, and the District of Columbia was higher than in New York. Unfortunately, southern urban

Table 6.3.   Life Expectancy for Blacks in Four Cities, 1880

City	At Birth	At Age 20	At Age 30	At Age 40
Baltimore	23.26	36.62	30.64	24.68
Charleston	21.82	31.60	27.14	21.51
New Orleans	25.56	30.63	26.98	22.49
Dist. of Columbia	25.25	35.34	30.22	24.63

blacks did not fare so well. Blacks in four southern cities had far less chance than whites of reaching old age—a gap of from twelve to seventeen years (see Table 6.3).[50] At birth a black had a life expectancy of 25.56 years in New Orleans, 25.25 in the District of Columbia, 23.26 in Baltimore, and 21.82 in Charleston. A large number of black children died before their first birthday. In Charleston infant deaths per thousand in 1880 for black males were 352.1 and for black females 323.2. Deaths per thousand in Charleston for white males and females were 146.8 and 118.8, respectively. By contrast, the death rates per thousand for infants of all races in Columbus, Ohio, a city of comparable size to Charleston, were 77.9 for males and 50.5 for females. In New York the death rate per thousand for all babies was 205.6 for males and 173.9 for females. The death rate in Charleston per thousand for whites was 26.2 for males and 21.7 for females. For black males it was 48.6 and for black females 42.2. The general pattern held throughout the South. Urban living was far more dangerous for blacks than for whites.

The threat of destructive fires added to the perils of city life in the South. Almost every place claimed to have experienced a great fire, resulting either from military action or other causes. The burning of Norfolk in the Revolution; of Washington's public buildings in the War of 1812; and of Atlanta, Columbia, and Richmond in the Civil War could not have been prevented by normal protective measures. The same was true of large conflagrations that stemmed from nonmilitary causes. In 1815 flames consumed 400 houses in Petersburg. A fire in Augusta in 1829 gutted between 400 and 500 buildings, causing $1 million in damages. The blaze that destroyed Louisville's commercial district in 1840 sparked a statewide movement for better fire protection. The flames that swept Savannah in 1796, 1820, and 1865 gave that city one of the South's worst fire-safety records. A fire that authorities believed threatened in its most serious stages to reach the magnitude of the Chicago fire of 1871 roared through Baltimore on 25 July 1873. The inferno ravaged 113 buildings, including schools, churches, and factories. Damage amounted to $750,000, of which insurance covered only a third.[51] Despite a string of such distressing occurrences and the ever-present threat of more disasters, many southern communities continued to rely on small and poorly funded fire departments.

By 1880 most cities had professional fire departments. An exception was the relatively new city of Chattanooga, which continued to depend on volunteers divided into three companies with a total of 102 men. The first company of 36 men, though, was a reserve unit. These volunteers had to make do with obsolete equipment—an old-fashioned fourth-class steamer, three hand-pulled hose carriages, and 950 feet of what an official referred to as "unreliable hose." The second company had a two-wheel hose carrier and 500 feet of "good hose." An elite first division of 30 men operated a hook-and-ladder truck. Departmental expenses for 1879 amounted to $5,400. Losses in eight fires totaled $15,500.[52] Chattanooga's volunteer department was fairly typical for a city in its population class. It was not uncommon, especially in the Northeast, for cities of around 100,000 to have volunteer departments.[53] As long as a system worked there seemed no compelling reason for change. Professional departments were not usually formed until after a disastrous fire that discredited the volunteers or, as fire fighting became more complicated, passed beyond the bucket-brigade era.

Several of the professional departments in the South were impressive statistically. Petersburg's force of 33 full-time firemen had at their disposal six hose reels, one hook-and-ladder truck, and 1,500 feet of "good hose." During 1879 the department responded to 31 alarms, only 3 of which were false. Fire losses came to $110,000. The cost of running the department for the year was $9,200. The Savannah Fire Department, with four steam fire engines, three one-horse hose reels, one hook-and-ladder truck, and 4,800 feet of hose, fought 32 fires in 1880, holding damage to $22,100. Charleston's fourteen steamer and three truck companies relied on 11,200 feet of hose; the department's budget was $26,000. The funding required to run a first-rate department increased markedly as a city expanded in population. The crucial need for a rapid response meant that a single central station was not adequate. Louisville's department had many line companies, funded by a yearly budget of $108,500. The Baltimore force had a $175,000 annual budget. A chief engineer with a salary of $2,000 a year and two assistant engineers receiving $1,400 annually supervised the daily activities of 208 firemen. Seventeen companies stayed on line, backed by five reserve units. The department had a great deal of apparatus, including thirteen steamers, twenty-six four-wheel hose carriages, ten steam heaters, four hook-and-ladder trucks, four fuel tenders, one supply wagon, twenty-four fire extinguishers, five covered wagons, one jagger wagon, 29,000 feet of hose, and a large reserve of four steamers and miscellaneous equipment. Seventeen fire horses were constantly on call. During 1880 the Baltimore Fire Department answered 343 alarms. Fire damage for the period was $580,300, with $320,500 caused by two large blazes.[54]

Efficient staffing and organization, modern equipment, and trust-worthy hoses helped to instill public confidence in the new profession-al departments. Yet little relationship existed between those factors and the amount of damage caused by fires. Success in fighting fires de-pended mainly on luck as well as fire-prevention programs and suffi-cient available water. The chief of the Washington Fire Department spoke for many of his colleagues when he used a specific example to plead for reform measures. "A special point in the city . . . is the Government Printing Office, a building which, in addition to the host of persons who are employed there day and night, contains so much valuable property," he said. "This building is old, illy constructed and, although crowded with inflammable material, was constructed with-out any regard to safety from fire. In its vicinity there are but few fire plugs, and they are small mains." He went on to note that the several hundred buildings, all built in rows and many without fire walls between them, in the vicinity of the printing office, were "liable to rapid destruction in the event of a fire without a full supply of water."[55] Few people took measures to prevent fires, and owners did not want fire inspectors to interfere with their property rights. As long as such attitudes prevailed, many blazes that should never have started caused serious damage.

Firemen ran considerable risks on the job in exchange for few benefits and privileges. Unlike most departments, the one in Baltimore had a benefit program. Men incapacitated on the job remained on full salary for up to a year. Families of fire fighters killed in the line of duty received $500. To keep qualified personnel the department allowed firemen to hold other jobs during off-duty hours.[56] Although this practice raised questions about how hard men worked when on duty, it was fairly common throughout the nation and was justified on the gounds that it saved money. Even with the move toward profession-alization, there remained a reluctance to think of firemen as full-time employees. The old volunteer tradition died hard. Still, fire fighters were generally held in high esteem by the public. The mayor of Louisville observed, "Our firemen, as they always have been, are active and fearless in discharge of their duties."[57] The statement would have applied equally well to the men in other departments in the South.

Civic authorities in the southern cities put much more time and effort into building police forces than fire departments. By the Gilded Age the "police idea" of forces organized along military lines had gained wide acceptance in the United States. Central to the concept was civilian control exercised through formal constitutional mechanisms. Usually, the mayor had the power to appoint the chief, subject to confirmation by the city council. Under a variation of this method, a police board had appointment powers. In actual practice, the boards, councils, and mayors left day-by-day administration to high-ranking police officers, although they maintained jurisdiction over budgetary matters.

In 1880, the high annual salaries paid high-ranking law enforcement officials demonstrated the importance given to police work. They were the highest paid public employees in the South. The superintendent of the metropolitan police in Washington made $2,610, the chief of police in New Orleans $3,480, and the marshal of the Baltimore force $2,500. The chiefs in Charleston and Atlanta made $1,800 and $1,500 respectively. The heads of police departments in Montgomery, Augusta, Chattanooga, and Macon received salaries in the $1,000 range. These pay rates were in keeping with national norms for towns of their size. Two southern cities had unique salary arrangements. In Newport, the chief had an $800 salary, plus an additional $400 in fees for such duties as transporting criminals and testifying in court. Norfolk's city marshal, who made $3 a day, had lucrative emoluments. Generally, southern chiefs of police received salaries comparable to and in many cases better than their counterparts in other parts of the country. The superintendent of the large Chicago department made $3,780 per annum. Chiefs in medium-sized Peoria, Fond du Lac, and Oshkosh had compensation rates ranging from $650 to $1,000.[58] Southern urban leaders were willing, despite continuing money problems, to pay high-ranking police officials well. A general consensus held that the leaders of the police needed large salaries to impress upon the general public the importance attached to the preservation of law and order.

The annual salaries of men in the lower ranks reflected the financial resources available to pay public employees in southern cities. Patrolmen seldom made as much as the national annual average of around $900. Police officers in Chattanoga, Augusta, and Macon received $600 and in Savannah $720. Charleston paid privates $576, Alexandria, $480. Patrolmen in Mobile made $40, in Atlanta $54, in Memphis $60, and in Montgomery $65 per month. Baltimore paid men on the beat $18 weekly and Norfolk $2 daily.[59] Many of the policemen were political appointees, and their efficiency varied greatly. The New Orleans police had a yearly base pay of $600. A local leader commented, "The police of New Orleans is well officered; but the entire force is ill-paid, and at times not paid; it is therefore deficient in *morale*, and is totally inadequate in point of numbers."[60] No cities had formal training programs for police officers. They learned on the job. Because of the nature of their work, police did not always enjoy high esteem in the community and sometimes met hostility. Although these attitudes may have caused psychological problems, police could take heart that they received higher salaries than most workers. Their average per capita annual wage of $175 in 1880 virtually assured political interference to win appointments as policemen but also guaranteed a constant stream of applicants.

Police departments in the South required officers to wear modified standard blue metropolitan police uniforms and to carry specified accouterments. In accordance with national standards, the men had to purchase their own uniforms and equipment. Some of the outfits were very elaborate. During winter months the Charleston police performed their duties outfitted in dark blue military frock coats adorned with black buttons stamped with the city crest and the words "Charleston Police." A black helmet added a distinctive touch. In summer the officers changed to blue flannel suits with sack coats and panama hats. In all seasons the members of the force had to wear white kid gloves while on duty. Every man had a rosewood baton, a five-pointed star, and a service revolver. Patrolmen in Norfolk walked their beats in New York–style dark blue uniforms. Their headgear in the summer was a white derby and in the winter a black one. This elaborate outfit cost $125. Police were armed with clubs, revolvers, nippers, and blackjacks. Lexington policemen had to purchase dark blue uniforms that cost $30 apiece and to furnish their own revolvers and clubs. The stylish Savannah police patrolled attired in dark blue frock coats with brass buttons, dark blue trousers, white belts, and regulation cork helmets. Less resplendent were the uniforms of the New Orleans and Vicksburg police. In hot months, New Orleans officers wore navy blue sack coats. In cold weather, double-breasted and single-breasted frock coats were the rule. The men carried clubs and whistles but no guns. Vicksburg's force was clothed in heavy blue uniforms and black hats in the winter, blue flannel garments and panama hats in summer.[61] Before the Civil War only a few police departments required uniforms because many Americans considered uniforms undemocratic. These prejudices broke down in the Civil War decade. Throughout the South in the Gilded Age, clearly identifiable uniforms and badges of authority helped to instill pride of office in the men charged with preserving the peace.

Beat and duty hours were long and hard. The police in many southern cities worked twelve hours daily, the national average. Norfolk policemen patrolled 26 miles of streets and lanes, performing their duties on schedules of six hours on and twelve off. Augusta police attempted to cover the entire city, walking six-hour beats, with only six hours of rest in between shifts. Macon officers toiled twelve hours on and twelve off, trying to protect 116 miles of thoroughfares.[62] Police everywhere devoted their primary efforts to protecting business property and keeping high crime districts under close surveillance. But the value of having police officers walk long hours on the beat provided more the semblance of a deterrent than an actual service that stopped crime in the streets.

Southern city dwellers tolerated heavier expenditures for police departments than for other urban services. In 1880 Baltimore spent $590,000 and Washington $302,000 for police protection. Many smaller cities had impressive funding levels. Charleston's budget was $68,600, Memphis's $35,000, and Augusta's $30,000. A number of other towns, including Atlanta, Norfolk, Mobile, Macon, Lexington, Chattanooga, Montgomery, and Vicksburg, spent roughly a dollar per resident on their police departments.[63] Expenditures for police services were generally higher in the South than elsewhere. Fear of what some white editors called the "black brute"[64] continued to permeate southern life. "A single day rarely passes that a case of lynching is not flashed over the wires and the cause is almost the same in each instance, the rape of a white woman or child by a big, burly negro," the *Nashville Banner* noted on 16 May 1881. "It is rape and hang. As often as it is done, that often will a devil swing off into eternity." A decade later, the editor of the *Alexandria Town Talk*, wrote that "whenever a negro or a white man rapes a woman that man dies. It is understood by both races that a proven case of rape means death."[65] Such inflammatory statements, repeated all across the South, added to white racial fears and furthered a law-and-order syndrome. By the 1880s, although some black city employees could be found in various patronage jobs, including firemen, there were few black police officers.[66]

Police blotters in the urban South detailed some of the successes and failures in the continuous battle against crime. Washington had a highly organized reporting system. In the year ending 30 June 1880 the police made 13,558 arrests—11,432 males and 2,126 females. The main causes were intoxication (4,391), ordinance violations (1,421), petty larceny (1,029), and assault and battery (1,020).[67] During 1880 the vast majority of arrests in southern towns were for minor offenses. Rape either went unreported or was listed under another category such as assault and battery. Although crimes of great violence happened—20 reported homicides in New Orleans, 10 in Louisville, 5 in Atlanta, 2 in Columbia, and 1 in Cumberland—police duty was usually routine. Macon patrolmen made 1,600 aprehensions, almost all for drunkenness, street fighting, and shooting guns within the city limits. These statistics were in line with those in the rest of the nation.[68]

But the statistics failed to show that blacks accounted for a disproportionately high number of total arrests. Some white leaders used the police as a means of harassing blacks to keep them aware of their place in society. Nashville policemen made regular weekend sweeps in which they automatically arrested all blacks encountered on suspicion. The blacks were held for a few days and then released without formal charges or a trial. During their short incarceration, they performed road work or other menial tasks.[69] The relationship between law enforcement and the perceived needs of the white majority in regard to the omnipresent race question was never officially admitted, nor was much written about it in annual reports.

Students of crime eschewed racial or sociological theories in explaining deviant behavior. Lawlessness was generally attributed to liquor saloons and houses of prostitution. In 1880 southern towns had both (see Table 6.4).[70] The available statistics failed to delineate the racial or economic characteristics of the establishments. Although no southern city had as many liquor saloons as New York (9,067) or San Francisco (8,694), they were present in abundance. Baltimore had one saloon for every 150 men, women, and children. Little Rock, only recently removed from the frontier, had 63 saloons. New Orleans, renowned for its French Quarter, had 429. Houses of prostitution were difficult to obtain information about because in most places they were illegal and hence unlicensed. New Orleans authorities readily admitted to having 365 houses. Such pleasure palaces were a significant factor in bringing visitors to the Crescent City. Large entertainment centers offered food, drink, gambling, and theatrical shows in addition to sexual attractions. Unlike other places, few persons in New Orleans felt guilty about the city's large number of brothels. Because they were good business, they were a source of pride.[71] Only Philadelphia, with an admitted national high of 517, had more. Four of the thirteen cities in the country that reported a hundred or more such houses were in the South. Baltimore tallied 300, Louisville 125, and Richmond 100. Such statistics—imperfect at best and collected at a time when intensive investigation into the reasons for crime was a new social science—provided further indication that the urban South had concerns similar to those in other parts of the country.

The cities of the New South continued to experience the same service and protective problems that plagued the Old South. The only real difference was that the problems had increased in magnitude as a consequence of growth. Just as before the war, not enough money was available to give a high level of support to a wide range of civic endeavors. Moreover, public safety took precedence over health and fire protection. As in so many other ways, the legacy of the peculiar institution continued as a significant factor in detemining policy in the cities. Beyond talk of law and order was the fear of black violence accentuated by the Reconstruction experience. Providing protection against blacks helped to deplete already hard-pressed city treasuries. None of the South's thirty largest communities in 1880—with the

Table 6.4.   Houses of Prostitution and Liquor
Saloons in Southern Cities, 1880

City	Houses of Prostitution	Liquor Saloons
Alabama		
Mobile	–	–
Montgomery	4	40
Arkansas		
Little Rock	6	63
Dist. of Columbia		
Georgetown	–	–
Washington	–	690
Georgia		
Atlanta	5	–
Augusta	15	156
Columbus	–	36
Macon	36	65
Savannah	25	–
Kentucky		
Covington	–	130
Lexington	20	37
Louisville	125	718
Newport	0	93
Louisiana		
New Orleans	365	429
Maryland		
Baltimore	300	2,100
Cumberland	4	167
Mississippi		
Vicksburg	–	–
North Carolina		
Wilmington	4	65
South Carolina		
Charleston	–	291
Columbia	20	40
Tennessee		
Chattanooga	–	–
Memphis	29	114
Nashville	–	–
Virginia		
Alexandria	–	–
Lynchburg	25	79
Norfolk	50	108
Petersburg	3	50
Portsmouth	–	–
Richmond	100	500

possible exception of debt-ridden Washington—had the public or private means to furnish residents with uniformly high levels of services. Thus Baltimore had a large waterworks but no comprehensive sewerage. Alexandria had a model municipal gas plant and a poor street-cleaning department. New Orleans expended more money on sidewalk repair and extensions than on draining household wastes. Lynchburg, which boasted a horse railroad, had few paved streets. Richmond did better at disposing of dead animals than removing garbage. Chattanooga had fewer telephones than privies. To a greater or lesser extent, all the cities tried to set priorities, always influenced by politics and immediate needs. The same considerations influenced policy all across the country, but in the South, the burdens of a depressed economy and race complicated matters. Attempts by southern city leaders to deal with problems ranging from sewerage to a harsh racial policy on law and order were further indication of a groping toward an urban society.

7

The Promise of Her
Great Destiny

Throughout the 1880s southern urban promoters sought to convey the impression that their section was progressing. A Birmingham resident, catching what he considered the spirit of events, wrote, "Why, men would come in at four o'clock in the morning and begin making trades; before breakfast. Property changed hands four and five times a day . . . Men went crazy two hours after getting here . . . A brand-new sensation was born every day." This exaggerated description, characteristic of claims made all across America about the wonders occurring in cities in the Gilded Age, contained more than a grain of truth. Birmingham was a bona fide "boom town" and a showcase of the New South. Chattanooga also had high hopes. The editor of the *Chattanooga Tradesman* wrote enthusiastically, as a zealous promoter must, that prospects were so good that American and European capitalists vied for the honor of investing funds in the area. "The great bulk of capital for the projects and people who buy the lots," he said, "come from the East and North, some of the money from England." Not to be outdone, a Virginian proclaimed that a town in his home state, Roanoke, had within a few short years been transformed from a "sleepy country village" into a southern version of a typical New England industrial town.[1] Roanoke, called Big Lick until 1882, was an old community revitalized by industrial progress.

Boomers claimed that riches lay for the taking all across Dixie. Middlesboro, Kentucky, was expected soon to reach metropolitan proportions, fueled by what the *Baltimore Manufacturers' Record* claimed was "fully $10,000,000" in English investment capital. Other promotional projects were the subject of similar extravagant claims. The builders of Cardiff, Tennessee, predicted amazing success for their "paper city," located in the "Richest and Most Inexhaustible Coal and Iron Region in the South."[2] Just as confidently, the editor of *Town Talk* in Alexandria, Louisiana, reported, "We have from a reliable source, that

Northern capital is now ready to erect at some point on Railroad between Loyds Bridge, and Alexandria, a Public Sugar Mill and Refinery, . . . All far reaching minds must see at once the importance of this enterprise, and how developing it will be to the Parish; and the valuable lands now laying idle will thus be made to yield handsome profit from cane raised, and sold per ton, to the public mill."[3] Richard Edmonds in his book *The South's Redemption from Poverty to Prosperity,* published in 1890, contended that unnamed New England capitalists planned to spend several million dollars to develop a gigantic industrial complex at Fort Payne, Alabama.[4] Across the South a new day of progress and prosperity appeared on the verge of dawning, or at least that was the message.

Land companies in dozens of southern towns worked hard to attract northen capital. These efforts spawned a land boom that did bring in some northern currency. The peak years were between 1887 and 1890,[5] when plungers gambled considerable sums by southern standards on new town sites touted as potential industrial complexes. True believers thought that the millennium was at hand. Right up to the close of his life, Henry Grady expressed only optimism about the future of the South. He wrote in *The New South,* "The promise of her great destiny, written in her fields, her quarries, her mines, her forests, and her rivers is no longer blurred or indistinct, and the world draws near to read."[6]

Actually, prosperity was spotty and selective. Most of the money went into the iron industry in Alabama, the lumbering operations in Louisiana, and the land boom in Florida. Enthusiastic promotional talk about huge investments in Cardiff and Middlesboro held no truth. Those two places like many others never even achieved the status of glorified villages. It became increasingly clear that the southern land boom was pale compared with those in other parts of the country during the same period. The real action was in the new cities of the West and in the great timber stands of the upper Midwest. For every dollar poured into the South, a thousand more went toward opening up the North Woods of Wisconsin, Minnesota, and Michigan.[7] On the banks of the Missouri River in Kansas City, land worth more than $70 million changed hands in a single year during a boom that lasted most of the 1880s.[8] Great booms in southern California transformed Los Angeles and San Diego from unimportant country towns into regional centers. Between 1880 and 1890 the population of Los Angeles grew from 11,200 to 50,400 and of San Diego from 2,600 to 16,200. In the Northwest, on Puget Sound, the arrival of rails from the East touched off a flurry of speculative activity. Seattle's population leaped from 3,500 to 42,800. Tacoma had 1,100 residents at the start of the decade and 34,900 at the end. Growth of this dimension was what the southern

cities, particularly the newer ones in the interior, needed. But the high
hopes of the 1880s gave way in the 1890s to a general feeling of despair
and frustration. The South failed to rise as the New South soothsayers
had predicted.

The results of the 1890 census made for very depressing reading in
most quarters south of the Mason and Dixon line. In the 1880s the
South actually lost rather than gained ground. During a decade of rapid
urbanization, the number of places with populations over 2,500, which
the census considered urban territory, increased from 939 to 1,348. At
the end of the 1880s only 192 of those communities were in the South.
Other urban statistics presented an even more depressing picture.
From 1880 to 1890 the number of places with populations with over
10,000 rose from 228 to 354, an overall increase of 126. The South added
only 18 such cities. Many American cities experienced rapid numerical
advances. A total of 117 cities added more than 10,000 inhabitants.
Only 16 of these were in the South.

Of special interest to the South were the large population increases
enjoyed by a number of medium-sized midwestern industrial cities.
For instance, Grand Rapids gained 28,300 people, Peoria 11,800,
Toledo 31,300, and Youngstown 17,800. None of these places achieved
metropolitan status, but they did develop into manufacturing towns
such as the men of the New South wanted for their section. As did
population, industy moved from east to west rather than north to
south. In the twelve states that the census considered as part of the
North Central division, the number of cities over 8,000 rose from 95 in
1880 to 152 in 1890. No comparable growth occurred in the South. The
number of places of more than 8,000 increased from 35 to 57. According
to census experts, there was a rough correlation between industrial and
urban expansion. Summing up the situation in the South, a census
official stated, "The industries of these states are mainly agricultural,
and while manufactures and mining are making some progress they
are still in their infancy . . . In certain of these states that proportion of
urban population is still trifling; thus, in Mississippi it constitutes but
2.64, in North Carolina but 3.87, and Arkansas but 4.89 per cent of the
total population."[9]

The census estimated that in 1890 $6.5 billion was invested in
American industry, more than double the figure of ten years earlier.
Total investments in the South reached $585 million, against $2 billion
for the North Central division alone. In 1890 only Maryland (fourteenth) and Kentucky (sixteenth) ranked in the leading twenty American manufacturing states in gross value of products. The amount of
money invested in southern manufacturing had increased markedly
from $234 million in 1880. In an era of almost no inflation, this increase
was impressive. Manufacturing capital in Georgia rose from $11 mil-

lion to $57 million, in Alabama from $11 million to $46 million. Yet these gains seemed small by national standards. Industrial investments outside the South rose by more than $3.5 billion. Manufacturing capitalization in the state of New York grew from $500 million to $1.3 billion. The additional $800 million added to New York's capital base was more than the total worth of all Dixie's industries.[10] The "industrial revolution" in the North generated so much money so quickly that the South could not catch up.

Only a few bright spots broke an otherwise depressing picture in the urban South. The capitalization of manufacturing in Baltimore rose from $38.6 million to $92.8 million. New Orleans ($26.3 million), Washington ($28.9 million), and Louisville ($36.1 million) all had fairly substantial capital bases upon which to build in the future. Yet these figures were small compared to Chicago's total of $359.7 million. In all, seventeen southern cities were among the top one hundred cities in aggregate capital. Richmond's capitalization more than doubled during the 1880s from $6.9 million to $16.8 million. In the same span the midwestern city of Columbus, Ohio, which had a heavy industrial base comparable to that of Richmond, enjoyed an increase in capital investment of from $5.4 million to $16.2 million. Except for Richmond and the South's four largest metropolitan areas, no city in the region had in excess of $10 million invested in manufacturing. Manufacturing in the piedmont was still in an early stage, although there had been some gains.

The highly publicized new interior manufacturing centers had made disappointingly little progress. Chattanooga did not even rank among the top one hundred cities. Atlanta had $9.5 million and Memphis $9.4 million in manufacturing capitalization in 1890. These increases were in excess of 300 percent, but so were those of many northern industrial centers. By contrast, the capital invested in Peoria, Illinois, plants jumped from $4.2 to $15.1 million, and it was only a cog in the midwestern manufacturing empire. Birmingham had yet to fulfill its promise. In 1890 the aggregate for all industries was $4.6 million and for iron and steel, $1.6 million. Racine, Wisconsin, a rising mill town with 5,000 fewer people than Birmingham, boasted $11.2 million in manufacturing capital. In Pittsburgh $48.2 million out of an industrial capitalization of $108.4 million was in iron and steel.[11] Clearly, the gloriously conceived attempt to raise the South to the level of the North had failed. The predictions of Grady and his colleagues turned to ashes.

During the 1890s the South stopped trying to compete with the North and turned inward. Widespread opposition developed to any policy that sought accommodation with the new northern industrial empire, although industrialism itself was not repudiated. Shortly after his untimely death, Grady came to be considered one of the South's fallen heroes. Henry Watterson continued to gain stature as a sectional leader. Edmonds's *Manufacturers' Record* remained the South's foremost commercial publication. Rather, the change in emphasis was directly related to the realities of sectional economic relations. Of particular significance was the growing perception that the North had lost interest in trying to influence the course of southern events.

The South underwent a period of retrenchment based on the recognition that there was continuity in southern history. In the 1850s, the delegates active in the southern commercial convention movement had reached the conclusion that the South could not compete with the North on its own terms. The premise followed that southern civilization was unique and should take its own distinctive path. Forty years later, after the Civil War, Reconstruction, and the aborted New South, a new generation of southern leaders reached much the same conclusion, although for somewhat different reasons. In the 1850s the main reason for retrenchment was economic. No one gave much thought to social problems because they were handled by the institution of human slavery. During the 1890s the main priority was to retain the supremacy of the white race. The result was legislation, including the Louisiana separate car act, sustained in 1896 by the United States Supreme Court in *Plessy v. Ferguson.* In later laws the South formulated a highly structured segregation system based on the separate but equal doctrine. In 1898, the U.S. Supreme Court in *Williams v. Mississippi* accepted the "Mississippi Plan,"[12] which called for the disfranchisement of black voters. A common thread between the 1850s and 1890s was that in both decades the North did not care about the development of an autonomous South. Few northerners had paid much attention to the full ramifications of the convention movement until it was too late. And no major outcry in the North arose to oppose the trend in the South toward white racial domination, even though the Jim Crow laws regulated race relations more completely and along the same lines as the discredited Black Codes. Northern attitudes were in sharp contrast to those of 1861. The circumstances were different—there was no Abraham Lincoln, and the peculiar institution was long dead. The rise of industry and the development of previously virgin areas had drastically changed northern priorities.

Agricultural discontent was another indication of the South's growing isolationism. Support of the Populist movement opposed the New South approach to solving economic problems. They wanted to eradicate rather than encourage what they perceived as outside domination of southern economic institutions. Although it generally went unrecognized at the time, there was a direct connection between the agrarian revolt and the South's historic inability to develop a great commercial and banking center able to control credit so as to offer farmers low interest rates, high prices, and other inducements. The leaders of the agrarian movement would have been perfectly at home at one of the prewar commercial conventions. Indeed, the Civil War was only an interlude in the quest of southern agrarians for more equitable commercial arrangements.

During the 1870s distressed farmers throughout the section had joined the Patrons of Husbandry. Local chapters numbered more than a thousand, but the southern Grangers had little impact beyond educating farmers about political action. The movement also spawned internal disharmony, which New South spokesmen ignored. The Grange gave way to a series of state-level farmers' alliances and local groups called agricultural wheels. Many of the members were tenant farmers and sharecroppers united in opposition to land barons. Out of this combination emerged the Southern Alliance, which advocated the cooperative marketing of farm products. Business opposition and a lack of capital doomed these plans. In response, the Southern Alliance went into politics. Rejecting overtures for a great national Populist party, Alliance leaders worked through the southern Democratic party, a bulwark of white supremacy. The Alliance, which initially claimed to have considerable black support, declined after agrarian Democrat William Jennings Bryan lost the 1896 presidential election. The bitter realities of abject poverty and racial strife bore down on Dixie's inhabitants.[13] As long as the rural South remained depressed and divided, the promise of southern life envisioned by the architects of the New South remained an impossible dream. The failed agrarian crusade was not an aberration but another frustrating episode in the South's economic inability to build an urban network that could have freed the section from outside domination.[14]

In the final analysis, the majority of southern urbanites responded negatively to the agrarian efforts, despite urban and rural interdependence. The prospect of black and white farmers banding together in a community of interest to achieve specific political ends frightened urban dwellers. The antiurbanism that culminated in Bryan's campaign pointed up divergent urban and rural interests. City people did not want to pay more than absolutely necessary for their food products. Rural folk felt gouged by urban businessmen at just about every conceivable level. Interest rates and shipping costs were causes of continual friction. On the other hand, few southern businessmen were willing to listen seriously to the proposals put forward by the Southern Alliance. Nor did they formulate counterproposals. More was involved than simply the protection of vested interests. Everyone agreed that southern agriculture was depressed long before the Panic of 1893. The failure of the rural South to recover from the Civil War assured its colonial status within an industrialized United States. Yet the traditional conservative nature of southern city building also meant that because of the South's consistent lack of investment capital, there was an unwillingness to take risks. The propagandists of the New South portrayed a section whose business leaders were wide awake to change. Although this may have been true in a few places, notably the rebuilt city of Atlanta and newly industrialized Birmingham, it did not extend to the urban South as a whole. The course of city building continued to flow along cautious traditional lines.

The thirty cities that had formed the backbone of the southern urban network in 1880 all experienced population gains during the following ten years (see Table 7.1).[15] Eight of the towns enjoyed increases in excess of the national average of 56.5 percent for all the people in the country living in urban territory. Seven ranked among the forty largest metropolises in the United States. Baltimore remained the nation's seventh largest city. New Orleans was twelfth, Washington fourteenth, and Louisville twentieth. The South's four largest cities continued as the section's only true metropolises. Richmond, in thirty-fourth place, and Nashville, in thirty-eighth, had respectable urban dimensions but fell short of metropolitan status. The precarious state of the southern economy precluded the building of instant cities such as were spinging to life in the West.[16]

The layer of southern cities that made the poorest showing, with certain marked exceptions, was that made up of the old Atlantic ports. Portsmouth and Alexandria, which grew by only 5 percent, struggled to retain their identities. Alexandria was becoming a Washington suburb. Georgetown had no official corporate existence. Since 1871 Congress had gradually stripped the city government of its powers. Yet the end for this old colonial village was dictated by progress rather than failure. As the country grew, necessitating larger government services, Washington continued to enjoy healthy progress. It added 52,800 inhabitants, and its percentage increase was at the national average. Vicissitudes of commerce affected the fortunes of the other key seacoast ports. Charleston rose by only 10 percent and Wilmington by 16 percent. Both cities continued to count the handling of cotton as crucial to their economic fortunes. Their leaders had found no way to alter their economics, and the depressed conditions in the hinterlands only added to the problems. Although Wilmington merchants deserved high marks for more than holding their own against increased competition and shifting marketing patterns, the time was past when the cotton trade could result in a swift advance in population. Savannah, which also enjoyed an impressive cotton trade, benefited from its increasing importance as a regional railroad center. Rapid urban growth in Georgia and the opening up of northeastern Florida gener-

Table 7.1.   Population Trends in Thirty Southern Cities, 1880-1890

City	Population		Increase	
	1880	1890	Number	Percent
Alabama				
Mobile	29,132	31,076	1,944	6.67
Montgomery	16,713	21,883	5,170	30.93
Arkansas				
Little Rock	13,138	25,874	12,736	96.94
Dist. of Columbia				
Washington	177,624	230,392	52,768	29.71
Georgetown	12,578	14,046	1,468	11.67
Georgia				
Atlanta	37,409	65,533	28,124	75.18
Augusta	21,891	33,300	11,409	52.12
Columbus	10,123	17,303	7,180	70.93
Macon	12,749	22,746	9,997	78.41
Savannah	30,709	43,189	12,480	40.64
Kentucky				
Covington	29,720	37,371	7,651	25.74
Lexington	16,656	21,567	4,911	29.48
Louisville	123,758	161,129	37,371	30.20
Newport	20,433	24,918	4,485	21.95
Louisiana				
New Orleans	216,090	242,039	25,949	12.01
Maryland				
Baltimore	332,313	434,439	102,126	30.73
Cumberland	10,693	12,729	2,036	19.04
Mississippi				
Vicksburg	11,814	13,373	1,559	13.20
North Carolina				
Wilmington	17,350	20,056	2,706	15.60
South Carolina				
Charleston	49,984	54,955	4,971	9.95
Columbia	10,036	15,353	5,317	52.98
Tennessee				
Chattanooga	12,892	29,100	16,208	125.72
Memphis	33,592	64,495	30,903	92.00
Nashville	43,350	76,168	32,818	75.70
Virginia				
Alexandria	13,659	14,339	680	4.98
Lynchburg	15,959	19,709	3,750	23.50
Norfolk	21,966	34,871	12,905	58.75
Petersburg	21,656	22,680	1,024	4.73
Portsmouth	11,390	13,268	1,878	16.49
Richmond	63,600	81,388	17,788	27.97

ated enough activities in the hinterlands so that Savannah added 12,500 inhabitants, a rise of 41 percent. In an era of sharper competition between cities, Savannah had fared well. Norfolk's success as a coal-exporting center—a direct consequence of decisions by northern railroad interests—sparked a boom. The number of residents jumped by 12,900, a rise of 59 percent.

Baltimore was the South's greatest success story. Its midwestern connections paid handsome dividends. The port of Baltimore remained prosperous throughout the 1880s. More than ever, the Monumental City dominated life in Maryland and Delaware. An augmentation of 31 percent translated into a spectacular population rise of 102,000. Only six other American cities added more than 100,000 persons. The Baltimore story served as an apt demonstration of the gradual evolution of city building in the South. Plans made before the Civil War led to railroad connections necessary in the nineteenth century to construct a national metropolis. The New South philosophy espoused in the pages of Richard Edmonds's Baltimore-based *Manufacturers' Record,* although inspirational, actually had little to do with the continued advance. The city's business community simply continued to follow a proven path to success.

Only two of the five old piedmont cities that had served as connecting links between the coast and the interior in antebellum days had growth rates in the 1880s in excess of the national average. Virginia's cities experienced disappointing growth. Petersburg added only 1,000 people, an increase of slightly under 5 percent and the lowest among the thirty cities that had formed the backbone of the southern urban system at the beginning of the decade. Petersburg's tobacco fims failed to keep pace with changing tastes brought about by the new popularity of cigarettes. Outside investors showed no interest in building manufacturing plants. So Petersburg languished off the beaten path of southern progress. Lynchburg, another Virginia tobacco town, had a modest 24 percent growth rate. Just as in Petersburg, the Lynchburg tobacco industry had failed to keep abreast with the times. If the New South propagandists had been right, both cities would have moved ahead rapidly, building upon a solid if modest manufacturing base. Instead, the opposite had happened. Because they relied on producing outmoded goods, the cities had limited future prospects. Richmond, which grew by 28 percent, slightly under the national average, added 17,800 residents, the largest total for any place in the Old Dominion. Richmond further cemented its role as the state's largest city. In addition to being a manufacturing and government town, Richmond emerged as one of the South's top banking centers. In South Carolina and Georgia, both Columbia and Augusta profited from increased industrialism. Columbia's growth rate was 53 percent and Augusta's only a percentage point lower. These rates were in line with the New South advocates' hopes. But although Augusta added 11,400 inhabitants and Columbia 5,300, neither place displayed the attributes of a boom town. They continued, as at the start of the decade, to function as medium-sized communities with increasingly solid industrial components. Taken as a whole, the original successful piedmont towns had not generated the speed of growth needed to serve as the heart of a southern factory system.

Of the cities in the South that had spearheaded the advance of civilization into the New West, six had more than 10,000 people in 1880. Two experienced considerable progress during the ensuing decade. Both drew upon the continued prosperity of the Louisville and Nashville Railroad. Louisville, the South's fourth largest city, had a growth rate of 30 percent, adding 37,400 inhabitants. Impressive transportation components had enabled Louisville to claim a place among the nation's regional metropolises. Nashville advanced in much the same way. A total of more than 32,900 new residents represented an increase of 76 percent. The population enlargements made Nashville and Louisville harbingers of the New South. Cumberland, Lexington, Newport, and Covington did not achieve such success. Cumberland, which grew by 19 percent, remained simply another railroad division point. Lexington, somewhat off the beaten path of commercial activity, grew by 29 percent. Much of the rise related to the agricultural base in the Kentucky Bluegrass region, one of the most prosperous in the South. Covington grew by 26 percent and Newport by 22 percent, but the two Cincinnati suburbs had virtually lost their remaining southern identity.

Unimpressive growth rates for the South's two major Gulf Coast ports reflected a combination of depressed regional markets and shifting national transportation patterns. New Orleans added 26,000 people, not a strong showing for a large city. The Crescent City's rate of increase of 12 percent was less than half that of any of the South's other three metropolitan centers. The leaders of New Orleans had given up hope of achieving urban greatness through domination of upriver trade. And as long as Louisiana and Mississippi remained in a state of agricultural stagnation, New Orleans could not advance appreciably by capitalizing on traditional regional trading areas. To compound matters, violent riots directed against Italians and New York's dominance as a receiving center for the massive flood of immigrants into the United States severely hurt New Orleans' role as a major immigrant reception center. In the Crescent City, it was a matter of hoping for the best by riding out an economic storm that had no foreseeable end. After J.D.B. DeBow died, the New South creed had no influential spokesman in New Orleans. Local leaders saw no reason to support a concept cloaked in regional terms that would help rival cities. New Orleans had no way of quickly realizing the promise predicted by Grady for the urban South. Survival rather than advance was the order of the day. The same conditions impaired Mobile's chances. In a period of recession, its carefully constructed regional railroad connections and its cotton marketing facilities were financial liabilities instead of strengths. Mobile added only 1,900 inhabitants, representing a poor growth rate of 7 percent. As long as Alabama continued to be dominated by an inefficient sharecropper economy there appeared little room for improvement. Mobile, a major part of a carefully constructed antebellum commercial urban system that had increasingly lost its forward thrust, would languish beside its beautiful bay.

The emerging interior cities of the South were crucial to the hopes of the New South promoters. "Magic cities" were expected to grow overnight from small country towns into great regional metropolises. Writing about the central South, Grady proclaimed, "The promise of her great destiny, written in her fields, her quarries, her mines, her forests, and her rivers, is no longer blurred or indistinct, and the world draws near to read."[17] As with so many statements about a New South on the march to greatness, the truth was somewhat different. The emerging interior cities had failed to grow at the pace necessary to challenge towns outside the South. All eight of the places in the southern interior with populations of over 10,000 inhabitants registered increases, but these gains were not large enough to have a national impact.

By southern norms the interior cities did very well. Only Vicksburg (13 percent) had a rate of growth under the national average. Both Vicksburg and Columbus (26 percent) were cotton-collecting points on natural river lines. Neither had the trunk railroad connections necessary to enlarge their commercial functions. Columbus, with its fine waterpower, still entertained hopes of developing into a large manufacturing center when the economy improved. But Vicksburg, though it remained a dominant city in Mississippi, had uninviting prospects at best. Vicksburg's citizens looked backward rather than forward, recalling the past glories of the Old South and the great siege of Civil War days. The promise of the New South never reached the town. Its inhabitants could only look with envy on a place where that promise was fulfilled—Atlanta.

In 1890 Atlanta had 28,100 more people than ten years earlier. This 75 percent increase was 46 percent above the national aveage. Atlanta's importance as a transportation and commercial hub in the Southeast increased over the decade. Grady served his city well, lecturing widely about its prospects in the North and filling the pages of his newspaper with favorable comments. Many of his promotional pieces were reprinted in smaller newspapers. In 1883, for example, the editor of the *Alexandria Town Talk* reported, "The Atlanta *Constitution* publishes a report showing that nearly $6,000,000 are invested in manufacturing industries in that city, and over $2,500,000—about half the capital invested—is paid out annually in wages."[18] Unlike most booster reports, the *Constitution* article was essentially correct. Atlanta was a city on the move.

During the 1880s, four other towns across the South's midsection registered even higher percentage increases. Population in Chattanooga advanced at a rate of 126 percent, Little Rock by 97 percent, Memphis by 92 percent, and Macon by 78 percent. Chattanooga added a number of new industries. Little Rock grew as plantation lands opened in central Arkansas. Memphis began to recover from the terrible epidemics of the 1870s. Macon benefited from solidifying its position as a subregional commercial hub. The absolute increases in population for all four cities were as impressive as the percentage figures. They all gained more than 10,000 people; Memphis added 30,900 residents. Another interior town, Montgomery, had a population rise of 5,100, an increase of 31 percent. But none of the five cities, upon which so much of the South's chances had hinged, achieved metropolitan status.

The 1890 population statistics for the thirty largest cities of the previous decade served as another indication of the continued gradual evolution of the southern urban system. Baltimore with 434,000 people and Washington with 230,400 kept their relative positions on the eastern seaboard. Savannah, which had 43,200 residents, continued to gain on Charleston, a city of 55,000. Norfolk, which had 34,900 people, was the second largest city and principal port in Virginia. A population of 20,000 cemented Wilmington's hold as North Carolina's number one port. Alexandria (14,300), Georgetown (14,000), and Portsmouth (13,000) were unimportant. Along the piedmont, Richmond's 81,400 persons continued to make it the largest fall line city. Neither Petersburg (22,700) nor Lynchburg (19,700) improved its position in Virginia. Columbia (15,400) remained the second largest city in South Carolina. Augusta (33,300) enhanced its industrial base. Louisville, a city of 161,000 inhabitants, moved ahead along expected lines. Lexington (21,600) continued on a downward slide that had started decades earlier. Covington (37,400), Newport (25,000), and Cumberland (12,700) had population figures that belied their significance in relationship to the southern urban network. Nashville, with 76,200 people, remained central Tennessee's leading urban center. New Orleans, despite a slow rate of increase, had 242,000 residents and was still the leading city of the lower South. Even with only the number of inhabitants added in the 1880s, it would still have been the nineteenth largest city in the South. Mobile (31,100), which remained in the shadow of

New Orleans, was still the second most important Gulf port. Long-established urban relationships remained unchanged.

Mixed growth rates in the interior of Dixie did not significantly alter the hierarchy of cities that had existed at the start of the decade. Atlanta's advanced to 65,500 people Chattanooga (29,100) and Little Rock (25,900) advanced as expected. Memphis (64,500) underwent a quicker recovery than predicted, mainly because of confidence in the sanitary reform program. Macon (22,800) rose along predictable lines; Montgomery (21,900) did not. Both retained their importance as cotton markets and added some manufacturing. Columbus boosters had expected their city to have more than its recorded 17,303 people in 1890, but Columbus remained an important subregional cotton center. So, at least temporarily, did Vicksburg, which with 13,400 residents was the largest city in Mississippi; it remained a connecting link in the downriver cotton trade. The interior cities continued to grow as part of a process mandated by decisions made many decades earlier.

Population trends in the eighteen southern cities that passed the 10,000 mark in the 1880s showed greater continuity than claimed by New South spokesmen (see Table 7.2).[19] Yet the statistics encouraged these men because they indicated a substantial flow of northern capital into some parts of Dixie. All eighteen cities registered growth rates in excess of the national average, understandable given their modest dimensions at the start of the decade. The pattern of new growth was generally predictable. No new seaport cities of importance arose from Maryland through South Carolina. In Florida, however, a combination of new settlement and the anticipation of a boom in the underdeveloped state led to urban growth. Both Jacksonville and Key West weathered serious yellow fever visitations and showed population growth. Jacksonville increased by 9,500 in population for a growth of 125 percent. The total number of inhabitants reached 17,200, and further increases seemed assured. A new cattle trade showed promise of diversifying Florida's agriculture. Key West and Pensacola, old naval bases that had prospered as a consequence of increased military and civilian efforts, hoped to benefit. A flourishing sponging trade helped Key West, which added 9,900 people, attain a population of 18,100. The addition of 4,900 residents made Pensacola a town of 11,800. No other new cities along the Gulf of Mexico became significant.

Developments in Florida harked well for the future. Northern capitalist Henry Morrison Flagler of the Standard Oil Company was a Sunshine State counterpart of empire builder James J. Hill in the Northwest. Flagler started land companies, newspapers, cattle ranches, citrus farms, and utilities in Florida. Ahead of his times in seeing the potential of tourism as a way to improve Florida's economy, Flagler built gigantic Victorian-style resort hotels, which tourists reached over

Table 7.2.   Population Trends in Eighteen Southern Cities That
Passed the 10,000 Mark, 1880-1890

| City | Population | | Increase | |
	1880	1890	Number	Percent
Alabama				
Birmingham	3,086	26,178	23,092	748.28
Arkansas				
Fort Smith	3,099	11,311	8,212	264.99
Florida				
Jacksonville	7,650	17,201	9,551	124.85
Key West	9,890	18,080	8,190	82.81
Pensacola	6,845	11,750	4,905	71.66
Kentucky				
Paducah	8,036	12,797	4,761	59.25
Louisiana				
Baton Rouge	7,197	10,478	3,281	45.59
Shreveport	8,009	11,979	3,970	49.57
Maryland				
Hagerstown	6,627	10,118	3,491	52.68
Mississippi				
Meridian	4,008	10,624	6,616	165.07
Natchez	7,058	10,101	3,043	43.11
North Carolina				
Asheville	2,616	10,235	7,619	291.25
Charlotte	7,094	11,557	4,463	62.91
Raleigh	9,265	12,678	3,413	36.84
Tennessee				
Jackson	5,377	10,039	4,662	86.70
Knoxville	9,693	22,535	12,842	132.49
Virginia				
Danville	7,526	10,305	2,779	36.93
Roanoke	669	16,159	15,490	2,315.40

a network of rails that ultimately extended to Key West via Flagler's Florida East Coast Railroad.[20] Grady said that by 1889 Flagler had already invested $7 million in Florida hotel properties and superb winter homes. "The tide of travel," Grady wrote, "is turning again, and Florida is not only confirmed as the winter garden of the Republic, but its sanitarium."[21] According to the 1890 census, Florida was the last frontier in the continental United States.[22] The men of the Old South had neither the capital nor the inclination to develop a remote, swampy region ill-suited to cotton production. Florida needed the capital resources coupled with a grand design that Flagler brought. A few unreconstructed southern nationalists denounced Flagler as another in a long line of northern rascals bent on keeping the South in colonial bondage. Of course, this evluation missed a fundamental point of the New South philosophy, the conception that the section could best be raised by attracting such men as Flagler. According to this viewpoint, the South desperately needed outside capital to break northern bondage.

In Louisiana and Mississippi many old river towns aspired to become great railroad centers. Predictions at the start of the 1880s that demands from overseas would generate a great cotton boom had proved a myth. Hence aspirations changed. In 1883 Edgar McCormick of the *Alexandria Town Talk* predicted a tremendous future for his village as a transportation center. "Here in Alexandria," he wrote, "it is a matter of little consequence to the merchants and people whether the river is high or low as the railroad facilities are unsurpassed. To-day flour is sold cheaper as it is in New Orleans. Alexandria is therefore headquarters for flour, and the merchants and people in the surrounding parishes . . . Our direct railroad connection with St. Louis enables us to buy without paying a profit to the middle men at New Orleans."[23] Despite such optimism, Alexandria was little more than a glorified village at the close of the decade. As a consequence of the agricultural depression, only a few river cities in the deep South achieved populations over 10,000. In Louisiana, Baton Rouge grew from 7,200 to 10,500 persons and Shreveport from 8,000 to 12,000. Impressive rates of increase—almost 50 percent for Shreveport and 46 percent for Baton Rouge—failed to hide lackluster records in other Louisiana towns. Results in Mississippi were much the same. Meridian rose by 165 percent, but it was still a farm marketing and railroad junction of 10,600 people in 1890. Few local residents entertained hope of major future progress. The prospects for Natchez were bleaker. In the ten-year span, its number of residents increased form 7,100 to 10,100. A temporary rise in river traffic had generated false hopes. Only hard times and decline appeared on the horizon. The economic environment was unpromising for city building.

Four cities that moved across the 10,000 mark in the 1880s would probably have done so if there had been no New South movement. These communities were on the periphery of the South, except for Jackson, Tennessee. A railroad division point, it had a growth rate of 87 percent, reflecting a population increase from 5,400 to 10,000. But an impressive percentage rise was not enough to make Jackson a major city. It never was prominent in plans for a New South. Nor was Fort Smith, Arkansas, on the edge of the Indian Territory in Oklahoma. The taming of the lawless area and the furthering of law and order by "Hanging Judge" Isaac Parker paved the way for land rushes into Oklahoma at the end of the decade. Fort Smith acquired a minor hinterland, advancing in the ten years from 3,100 to 11,300 people. The town's progress was an unexpected plus to the hopes of advocates of rapid southern urbanization. How well Fort Smith would do in the future, however, was tied in more with western development than with that of the South. Fort Smith was a southern city only because of its Arkansas location. So was the Kentucky river city of Paducah. A gain of close to 5,000 inhabitants brought its population to 12,800, but Paducah's prosperity rested on building a hinterland directly to the north in Illinois. Hagerstown, Maryland, was another of many places that grew as a railroad junction. It had 10,100 residents, and its proximity to Baltimore and Washington gave it no chance of building a large marketing area. Hagerstown and Jackson were important for limited transportation reasons. Paducah was a river town with small ambitions in the post-steamboat era. Fort Smith was a glorified military post. Although these places afforded further evidence of gradual progress, they were not crucial to the building of an urban South.

Industrial progress, significant by southern standards, led to the rise of some piedmont mill towns. Big Lick, Virginia, had 669 residents at the start of the 1880s. The opening of textile factories financed by Yankee capitalists ushered in a boom. Under the new name of Roanoke, the place in 1890 had 16,200 inhabitants, making it the fourth largest city in Virginia.[24] Roanoke had a 2,315 percent rate of growth. Of all the cities in the country over 2,500 population, only three had greater growth percentages: the Oregon lumber town of Albina (3,487 percent) and the two Washington centers of Tacoma (3,179 percent) and Spokane (5,592 percent). None of the other new piedmont towns came close to duplicating the showing of Roanoke, although four did rather well. Danville, Virginia, had a 37 percent rate of increase, going from 7,500 to 10,300 persons. In North Carolina, textile and cigarette manufacturing led to major advances. Charlotte and Raleigh continued down paths set earlier. Their New South boosters pointed with pride to an increase of 63 percent for Charlotte and 37 percent for

Raleigh. In 1890 the former had 11,600 people and the latter 12,700. Asheville, a country village of 2,600 in 1880, served as still another example of how the coming of industry could lead to a sharp rise in population. As a consequence of a 291 percentage increase, the town had 10,200 inhabitants in 1890. Along with Roanoke, Danville, Charlotte, and Raleigh, it had bright prospects. But despite the dramatic changes under way in the tobacco industry, coupled with the luring of New England textile manufacturers, none of the cities appeared to have the remotest chance of duplicating the overnight success of Chicago or San Francisco. Still, if twenty other cities had done as well in the 1880s as Roanoke or even Danville, the section would have quickly gained urban parity with the rest of the nation. Perhaps, then, the visions of the New South advocates and the agrarian crusaders for an independent self-sufficient South might have come true.

Two cities more than two hundred miles apart, one old and one new, personified attributes associated with the rise of a New South. In Tennessee, Knoxville, which began as a frontier outpost in the New West in the previous century, finally started to display the success predicted by its early promoters. During the 1880s, Knoxville, helped by an infusion of industry, especially a large trash can factory, more than doubled in population from 9,700 to 22,500. Unlike many other southern cities, Knoxville had significant suburban characteristics. Census statisticians noted that roughly 40,000 persons lived in the Knoxville area, most along the pikes and creek valleys that spread out from the city in all directions.[25] Despite its success, Knoxville had the disadvantage of being a rival of Atlanta. Henry Grady ignored Knoxville when he listed cities in the forefront of the New South movement. Birmingham was another case. Grady, who envisioned the new "Vulcan" as the next Pittsburgh, saw Birmingham as both a fitting symbol of the New South and a junior partner of Atlanta. The population of Birmingham increased in the 1880s from 3,100 to 26,200, a rise of 748 percent. Within a few years the Alabama city had acquired promising demographic dimensions.

Birmingham hoped to become a regional metropolis. The Louisville and Nashville Railroad connected Birmingham with a number of neighboring iron and coal-producing towns, including Bessemer, Talladega, and Anniston. According to promotional literature, there were thirty-two iron furnaces in and around Birmingham. The editor of the *Birmingham Iron Age* proclaimed that more outside capitalists arrived every week. By 1890 Alabama produced more iron and steel than any other southern state. This progress caused Andrew Carnegie to remark that the South was the "most formidable industrial enemy" that Pennsylvania encountered in the struggle for control of the American iron industry.[26] Northern money, some of it supplied by

Carnegie, had provided the necessary resources for the start of a boom. Unfortunately for its future aspirations, more than outside money and a few small towns with furnaces and mines was needed to make Birmingham a great city. Hinterland agricultural connections were of crucial importance, and as long as the farm lands around Birmingham remained depressed, the city was bound to have problems sustaining the rapid growth needed to make it an important center. Birmingham did not fit neatly into the southern urban system. Dixie's fragile agricultural economy did not require a proliferation of competing cities. After the mills were built and staffed, Birmingham, like the new industrial towns in the piedmont, faced competition from already existing cities that had long-established local agricultural connections. Despite the New South propaganda, the horrendous financial difficulties that helped spawn the agrarian revolt meant that there remained as before the Civil War an unpromising environment for "instant cities." Even with some outside help and a boldly stated program for industrial progress, city builders continued to encounter serious challenges.

Because the South was not immune to national developments, in the 1890s urban progress was one of the section's few economic bright spots. In 1900 the South contained nine more cities with populations over 10,000 than it had ten years earlier, but none of these cities posed any immediate threat to the existing orderly southern network of cities. The largest of these, Newport News, Virginia, which advanced from 4,400 to 19,600 inhabitants, was actually a part of the complex of ports surrounding Norfolk. A port with an independent existence, Tampa, Florida, added 15,800 people and could expect future growth in relationship to the development of Florida's west coast. Two interior river towns enjoyed moderate success. Owensboro, Kentucky, on the Ohio River between Paducah and Louisville, reached 13,200. Pine Bluff, Arkansas, on the Arkansas River, grew apace with the development of the rice industry on the Grand Prairie in east central Arkansas. Pine Bluff had 11,500 residents but little immediate hope of being more than a farm marketing town. The chances of the agricultural and educational community of Athens, Georgia, which reached a population of 10,200 in 1900, were little better. The four other places that crossed the 10,000 line were mill towns. In North Carolina, Greensboro and Winston-Salem both had 10,000 inhabitants. The rise of the South Carolina cities of Greenville (11,900) and Spartanburg (11,400) portended further industrial advances in the Palmetto State. But the fact that the South added only four new industrial towns reflected the general slowdown in the national economy that followed the Panic of 1893. The more industry the South acquired, the more the section's economy depended on outside forces.

The urbanization process in the South continued to move forward along well-established lines. The development of Newport News improved Atlantic coast port facilities. Economic enhancement of this nature had been under way since the earliest days of settlement. Owensboro was another junction point along the South's northern rim. Pine Bluff and Athens constituted additions to the layer of interior cities. Growth in Greensboro, Winston-Salem, Greenville, and Spartanburg was a logical consequence of the program to bring manufacturing to the piedmont. Tampa was a product of the opening of Florida. The Sunshine State contained the last layer of southern cities raised up in the nineteenth century. Events in Florida and elsewhere gave moot evidence of the strong spirit of urban enterprise that prevailed in the South. Critics noted that in the 1890s the rest of the nation added seventy-six cities of more than 10,000, clouding the significance of that figure as a dividing line between large and small communities. Yet what at first glance was a sorry showing in the South missed a fundamental point: the necessity to evaluate southern urbanization on its own merits.

The layering process was a logical response to the needs of an agrarian society. The layers of cities evolved as new lands, farther away from the eastern seaboard, opened for settlement. The procedure was a recognition that although the Old South needed commercial cities, it did not require nor did it have the strength to construct cities helter-skelter as long as it continued to operate under the restraints imposed by the plantation system. The Civil War brought a temporary halt to layering. It began again during Reconstruction and continued into the twentieth century in the resort cities of Florida and the mill towns of the piedmont. The New South movement, with the clairon call for manufacturing and the exhortations about the opportunities that awaited investors, clouded the issues. Except for a few triumphs southern urbanization continued about as before. This is not to say that things could not have been better. Entrepreneurs made bad decisions and missed opportunities. The realities of southern economics necessitated a very conservative approach to risk taking. Southern urban capitalists could not afford to risk their limited cash balances on a single decision.

The South entered the twentieth century with a clearly defined and orderly urban system. The Atlantic and Gulf ports continued to serve as the cornerstone of the network. Baltimore had come close to becoming the great commercial city dreamed about by the nationalists of the Old South. It had the twin advantages of having southern marketing areas outside the depressed cotton South and excellent connections with midwestern grain markets. Baltimore's success made it controversial, and the city's Midwest railroad strategy had hurt trade on the Mississippi River. Foes continued to claim that Baltimore was no longer southern, ignoring that it was one of the region's oldest cities. Washington, a northern city to southerners and a southern one to northerners, had 279,000 people. It was the only seaport of signficant size along the Atlantic coast that did not owe its success to maritime commerce. Although some observers felt that Washington lacked the cultural refinements necessary for a national capital, it had evolved into a pleasant town suited to the needs of the government of a nation of 90 million people.

Down the Virginia coast, Norfolk's ascendancy as a coal-exporting cnter had turned it into an important Atlantic port. Norfolk had 46,600 inhabitants, and another 21,000 lived in Newport News and Portsmouth. In North Carolina, Wilmington (21,000) experienced limited progress as a cotton-shipping port. Although Charleston, which had 56,800 people, remained important, it was no longer a pace setter for the South. An old rival, Savannah (54,200), approached Charleston in size. The Georgia city's railroads supplied good hinterland connections. Jacksonville (28,400) owed its growth to the development of regional markets in Florida. So did the other chief Florida ports: Key West (17,000), Tampa (15,800), and Pensacola (17,700). Mobile (38,500), with a weak marketing area, had to contend with increasingly stiff opposition from the other Gulf ports. Even in a decade of depression and social unrest, New Orleans added 45,100 people. The South's second largest city had a population of 287,100, remaining—as it had for decades—a great cotton-shipping port.

With New Orleans and Baltimore as cornerstones, the general contours of coastal urbanization in the South were not appreciably different than they had been in the Early National period. The only exception was the rise of the Florida cities, but even they had been important in the fishing village economy that had characterized Florida under Spanish rule.

The 1900 census showed no significant changes in long-standing relationships among the old piedmont and New West layers of cities. None of the cities built in the Gilded Age yet posed a threat to established relationships. Richmond had 85,100 residents, but no other interior city in Virginia had as many as 20,000 people. The same was true in North Carolina. Charlotte, the largest of the state's new mill towns, with 18,100 residents, hardly qualified as an industrial giant. South Carolina's primary interior town, Columbia, had 21,000 inhabitants. Augusta, which had a listed population of 39,400, was a successful commercial and mill town but far from a metropolis. A significant feature of the industrial movement in the piedmont was that the old established places with good railroad connections maintained their dominate positions, despite the addition of a few more mill towns. Railroads had helped cities cement their positions. Louisville entered the twentieth century with 204,700 persons and Nashville with 80,900. Both centers continued to dominate and further to consolidate large marketing areas. Populist orators correctly charged that the Louisville and Nashville Railroad was ultimately controlled by eastern capital, but so were the main railroad lines that ran out of Chicago. The amount of business that a great railroad system generated for a terminal was far more important in the long run than the origin of the capital. Certainly, there was a need to formulate an aggressive community urban railroad policy at the earliest possible date, even when future prospects appeared bleak. No city, not even Chicago, had the resources to construct its own trunk railroads. From Richmond to Augusta and Louisville to Nashville, places that had advanced quickly because of decisions made in the Old South continued to be dominant into the twentieth century.

Birmingham was the only "instant city" of major stature spawned in the Gilded Age. Birmingham contained 38,400 residents in 1900, and 10,000 more lived in its suburbs, especially outlying Bessemer. Birmingham had advanced impressively since its founding thirty years earlier. In a similar time span, between the 1830s and the 1860s, Chicago's population grew from a few people to more than 100,000. In the 1890s, when Birmingham grew by close to 12,000 inhabitants, Chicago added close to a million. Birmingham and other cities in the South's interior had no way of competing directly with a city such as Chicago for people. The New South propagandists did the South a disservice by claiming that the adoption of an urban and industrial program would soon allow Dixie to build a series of monster metropolises. It made substantial achievements appear almost as failures.

Within southern parameters, many of the interior cities had done very well. Memphis, despite the stigma of frequent yellow fever outbreaks, moved forward in impressive fashion, helped by the creation of new markets in eastern Arkansas. The city had 102,300 residents in 1900, having added 37,800 in ten years. Atlanta increased by 24,000 people. The jewel of the New South had 89,900 residents at the close of the 1890s. Its role as a banking and trading center assured future growth. If the Peach State's agricultural economy ever prospered, regional dominance seemed in reach. Several places in the cotton South entered the twentieth century as medium-sized towns built upon solid foundations: Columbus (17,600), Macon (23,300), Montgomery (30,300), and Meridian (14,100), to name a few. The contours of the interior layer of cities were in place.

The 1900 census demonstrated that at best the South had only slightly improved its urban position in the United States during the Gilded Age. In 1900 there were 400 cities with more than 10,000 people in the United States. Only 57 of those were in the South. Twenty years earlier, 30 out of 228 such cities had been in the South. Other indexes nullified that slight gain. Of 82 American cities in 1900 in the 25,000 to 50,000 population group, only 10 were in the South. Of 40 cities of from 50,000 to 100,000, the South had but 5. Of 38 cities in excess of 100,000, there were 5 in the South. Dixie had added only 1 city in that category in twenty years; the rest of the country had 17 more. The South, however, did have Baltimore, which kept its hold on sixth place nationally. Moreover, the figures failed to convey a fundamental point about the southern urban network: as throughout much of its history, the South entered the new century with cities designed to serve sectional commercial needs. That was the best the South could do, given its inability to build up a city capable of combating New York. The South never had the means of controlling its own credit. For that reason and because of the nature of the agricultural system, most southerners approached city building reasonably and realistically. Dixie's urban network has to be considered on its own merits. A statistical lag was inevitable, given the circumstances.

Southern urbanization in the Gilded Age underscored the continuity of the section's experience. Economic, social, religious, and political attitudes all had antebellum roots. Neither the Civil War nor Reconstruction had much more than a temporary disruptive impact on southern cities. Indeed, there was little need to transform them in northern images because they had mirrored national urban values since colonial times. The manner of their construction and their attempt to garner markets though transportation systems were all in the prevailing direction of American city making. It went without saying that there was more sophisticated social life in New Orleans than in Scranton, Pennsylvania, and that similar disparities gave life a flavor in Columbia distinct from that in Little Rock. Yet, allowing for differences in style and taste, tempered by geography and climate, one city was much the same as another. Urbanity was basically a matter of degree.

The realization that the South lacked the resources to achieve urban and hence economic parity with the rest of America in a short time dulled the spirit of many white southerners. An inferior agricultural system militated against a quick recovery. In the wake of the failed agrarian crusade, southern leaders concentrated on maintaining segregation and remembering the Lost Cause. A general acceptance of second-class status in the Union in exchange for a measure of social control over internal affairs gave the South the appearance of a failed and conservative bastion. Fundamentalist religious bodies deplored modernist values such as evolution. The gradual rise of the Ku Klux Klan, along with frequent lynchings, provided further indication to the rest of the nation that the South was a place apart. The region's intellectuals defended Dixie by attacking the intrusion of Yankee values and conjuring up visions of an idealized agrarian society. Through it all, the cities remained the best hope for a progressive South. Indeed, they continued to grow along logical lines—the next urban layer coming in Florida.

The failure of the plans of the New South leaders clouded the continuity and the progress made in southern city building. At the same time they provided, as for J. D. B. DeBow in antebellum days, a rationale for building the very kind of urban society about which Jefferson had expressed ambivalence. In the twentieth century, a new generation of civic boosters called for advancement of their particular towns. It made little difference that northern money fueled the Alabama steel industry, the piedmont textile mills, or the Florida land boom; it was all part of a continuing process. A potential remained for urban advance on the model of Chicago. The South experienced an "urban ethos" in the 1920s, a calamity along with the rest of the country in the 1930s, an infusion of federal money in the 1940s, and a great boom in the following decades. By 1985 the region had achieved many of the goals of the New South. Given the manner in which southerners had built their cities, the results represented the completion of a logical urbanization policy that brought about parity with the rest of the nation. Cities enabled the South to regain the status in the Union that it had enjoyed early in the nineteenth century.

The picture of castles in the sky painted by the men of the New South creed requires viewing from within rather than from outside the South. They were keepers of the faith, honorable heirs to an ambivalence on the part of southerners over the nature of the cities they wanted. During a time of trial for Dixie, they held out a vision of a South of cities built with northern money but under southern direction. But schemes went sour and goals were overreached. Southerners' views on race were distasteful to many of their northern contemporaries. Yet once southern attitudes changed, and vast quantities of northern and federal money flowed South, the visions of the men of the New South came true. A hundred years after the promulgation of the creed, numerous ornaments attested to the South's urban condition: the high-rise buildings of Birmingham, the Metro subway of Washington, the condominiums of Fort Lauderdale, and the Super Dome of New Orleans. None seemed as appropriate as a monument at Marietta and Forsyth streets in downtown Atlanta. It was a statue of Henry Grady.

Notes

1. A Wider Field Both for Virtue and Vice

1. There is valuable material on the "Sunbelt" concept in David C. Perry and Alfred J. Watkins, eds., *The Rise of the Sunbelt Cities*, Urban Affairs Annual Reviews, vol. 14 (Beverly Hills, 1977). See also Carl Abbott, *The New Urban America: Growth and Politics in Sunbelt Cities* (Chapel Hill, 1981); Don Doyle, "The Urbanization of Dixie," *Journal of Urban History* 7 (November 1980): 83-91; Richard M. Bernard and Bradley R. Rice, eds., *Sunbelt Cities: Politics and Growth since World War II* (Austin, 1983).

2. See, for example, Carl N. Degler, *Place over Time: The Continuity of Southern Distinctiveness* (Baton Rouge, 1977), 145-47. David R. Goldfield, *Cotton Fields and Skyscrapers: Southern City and Region, 1607-1980* (Baton Rouge, 1982), claims that after four centuries southern cities are closer in spirit to antebellum plantations than to New York and Chicago.

3. Thomas Jefferson, *Notes on the State of Virginia*, ed. William Peden (Chapel Hill, 1955), 165. Morton White and Lucia White, *The Intellectual versus the City: From Thomas Jefferson to Frank Lloyd Wright* (Cambridge, Mass., 1962), places Jefferson in the mainstream of intellectual thought. For a different approach see Charles N. Glaab, "The Historian and the American Urban Tradition," *Wisconsin Magazine of History* 47 (Autumn 1963): 12-25.

4. Thomas Jefferson to James Madison, 21 December 1787, in Julian P. Boyd et al., eds., *The Papers of Thomas Jefferson*, 21 vols. (Princeton, 1950-1983), 12:442.

5. Jefferson to Benjamin Rush, 23 September 1800; Jefferson to C.F.C. DeVolney, 8 February 1805; Jefferson to Benjamin Austin, 9 January 1816; Jefferson to William Short, 2 September 1823, *The Writings of Thomas Jefferson*, Andrew Lipscomb and Andrew Bergh, eds., 20 vols. (Washington, 1903), 10:173, 11:66-67, 13:387-393, 13:469. While he was president, Jefferson confidently predicted that Norfolk in his native Virginia would eventually surpass New York as a great seaport. See John Melish, *Travels through the United States of America in the Years 1806 and 1807, and 1809, 1810, and 1811, Including an Account of Passages betwixt America and Britain, and Travels through Various Parts of Great Britain, Ireland and Upper Canada*, 2 vols. (Philadelphia, 1818), 1:201-2.

6. For an elaboration on this theme in a different context see Henry D. Shapiro, *Appalachia on Our Mind: The Southern Mountains and Mountaineers in the American Consciousness, 1870-1920* (Chapel Hill, 1978).

7. Ellwood Fisher, "The North and the South," *DeBow's Review* 7 (September 1849): 264.

8. See Robert V. Remini, *Andrew Jackson and the Course of American Empire, 1767-1821* (New York, 1977), 86-135; Clement Eaton, *Jefferson Davis* (New York, 1977); John F. Stover, *The Railroads of the South, 1865-1900: A Study in Finance and Control* (Chapel Hill, 1955), 9,

17. See Lyle W. Dorsett and Arthur H. Shaffer, "Was the Antebellum South Antiurban? A Suggestion," *Journal of Southern History* 38 (February 1972): 93-100; Blaine A. Brownell, *The Urban Ethos in the South, 1920-1930* (Baton Rouge, 1975).

9. George Tucker, *Progress of the United States in Population and Wealth* (New York, 1843), 127.

10. See Charles N. Glaab and A. Theodore Brown, rev. by Charles N. Glaab. *A History of Urban America*, 2 ed. (New York, 1976), 45-65.

11. Both quotes are from Philip S. Foner, *Business and Slavery: The New York Merchants and the Irrepressible Conflict* (Chapel Hill, 1941), 10. On page 4 of the same book, DeBow is quoted as stating, "What would New York be without slavery?"

12. The standard work on colonial urbanization is Carl Bridenbaugh, *Cities in the Wilderness: The First Century of Urban Life in America* (1938; rpr. New York, 1955). There is a good synthesis in Carville Earle and Ronald Hoffman, "The Urban South: The First Two Centuries," in Blaine A. Brownell and David R. Goldfield, eds., *The City in Southern History: The Growth of Urban Civilization in the South*, National University Publications Interdisciplinary Urban Series (Port Washington, N.Y., 1977), 23-51. A general account of cities in the new nation can be found in difficult-to-digest monographs by Allan R. Pred, both in the Harvard Studies in Urban History, *Urban Growth and the Circulation of Information: The United States System of Cities, 1790-1840* (Cambridge, Mass., 1973), and *Urban Growth and City-Systems in the United States, 1840-1860* (Cambridge, Mass., 1980).

13. Urban conditions in antebellum days are analyzed in David R. Goldfield, "Pursuing the American Urban Dream: Cities in the Old South," in Brownell and Goldfield, eds., *The City in Southern History*, 52-91. See also Leonard P. Curry, "Urbanization and Urbanism in the Old South: A Comparative View," *Journal of Southern History* 40 (February 1974): 43-60. John C. Calhoun at first supported the American System. In the early 1820s, when it increasingly appeared that the South did not fit in with the rest of the nation, he anonymously wrote the *South Carolina Exposition and Protest* (1828), which detailed the mechanics of nullification. In 1832 he resigned as vice-president, turned his back on his national political ambitions, and became a sectional spokesman. The most comprehensive account of New York's 1817 decisions and their ramifications can be found in Robert Greehalgh Albion, *The Rise of the Port of New York [1815-1860]* (New York, 1939). The basic study of the race for western markets is Julius Rubin, *Canal or Railroad? Imitation and Innovation in the Response to the Erie Canal in Philadelphia, Baltimore, and Boston, Transactions of the American Philosophical Society*, n.s., vol. 51, pt. 3 (Philadelphia, 1961). William Best Hesseltine, "Regions, Classes and Sections in American History," *Journal of Land and Public Utilities Economics* 1 (February 1944): 35-44, saw the battle for regions as a key element in the American experience. He wrote, "Control of a region's political and intellectual institutions is merely ancillary to the control of the purely economic institutions which lie at the foundation of a region's life. The ownership of the banks and the direction of credit facilities; the control of railroads, harbors, shipping facilities, and warehouses; and the domination of employers' associations, chambers of commerce, and labor organizations are the major objectives of a ruling group" (p. 39).

14. See Philip D. Jordan, *The National Road*, American Travel Series (Indianapolis, n.d.).

15. A convention, held in Knoxville, planned the Louisville, Cincinnati and Charleston Railroad. See Edward Ingle, *Southern Sidelights: A Picture of Social and Economic Life in the South a Generation before the War* (New York, 1896), 98.

16. There is a detailed economic analysis of Baltimore's strategy in Rubin, *Canal or Railroad?* The building of the railroad is detailed in the first volume of a still standard work, Edward Hungerford, *The Story of the Baltimore and Ohio Railroad, 1827-1927*, 2 vols. (New York, 1928).

17. Urban rivalries were responsible for these claims. In 1853 an editorial writer in the

Richmond Daily Dispatch warned, "Our legislature should not give away the State to Baltimore, a Northern city, having no sympathy with us." In 1857 a journalist in the *Alexandria Gazette*, concerned about a possible railroad alliance between Richmond and Baltimore, claimed, "Our citizens cannot but view with alarm a scheme calculated to divert the long sought trade from their city and railroad to Baltimore, a foreign city." Of course, neither Richmond nor Alexandria had any objection to trying to obtain northern trade connections. The quotes are from David R. Goldfield, *Urban Growth in the Age of Sectionalism: Virginia, 1847-1861* (Baton Rouge, 1977), 207-8. C. Vann Woodward, in *Origins of the New South, 1877-1913*, A History of the South, vol. 9 (Baton Rouge, 1951), 162, wrote, "Baltimore was at one and the same time the last refuge of the Confederate spirit in exile and a lying-in hospital for the birth of the New Order."

18. Stover, *Railroads of the South*, 25-27.

19. Developments in Virginia are covered in Goldfield, *Urban Growth*. Considerable attention is given to Washington canal activities in Rubin, *Canal or Railroad?* See also Goldfield and Brownell, *The City in Southern History*, 53-56; David T. Gilchrist, ed., *The Growth of the Seaport Towns: 1790-1825* (Charlottesville, 1967); Louis D. Rubin, Jr., *Virginia: A Bicentennial History* (New York, 1977), 93-121. Goldfield stresses the mutual interests between planters and commercial interests in "Urban-Rural Relations in the Old South: The Example of Virginia," *Journal of Urban History* (February 1976): 146-68.

20. The *Savannah* crossed the Atlantic between 24 May and 20 June 1819; converted to a regular sailing ship, it sunk in a storm off Long Island in 1822 (*Georgia: A Guide to Its Towns and Countryside*, American Guide Series [Athens, 1940]). Valuable material on Savannah can be found in J. E. Tuel, *The Steam Marine of the Port of New York, Examined in Its Connection with the Southern Ports of the United States and the West Indies; and in Its Communication with the Atlantic and Pacific Ocean* (Albany, 1853), 3-23. See also Albion, *Rise of New York Port*, 312-35.

21. The progress of the grain trade in the Midwest is delineated in John G. Clark, *The Grain Trade in the Old Northwest* (Urbana, 1966). See also Charles N. Glaab and Lawrence H. Larsen, "Neenah-Menasha in the 1870's," *Wisconsin Magazine of History* 52 (Autumn 1968): 19-34.

22. "Commercial Delusions'—Speculations," *American Review* 2 (October 1845): 341-57, tells the story of an unsuccessful speculation.

23. See G. W. Stephens, "Some Aspects of Early Intersectional Rivalry for the Commerce of the Upper Mississippi River Valley," *Washington University Studies* 10 (1923):277-300, and Lawrence H. Larsen, "Chicago's Midwest Rivals: Cincinnati, St. Louis, and Milwaukee," *Chicago History: The Magazine of the Chicago Historical Society* 5 (Fall 1976): 151-61. Early settlement patterns and the emergence of major cities are described in Richard Wade, *The Urban Frontier: Pioneer Life in Early Pittsburgh, Cincinnati, Lexington, Louisville, and St. Louis* (Chicago, 1959). The role of St. Louis is detailed in Neil Primm, *St. Louis: Lion of the Valley* (Boulder, 1981). Louisville's southward turn is documented in Maury Klein, *History of the Louisville and Nashville Railroad* (New York, 1972), 5. Cincinnati did not entirely give up its southern trade ambitions; see William Alexander Mabry, "Ante-Bellum Cincinnati and Its Southern Trade," in David Kelley Jackson, ed., *American Studies in Honor of William Kenneth Boyd* (1940; rpr. Freeport, N.Y., 1968), 60-85. The most detailed study of the Chicago and St. Louis rivalry is Wyatt Belcher, *The Economic Rivalry between St. Louis and Chicago, 1850-1880* (New York, 1947). New light on the economic struggle is shed in J. Christopher Schnell, "Chicago versus St. Louis: A Reassessment of the Great Rivalry," *Missouri Historical Review* 71 (April 1977): 245-65, and John F. Stover, *History of the Illinois Central Railroad* (New York, 1975). A contemporary analysis is in "A System of Internal Improvement for the West," *Western Journal* 2 (January 1849): 1-8.

24. William M. Burwell, "Virginia Commercial Convention," 12 (January 1853): 30; J.

D. B. DeBow, "Contests for the Trade of the Mississippi Valley," 3 (February 1847):98; Jesup W. Scott, "The Great West," 15 (July 1853): 51-53, all in *DeBow's Review.* See also Dorsett and Shaffer, "Was the Antebellum South Antiurban?"; Blaine Brownell, "Urbanization in the South: A Unique Experience," *Mississippi Quarterly* 26 (Spring 1973):105-20; David R. Goldfield, "The Urban South: A Regional Framework," *American Historical Review* 86 (December 1981):1009-34.

25. Quoted in Goldfield and Brownell, *The City in Southern History,* 59.

26. Quoted in *Dictionary of American Biography,* s.v., "DeBow, James Dunwoody Brownson."

27. George Fitzhugh, "Washington City and Its Characteristics," *DeBow's Review* 4 (June 1858):502-3.

28. Hinton Rowan Helper, *The Impending Crisis of the South: How to Meet It* (New York, 1857), 331-34.

29. Quoted in Weymouth T. Jordan, *Ante-Bellum Alabama Town and Country* (Tallahassee, 1957), 21.

30. Quoted in Woodward, *Origins of the New South,* 107.

31. Quoted in Paul M. Gaston, *The New South Creed: A Study in Southern Mythmaking* (New York, 1970), 25.

32. The most comprehensive summary of their views can be found in ibid. See also Woodward, *Origins of the New South,* 145-47.

33. The number of weeklies in the South rose from 182 in 1865 to 499 in 1868 and 1,827 in 1885 (Thomas D. Clark, "The Country Newspaper: A Factor in Southern Opinion, 1865-1930," *Journal of Southern History* 14 [February 1948]:3-33).

34. Dawson is quoted in Gaston, *New South Creed,* 38; Watterson in Woodward, *Origins of the New South,* 7. Page never stressed industrial development. See John Milton Cooper, Jr., *Walter Hines Page: The Southerner as American, 1855-1918* (Chapel Hill, 1977), 54-55.

35. Van Horn's role as an urban promoter is discussed in Charles N. Glaab, *Kansas City and the Railroads: A Study in Community Policy* (Madison, 1962).

36. This quotation is from a "character sketch" of Grady by Oliver Dyer in Henry W. Grady, *The New South* (New York, 1890), 19-20.

37. A useful biography is Raymond Nixon, *Henry Grady: Spokesman of the New South* (New York, 1943). See also the sketch in Donald Davidson, ed., *Selected Essays and Other Writings of John Donald Wade* (Athens, Ga., 1966), 120-48.

38. Grady, *New South,* 25.

39. Ibid., 97-98.

40. Gaston, *New South Creed,* 180-83.

41. Grady, *New South,* 104.

42. Quoted in Gaston, *New South Creed,* 117, 126.

43. Quoted in Lawrence J. Friedman, *The White Savage: Racial Fantasies in the Postbellum South* (Englewood Cliffs, N.J., 1970), 40, 54. See also Henry Watterson, *The Compromises of Life* (New York, 1903). Watterson is the subject of two biographies, Isaac Marcosson, *"Marse Henry": A Biography of Henry Watterson* (New York, 1951); Joseph Wall, *Henry Watterson: Reconstructed Rebel* (New York, 1956).

44. Quoted in Friedman, *White Savage,* 43.

45. The southern acceptance of northern economic values is detailed in Grady McWhiney, *Southerners and Other Americans* (New York, 1973). See also the classic study, W. J. Cash, *The Mind of the South* (New York, 1941).

46. Grady, *New South,* 91-92.

47. Quoted in Gaston, *New South Creed,* 1.

48. Quoted in William B. Hesseltine and David L. Smiley, *The South in American History* (Englewood Cliffs, N.J., 1960), 393.

49. See Sheldon Hackney, "Origins of the New South in Retrospect," *Journal of Southern History* 38 (May 1972):191-216; Herbert Collins, "The Idea of a Cotton Textile Industry in Post-Bellum North Carolina, 1870-1900," *North Carolina Historical Quarterly* 34 (July 1927):358-92; Patrick J. Hearden, *Independence and Empire: The New South's Cotton Mill Campaign, 1865-1901* (DeKalb, Ill., 1982).

50. Quoted in Albert Bushnell Hart, *The Southern South* (New York, 1910), 231-32.

2. A Victory of Plenty

1. *Atlanta: A City of the Modern South,* American Guide Series (1942; rpr. St. Clair Shores, Mich., 1973), 23.

2. Henry W. Grady, *The New South* (New York, 1890), 166-67.

3. Southern railroad gauges were three inches wider than those in the North. Most southern lines were adjusted to standard in 1886 (C. Vann Woodward, *Origins of the New South, 1877-1913,* A History of the South, vol. 9 [Baton Rouge, 1951], 123-24).

4. Quoted in Paul M. Gaston, *The New South Creed: A Study in Southern Mythmaking* (New York, 1970), 76. For an account of the building of the urban net, see Howard N. Rabinowitz, "Continuity and Change: Southern Urban Development, 1860-1900," in Blaine A. Brownell and David R. Goldfield, eds., *The City in Southern History: The Growth of Urban Civilization in the South* (Port Washington, N.Y., 1977), 92-122.

5. Quoted in Woodward, *Origins of the New South,* 112.

6. Quoted in Gaston, *New South Creed,* 43.

7. Grady, *New South,* 162, 229.

8. The characteristics of southern cities are detailed in George E. Waring, Jr., comp., "The Southern and the Western States," *Report on the Social Statistics of Cities, Tenth Census of the United States, 1880,* vol. 10, pt. 2 (Washington, 1886-1887), 3-15. Volume 9, part 1 is entitled "The New England and the Middle States." This source is cited in this and ensuing chapters as *Social Statistics of Cities,* pt. 1 or pt. 2. This two-part volume is the basic source of information on the characteristics of 222 cities with populations of 10,000 or more in 1880, plus smaller cities of regional importance. Detailed information is given on such topics as location, railroad communications, waterworks, places of amusement, drainage, municipal sanitation, police, fire protection, public schools, cemeteries, and historical background. Zane Miller, "The Rise of the City," *Hayes Historical Journal* 3 (Spring and Fall 1980): 73-84, shows how Waring placed cities in a sectional context while also illustrating their national similarities.

9. Despite the importance of Charleston in American history, there is no scholarly urban biography of the city. Books about Charleston include De Saussure and J. L. Dawson, *Census of the City of Charleston, for the Year 1848: Exhibiting the Condition and Prospects of the City, Illustrated by Many Statistical Details, Prepared under the Authority of the City Council* (Charleston, 1849); Charles Fraser, *Reminiscences of Charleston: Lately Published in the Charleston Courier and Now Revised and Enlarged by the Author* (Charleston, 1854); Jacob Cardozo, *Reminiscences of Charleston* (Charleston, 1866); Harriet Leiding, *Charleston: Historic and Romantic* (Philadelphia, 1931); Robert Rhett, *Charleston: An Epic of Carolina* (Richmond, 1940); Robert Molloy, *Charleston: A Gracious Heritage* (New York, 1947); and George Rogers, Jr., *Charleston in the Age of the Pinckneys* (Norman, 1969).

A detailed history of Baltimore by Robert Luce is in *Social Statistics of Cities,* 2:3-15. Two readable popular histories are Hamilton Owens, *Baltimore and Chesapeake* (New York, 1941), and Francis F. Beirne, *The Amiable Baltimoreans* (1951; rpr. Hatboro, Pa., 1968). Local histories of the "Monumental City" include *Baltimore: Past and Present, with Biographical Sketches of Its Representative Men . . .* (Philadelphia, 1881); J. Thomas Scharf, *History of Baltimore City and County . . .* (Philadelphia, 1881); Henry Elliott Shepherd, ed., *History of Baltimore from Its Founding as a Town to the Current Year, 1729-1898, Including Its Early*

Settlement and Development; A Description of Its Historic and Interesting Localities: Political, Military, Civil, and Religious Statistics; Biographies of Representative Citizens, etc., etc. (Uniontown, Pa., 1898); Clayton Colman Hall, ed., *Baltimore: Its History and Its People*, 3 vols. (New York, 1912); and Charles Hirschfield, *Baltimore, 1870-1900; Studies in Social History* (Baltimore, 1941); Sherry Olson, *Baltimore: The Building of an American City* (Baltimore, 1980). There is excellent bibliographical data on Baltimore in James B. Crooks, *Politics and Progress: The Rise of Urban Progressivism in Baltimore, 1895 to 1911* (Baton Rouge, 1968), 237-46.

Important to understanding Baltimore's internal improvement schemes are Milton Reizenstein, *The Economic History of the Baltimore and Ohio Railroad*, Johns Hopkins University Studies in Historical and Political Science, Fifteenth Series, vols. 7-8 (Baltimore, 1897); James Livingood, *The Philadelphia-Baltimore Trade Rivalry, 1780-1860* (Harrisburg, 1947); and Julius Rubin, *Canal or Railroad? Imitation and Innovation in the Response to the Erie Canal in Philadelphia, Baltimore, and Boston, Transactions of the American Philosophical Society*, n.s., vol. 51, pt. 3 (Philadelphia, 1961), 63-79; Gary Browne, *Baltimore in the Nation, 1789-1861* (Chapel Hill, 1980).

Washington is the subject of Constance McLaughlin Green's fine two-volume urban biography, *Washington*, vol. 1, *Village and Capital, 1800-1878* (Princeton, 1962), and *Washington*, vol. 2, *Capital City, 1879-1950* (Princeton, 1963). Among the many books about Washington are John Porter, *The City of Washington: Its Origin and Administration* (Washington, 1885); Charles Todd, *The Story of Washington: The National Capital* (New York, 1889); Rufus Wilson, *Washington, the Capital City, and Its Part in the History of the Nation* (Philadelphia, 1901); William Tindall, *Standard History of the City of Washington from a Study of Original Sources* (Knoxville, 1914); William Howard Taft and James Bryce, *Washington: The Nation's Capital* (Washington, 1915); Charles Moore, *Washington: Past and Present* (New York, 1929); *Washington: City and Capital*, American Guide Series (Washington, 1937); William Stevens, *Washington: The Cinderella City* . . . (New York, 1943); and Donald L. Lewis, *District of Columbia: A Bicentennial History* (New York, 1976). There are many period works ranging from the older Noah Brooks, *Washington in Lincoln's Time* (New York, 1895), to the newer James Whyte, *The Uncivil War: Washington during the Reconstruction, 1865-1878* (New York, 1958).

Georgetown is included in all the general accounts of Washington's history. See also Richard Jackson, *The Chronicles of Georgetown, D.C., from 1751 to 1878* (Washington, 1878); Grace Ecker, *A Portrait of Old Georgetown* (Richmond, 1933). For Alexandria see Mary Powell, *The History of Old Alexandria, Virginia: From July 13, 1749, to May 24, 1861* (Richmond, 1928); Nettie Voges, *Old Alexandria: Where America's Past is Present* (McLean, Va., 1975). There is considerable information on Alexandria in David R. Goldfield, *Urban Growth in the Age of Sectionalism: Virginia, 1847-1861* (Baton Rouge, 1977). Norfolk's role in the New South is discussed in a pioneering urban biography, Thomas J. Wertenbaker, *Norfolk: Historic Southern Port*, ed. Marvin Schlegel (1931; rpr. Durham, 1962). For other accounts see H. W. Burton, *History of Norfolk, Virginia: A Review of Important Events and Incidents Which Occurred from 1736 to 1877; Also a Record, Personal Reminiscences and Political, Economical, and Curious Facts* (Norfolk, 1874); George Holbert Tucker, *Norfolk Highlights, 1854-1881* (Norfolk, 1940). For Portsmouth see Marshall Butt, *Portsmouth under Four Flags, 1752-1961* (Portsmouth, 1961). Wilmington's heritage is covered in James Sprunt, *Chronicles of the Cape Fear River, 1660-1916* (1914; rpr. Raleigh, 1916); Andrew Jackson Howell, *The Book of Wilmington* (n.p., 1930); Henry Bacon McKoy, *Wilmington, N.C.—Do You Remember When?* (Greenville, S.C., 1957). Books on Savannah include William Harden, *A History of Savannah and South Georgia*, 2 vols. (Chicago, 1913); Mills Lane, *Savannah Revisited: A Pictorial History* (Savannah, 1973); Cliff Sewell, *Savannah: Now and Then* (Savannah, 1974); and Betsy Fancher, *Savannah: A Renaissance of the Heart* (Garden City, 1976).

10. Quoted in Woodward, *Origins of the New South*, 107.

11. Quoted in *Social Statistics of Cities*, 2:182.

12. Quoted in Gaston, *New South Creed*, 72-3. See Broadus Mitchell, *The Rise of Cotton Mills in the South*, John Hopkins University Studies in Historical and Political Science, ser. 39, no. 2 (Baltimore, 1921).

13. Ernest McPherson Lander, Jr., *A History of South Carolina, 1865-1960* (Chapel Hill, 1960), 82; Broadus Mitchell, *William Gregg: Factory Master of the Old South* (Chapel Hill, 1928), and Fletcher M. Green, "Duff Green: Industrial Promoter," *Journal of Southern History* 2 (February 1936): 29-42. See also Herbert Collins, "The Southern Industrial Gospel before 1860," *Journal of Southern History* 12 (August 1946):383-402; Robert S. Cotterill, "The Old South to the New," *Journal of Southern History* 15 (February 1949):3-8; Diffee W. Standard and Richard Griffin, "The Cotton Textile Industry in Ante-Bellum North Carolina," *North Carolina Historical Review* 34 (January 1957):15-37, 34 (April 1957):131-66; Weymouth T. Jordan, *Ante-Bellum Alabama: Town and Country*, Florida State University Studies, no. 27 (Tallahassee, 1957), 140-66; Charles D. Dew, *Ironmaker for the Confederacy: Joseph R. Anderson and the Tredegar Iron Works* (New Haven, 1966).

Books that cover the history of Richmond include Samuel Mordecai, *Virginia, Especially Richmond in By-gone Days, with a Glance at the Present, Being Reminiscences and Last Words of an Old Citizen*, 2d ed. (Richmond, 1860); William Christian, *Richmond: Its People and Its Story* (Philadelphia, 1923); John P. Little, *History of Richmond* (Richmond, 1933); John Abram, *Memories of Old Richmond, 1881-1944* (White Marsh, Va., 1973); Virginius Dabney, *Richmond: The Story of a City* (Garden City, 1976). Harry N. Ward and Harold E. Greer, Jr., *Richmond during the Revolution 1775-83* (Charlottesville, 1979) deals with a crucial period. Goldfield, *Urban Growth*, has material on the antebellum period. For Petersburg see James G. Scott and Edward A. Wyatt IV, *Petersburg's Story: A History* (Petersburg, 1960). Catherine Copeland, *Bravest Surrender: A Petersburg Patchwork* (Richmond, 1961), covers the Civil War period. For Lynchburg see Margaret Couch Cabell, *Sketches and Recollections of Lynchburg* (Richmond, 1858); William Christian, *Lynchburg and Its People* (Lynchburg, 1900); Rosa Faulkner Yancey, *Lynchburg and Its Neighbors* (Richmond, 1935); Dorothy T. Potter and Clifton W. Potter, Jr., *Lynchburg: "The Most Interesting Spot"* (Lynchburg, 1976). Lynchburg is one of the cities covered in a fine dissertation by Thomas Armstrong, "Urban Vision in Virginia: A Comparative Study of Ante-bellum Fredericksburg, Lynchburg, and Staunton" (Ph.D. dissertation, University of Virginia, 1974). Representative histories of Columbia include Columbia Chamber of Commerce, *Columbia South Carolina Chronicles and Comments, 1786-1913* (Columbia, 1913); Helen Kohn Hennig, ed., *Columbia: Capital City of South Carolina, 1786-1936* (Columbia, 1936); Julian A. Selby, *Memorabilia and Ancedotal Reminiscences of South Carolina and Incidents Connected Therewith* (Columbia, 1905). For the terrible consequences of the Civil War in Columbia see Marvin Lucas, *Sherman and the Burning of Columbia* (College Station, 1976), and Earl Schenck Miers, ed., *When the World Ended: The Diary of Emma LeConte* (New York, 1957). Aspects of Augusta's past are discussed in Edward J. Cashin, *The Story of Augusta* (Augusta, 1980); Charles Nash, *The History of Augusta, First Settlements and Early Days as a Town, Including the Diary of Mrs. Martha Moore Ballard (1785-1812)* (Augusta, 1904); Ray Rowland and H. Callahan, *Yesterday's Augusta*, Seeman's Historic City Series, no. 27 (Miami, 1976); Florence Corley, *Confederate City: Augusta, Georgia, 1860-1865* (Columbia, 1960); Barry Fleming, *Autobiography of a City in Arms: Augusta, Georgia, 1861-1865* (Augusta, 1975); Augusta Unit, Federal Writers' Project in Georgia, Works Projects Administration, *Augusta* (Augusta, 1938).

14. Louisville is discussed in a provocative essay, "An American Museum Piece," in George R. Leighton, *Five Cities: The Story of Their Youth and Old Age* (New York, 1939), 49-99. Three old histories are Benjamin Casseday, *The History of Louisville from Its Earliest Settlement till the Year 1852* (Louisville, 1852); *History of Ohio Falls Cities and Their Counties, with Illustrations and Bibliographical Sketches* (Cleveland, 1882); and Josiah Johnston, ed.,

Memorial History of Louisville from Its First Settlement to the Year 1896, 2 vols. (Chicago, 1896). Of more recent vintage is Isabella McMeekin, *Louisville: The Gateway City* (New York, 1946). The Louisville story to 1830 is told in a scholarly work, Richard Wade, *The Urban Frontier: Pioneer Life in Early Pittsburgh, Cincinnati, Lexington, Louisville, and St. Louis* (1959; rpr. Chicago, 1976). See as well Henry McMurtrie, *Sketches of Louisville and Its Environs: Including, among a Great Variety of Miscellaneous Matter, and Florula Louisvillensis, or A Catalogue of Nearly 400 Genera and 600 Species of Plants, That Grow in the Vicinity of the Town, Exhibiting Their Generic, Specific, and Vulgar English Names* (Louisville, 1819).

Kentucky: A Guide to the Bluegrass State, American Guide Series (New York, 1939), has data on Lexington, Newport, and Covington. Wade, *Urban Frontier,* has much information on Lexington. The city's pioneer period is covered in Richard Staples, *The History of Pioneer Lexington, (Kentucky); 1779-1806* (Lexington, 1939). Civil War times are covered in John Coleman, *Lexington during the Civil War,* rev. ed. (Lexington, 1939). Local histories include George Ranck, *History of Lexington, Kentucky: Its Early Annals and Recent Progress, Including Biographical Sketches and Personal Reminiscences of the Pioneer Settlers, Notices of Prominent Citizens, etc., etc.* (Cincinnati, 1872), and John D. Wright, *Lexington: Heart of the Bluegrass* (Lexington, 1982). For short historical sketches of Covington and Newport see *Social Statistics of Cities,* 2:111-12, 131-32.

For Maryland, see *Maryland: A Guide to the Old Line State,* American Guide Series (New York, 1940), 263-66. See also William Loudermilk, *History of Cumberland from the Time of the Indian Town, Caiuctucuc in 1728, up to the Present Day, Embracing an Account of Washington's First Campaign and Battle of Fort Necessity, Together with a History of Braddock's Expedition* (rpr. Baltimore, 1971).

Among many books on Nashville are John Wooldridge, ed., *History of Nashville, Tenn., with Full Outline of the Natural Advantages . . . History of the City Down to the Present Time* (Nashville, 1890); William McRaven, *Nashville: "Athens of the South"* (Chapel Hill, 1949); Jesse Burt, *Nashville: Its Life and Times* (Nashville, 1959); Alfred Crabbe, *Nashville: Personality of a City* (Indianapolis, 1960); Wilbur Creighton, *Building of Nashville* (Nashville, 1969); Eleanor Graham, ed., *Nashville: A Short History and Selected Buildings* (Nashville, 1974); and Carl Zilbart, *Yesterday's Nashville* (Miami, 1976).

15. George W. Cable, whose views in favor of racial equality made him a troublesome figure in the New South, wrote what census officials called a "careful and elaborate" account of the history of New Orleans in *Social Statistics of Cities,* 2:213-67. His book *The Creoles of Louisiana* (New York, 1884) received a controversial reception; it is discussed in Clement Eaton, *The Waning of the Old South Civilization, 1860-1880's,* Mercer University Lamar Memorial Lectures, no. 10 (Athens, 1968), 145-48. The many popular histories of New Orleans include Henry Rightor, *Standard History of New Orleans, Louisiana* (Chicago, 1900); John Sakendall, *History of New Orleans,* 3 vols. (New York, 1952); Lyle Saxon, *Fabulous New Orleans* (Chicago, 1928); Harriet Kane, *Queen New Orleans: City by the River* (New York, 1949); Oliver Evans, *New Orleans* (New York, 1959); Hodding Carter, ed., *The Past as Prelude: New Orleans, 1718-1968* (New Orleans, 1968). There is material on specific periods in Albert Fossier, *New Orleans: The Glamour Period, 1800-1840 . . .* (New Orleans, 1957); Theodore Clapp, *Autobiographical Sketches and Recollections during a Thirty-Five Year's Residence in New Orleans* (Boston, 1857); Robert C. Reinders, *End of an Era: New Orleans, 1850-1860* (New York, 1964); Gerald M. Capers, *Occupied City: New Orleans under the Federals, 1862-1865* (Lexington, 1965); and Joy J. Jackson, *New Orleans in the Gilded Age* (Baton Rouge, 1969). A valuable compilation is *New Orleans City Guide,* American Guide Series (Boston, 1938).

For Mobile, see Peter Hamilton, *Mobile of the Five Flags: The Story of the River Basin and Coast about Mobile from the Earliest Times to the Present* (Mobile, 1913); Charles Summersell, *Mobile: History of a Seaport Town* (University, Ala., 1949); and Caldwell Delaney, *The Story of Mobile* (Mobile, 1953). An old account is Peter Hamilton, *Colonial Mobile: An Historical*

Study, Largely from Original Sources, of the Alabama-Tombigbee Basin from the Discovery of Mobile Bay in 1519 until the Demolition of Fort Charlotte in 1821 (Boston and New York, 1897). Information on Mobile can also be found in Weymouth T. Jordan, *Ante-Bellum Alabama: Town and Country*.

16. See Lawrence H. Larsen, *The Urban West at the End of the Frontier* (Lawrence, 1978).

17. Quoted in Gaston, *New South Creed*, 79.

18. Quoted in Grady, *New South*, 195.

19. Material on the various towns can be found in the appropriate American Guide Series compilations: *Georgia: A Guide to Its Towns and Countryside* (Athens, 1940); *Mississippi: A Guide to the Magnolia State* (New York, 1938); *Arkansas: A Guide to the State* (New York, 1941). For Columbus see John Martin, *Columbus, Geo. from its Selection as a "Trading Town" in 1827, to its Partial Destruction by Wilson's Raid in 1865: History-Incident-Personality* (Columbus, 1874); Nancy Telfair, *A History of Columbus, Georgia, 1828-1928* (Columbus, 1929); Etta Blanchard Worsley, *Columbus on the Chattahoochee* (Columbus, 1951). For Macon see James H. Stone, "Economic Conditions in Macon, Georgia, in the 1830's," *Georgia Historical Quarterly* 54 (Summer 1970):209-25; Bowling Gates, "Macon, Georgia, Inland Trading Center, 1826-1836," *Georgia Historical Quarterly* 55 (Fall 1971):365-77; John Butler, *Historical Record of Macon and Central Georgia* (1879; rpr. Macon, 1950); Ida Young, *History of Macon, Georgia* (Macon, 1950). For Vicksburg, where the great siege was a central event, see Mary Loughborough, *My Cave Life in Vicksburg: With Letters of Trial and Travail* (Little Rock, 1882); Osborn Oldroyd, *A Soldier's Story of the Siege of Vicksburg* (Springfield, Ill., 1885); William Everhart, *Vicksburg National Military Park, Mississippi*, National Park Service Historical Handbook Series no. 21 (Washington, 1954); Peter Walker, *Vicksburg: A People at War, 1860-1865* (Chapel Hill, 1960); John Milligan, *Gunboats Down the Mississippi* (Annapolis, 1965); Adolph Hoehing and the editors of the Army *Times* Publishing Co., *Vicksburg: 47 Days of Siege* (Englewood Cliffs, N.J., 1969). For Little Rock see Dallas Herndon, *Why Little Rock Was Born* (Little Rock, 1933); Ira Richards, *Story of a Rivertown: Little Rock in the Nineteenth Century* (Benton, Ark., 1969). For Memphis see Gerald Capers, *The Biography of a Rivertown: Memphis, Its Heroic Age* (Chapel Hill, 1939); James Davis, *The History of Memphis* (Memphis, 1873); John Keating, *History of the City of Memphis and Shelby County, Tennessee, with Illustrations and Biographical Sketches of Some of Its Prominent Citizens* (Syracuse, 1888); Samuel Cole Williams, *Beginnings of West Tennessee: In the Land of the Chickasaws, 1541-1841* (Johnson City, Tenn., 1930). For Atlanta see *Atlanta: A City of the Modern South*, American Guide Series (1942; St. Clair Shores, Mich., 1973). Some of the many books on Atlanta are Edward Clarke, *Illustrated History of Atlanta, Containing Glances at its Population, Business, Manufactures, Industries, Institutions . . . and Advantages Generally, with Nearly One Hundred Illustrations, and a Lithographic Map of the City* (Atlanta, 1878); Wallace Reed, *History of Atlanta, with Illustrations and Bibliographical Sketches and Some of its Prominent Men and Pioneers* (Syracuse, 1889); Thomas Martin, *Atlanta and its Builders: A Comprehensive History of the Gate City of the South* (New York, 1902); *Pioneer Citizens' History of Atlanta*, Pioneer Citizens' Association (Atlanta, 1902); Walter Cooper, *Official History of Fulton County* (Atlanta, 1934); and Franklin Garrett, *Yesterday's Atlanta*, Seeman's Historic Cities Series No. 8 (Miami, 1974). For Chattanooga, see such local studies as *Past, Present, and Future of Chattanooga, Tennessee, "The Industrial Center of the South": Its Superior Resources and Advantages, and the Inducements it Offers for Capital and Labor in Farming, Manufacturing, Mining, and Commerce* (Chattanooga, 1885); *Chattanooga: Its History and Growth*, Chattanooga Community Association (Chattanooga, 1930); Zella Armstrong, *The History of Chattanooga County and Chattanooga, Tennessee*, 2 vols. (Chattanooga, 1931-1940); and Gilbert Govan and James Livingood, *The Chattanooga Country, 1540-1915: From Tomahawks to TVA* (1952; Chapel Hill, 1967).

A good starting point for studying Montgomery is Virginia Van der Veer Hamilton, *Alabama: A Bicentennial History* (New York, 1977), 120-21. An old local history is H. G.

McCall, *A Sketch, Historical and Statistical of the City of Montgomery, Outlining Its History, Location, Climate, Health . . .* (Montgomery, 1885). Of more recent vintage is *Montgomery, City of Progress: Yesterday and Today,* Montgomery Chamber of Commerce (Montgomery, 1937).

20. Quoted in Gaston, *New South Creed,* 1, 68.

21. Quoted in ibid., 43.

22. E. Merton Coulter, in a pioneering analysis of postbellum southern urbanization, noted that although the precentage of urban growth remained very small, the New South went far by southern standards toward urbanization. See *The South during Reconstruction, 1865-1877,* A History of the South, vol. 8 (Baton Rouge, 1947), 252-74.

3. Cogs in the Great Machine

1. The Civil War clouded over the many similarities between whites in both sections. They shared such American values as capitalism, economic and social mobility, materialism, democracy, evangelical religion, patriotic nationalism, consensus politics, racial prejudice, and utilitarianism. See Grady McWhiney, *Southerners and Other Americans* (New York, 1973), vii. Adverse accounts by northern antislavery forces in the antebellum period had helped condition people in the North to expect the worst of southerners and their intentions. William Lloyd Garrison, *The New 'Reign of Terror' in the Slaveholding States, for 1859-1860* (New York, 1860), is a case in point. See also Edward Ingle, *Southern Sidelights: A Picture of Social and Economic Life in the South a Generation before the War* (New York, 1896).

2. A standard work is C. Vann Woodward, *The Strange Career of Jim Crow* (New York, 1966).

3. See Roger L. Ransom and Richard Sutch, *One Kind of Freedom: The Economic Consequences of Emancipation* (Cambridge, Eng., 1977).

4. King's career and the salient points in his study are analyzed by the editors in Edward King, *The Great South,* ed. W. Magruder Drake and Robert R. Jones (1879; rpr. Baton Rouge, 1972), xxi-xxii.

5. King, *Great South,* 426 (Beaufort), 322 (Mobile), 739 (Wedverton), 801 (Strasburg).

6. King was one of several northern journalists who wrote about the South in the 1870s. Some of the others were James S. Pike, Charles Nordoff, and Robert Somers. Along with King, they argued that sectional bitterness was on the wane and would vanish as soon as the North reversed its Reconstruction policies (Paul M. Gaston, *The New South Creed: A Study in Southern Mythmaking* [New York, 1970], 39-40).

7. King, *Great South,* 347 (Augusta), 363 (Savannah), 438 (Charleston), 472 (Wilmington), 373 (Columbus), 555 (Lynchburg), 631 (Richmond), 707 (Louisville), 53 (New Orleans), 530 (Chattanooga).

8. Ibid., 707.

9. Ibid., 428.

10. The repast is described and Grady is quoted in Gaston, *New South Creed,* 87-90.

11. For an example of northern views about the South see the novel by Albion Winegard Tourgée, *A Fool's Errand, by One of the Fools* (New York, 1880).

12. For the rise of Chicago see Bessie L. Pierce, *A History of Chicago,* 3 vols. (New York, 1937-57).

13. See the text and bibliography of Lawrence H. Larsen, *The Urban West at the End of the Frontier* (Lawrence, 1978).

14. Quoted in Gaston, *New South Creed,* 89.

15. Henry W. Grady, *The New South* (New York, 1890), 184-85.

16. Quoted in Gaston, *New South Creed,* 76.

17. Quoted in ibid., 77.

18. Eaton, *Old South Civilization*, 160-61.

19. "Statistics of the Place of Birth of the Population of the United States," *Statistics of the Population of the United States, Tenth Census of the United States, 1880* (Washington, 1883), 1:464.

20. Quoted in Gaston, *New South Creed*, 16.

21. Table IX, "Population, as Native and Foreign-born, of Cities and Towns of 4,000 Inhabitants and Upward: 1880 and 1870," *Statistics of the Population*, 447 (Alabama and Arkansas), 448 (District of Columbia and Georgia), 449 (Kentucky and Louisiana), 450 (Maryland), 451 (Mississippi), 453 (North Carolina), 455 (South Carolina and Tennessee), 456 (Virginia); Table VI, "Population, by Race, of Cities and Towns of 4,000 Inhabitants and Upward: 1880 and 1870," ibid., 416 (Alabama and Arkansas), 417 (District of Columbia and Georgia), 418 (Kentucky and Louisiana), 419 (Maryland), 421 (Mississippi), 422 (North Carolina), 424 (South Carolina and Tennessee), 425 (Virginia).

22. Quoted in Howard N. Rabinowitz, *Race Relations in the Urban South, 1865-1890*, History of Urban America Series (New York, 1978), 24.

23. The pioneering study of urban slavery is Richard Wade, *Slavery in the Cities: The South, 1820-1860* (New York, 1964). See also Claudia Dale Golden, *Urban Slavery in the American South, 1820-1860: A Quantitative History* (Chicago, 1976); John S. Kendall, "New Orleans 'Peculiar Institution,' " *Louisiana Historical Quarterly* 23 (July 1946):864-86; Robert S. Starobin, *Industrial Slavery in the Old South* (New York, 1970); Ira Berlin, *Slaves without Masters: The Free Negro in the Antebellum South* (New York, 1974); Leonard P. Curry, *The Free Black in Urban America, 1800-1850: The Shadow of the Dream* (Chicago, 1981).

24. The black and immigrant employment picture in New Orleans is discussed in Fredrick Marcel Spletstoser, "Back Door to the Land of Plenty: New Orleans as an Immigrant Port, 1820-1860," 2 vols. (Ph.D. dissertation, Louisiana State University, 1978). See the following articles in the *Journal of Negro History:* L. P. Jackson, "Free Negroes of Petersburg, Virginia," 12 (July 1927):365-88; E. Horace Fitchett, "The Origin and Growth of the Free Negro Population of Charleston, South Carolina," 26 (October 1941):421-37; Dorothy Provine, "The Economic Position of Free Blacks in the District of Columbia," 58 (January 1973):61-72. A useful case study is Whittington B. Johnson, "Free Blacks in Antebellum Savannah: An Economic Profile," *Georgia Historical Quarterly* 64 (Winter 1980):418-31.

25. Quoted in Rabinowitz, *Race Relations*, 22.

26. Free Negroes played important roles in the establishment of stable black communities in southern cities after the Civil War. See John W. Blassingame, *Black New Orleans, 1860-1880* (Chicago, 1973); Constance M. Green, *The Secret City: A History of Race Relations in the Nation's Capital* (Princeton, 1967); Dale Somers, "Black and White in New Orleans: A Survey of Urban Race Relations, 1865-1900," *Journal of Southern History* 40 (February 1974):19-42; Robert E. Perdue, *The Negro in Savannah, 1865-1900* (New York, 1973).

27. King, *Great South*, 580.

28. See Spletstoser, "Back Door to the Land of Plenty."

29. See Stephen Byrne, *Irish Emigration to the United States: What It Has Been, and What It Is* (New York, 1873); Albert Faust, *The Geman Element in the United States*, 2 vols. (New York, 1912). A good general summary remains Carl Wittke, *We Who Built America: The Saga of the Immigrant* (Cleveland, 1939).

30. See Thomas D. Clark, *Kentucky: Land of Contrast* (New York, 1968).

31. For general background of the rise of nativist thought in America see Ray Allen Billington, *The Protestant Crusade, 1800-1860: A Study of the Origins of American Nativism* (New York, 1938).

32. Quoted in Spletstoser, "Back Door to the Land of Plenty," 1: 240-43. See Darrell Overdyke, *The Know-Nothing Party in the South* (Baton Rouge, 1950).

33. Clark, *Kentucky*, 122.

34. C. Vann Woodward, *Origins of the New South, 1877-1913,* A History of the South, vol. 9 (Baton Rouge, 1951), 297-99.

35. Table XVI, "Foreign-born Population of Fifty Principal Cities, Distributed, According to Place of Birth, among the Various Foreign Countries: 1880," *Statistics of the Population,* 538-41. Little has been written about southern immigrants. Dieter Cunz, *The Maryland Germans: A History* (1948 rpr. Port Washington, N.Y., 1972), has considerable information about the Germans of Baltimore. The Irish experience in New Orleans in antebellum times is covered in Earl Niehaus, *The Irish in New Orleans, 1800-1860* (Baton Rouge, 1965). See also Spletstoser, "Back Door to the Land of Plenty." Two articles on Germans are Robert T. Clark, "Reconstruction and the New Orleans German Colony," *Louisiana Historical Quarterly* 23 (April 1940):501-24, and Bob Cyrus Rauchle, "The Political Life of the Germans in Memphis, 1848-1900," *Louisiana Historical Quarterly* 28 (Summer 1968):165-75. There is valuable general material in Stephen Thernstrom, ed., *Harvard Encyclopedia of American Ethnic Groups* (Cambridge, Mass., 1980).

36. See Stanley C. Johnson, *A History of Emigration from the United Kingdom to North America, 1763-1912* (London, 1913).

37. *Statistics of the Population,* 460.

38. Ibid., 467.

39. King, *Great South,* 30-31.

40. See Joy J. Jackson, *New Orleans in the Gilded Age* (Baton Rouge, 1969).

41. Table XV, "Native Population of Fifty Principal Cities, Distributed According to States and Territories of Birth: 1880," *Statistics of the Population,* 536-37.

42. Ibid., 472.

43. *Social Statistics of Cities,* 2:191 (Mobile), 199 (Montgomery), 211 (Little Rock), 53 (Georgetown), 27 (Washington), 157 (Atlanta), 163 (Augusta), 169 (Macon), 173 (Savannah), 111 (Covington), 117 (Lexington), 122 (Louisville), 131 (Newport), 213 (New Orleans), 3 (Baltimore), 209 (Vicksburg), 93 (Wilmington), 95 (Charleston), 105 (Columbia), 135 (Chattanooga), 140 (Memphis), 151 (Nashville), 55 (Alexandria), 60 (Lynchburg), 65 (Norfolk), 71 (Petersburg), 75 (Portsmouth), 79 (Richmond). The total numbers of males and females appear in the *Social Statistics of Cities,* but in no other printed volume of the 1880 census. Columbus and Cumberland are not included in the *Social Statistics of Cities.* The totals for those cities obtained from the manuscript census schedules are very low— 2,168 women in Cumberland and 1,338 in Columbus—indicating that many sheets are missing. (1880 Population Schedules, Georgia, Montgomery, Morgan, Murray, and Muscogee counties, Microfilm T-9, Roll No. 159, Kansas City Federal Archives and Records Center; 1880 Population Schedules, Maryland, Allegany County, Micrfilm T-9, Roll No. 493, ibid.). For conclusions about the excess number of women in most places see Adna Ferrin Weber, *The Growth of Cities in the Nineteenth Century: A Study in Statistics* (1899; rpr. Ithaca, N.Y., 1963), 278-84.

44. Table XXXV, "Number of Persons in Fifty Principal Cities Engaged in Each Class of Occupations, with Distinction of Age and Sex and of Nativity: 1880," *Statistics of the Population,* 855.

45. Ibid.

46. Quoted in Gaston, *New South Creed,* 134.

47. Eaton, *Old South Civilization,* 128-29.

48. Quoted in Gaston, *New South Creed,* 147.

49. King, *Great South,* 556-57.

50. *Statistics of the Population,* 855.

51. The quotes are from Gaston, *New South Creed,* 111-13.

52. Grady, *New South,* 184-86.

53. Table 1, "Summary of Denominations for 124 Cities, by Cities," *Report on Statistics of Churches in the United States, Eleventh Census of the United States, 1890* (Washington, 1894), 9:91.

54. Introduction, ibid., xx, xxvi.

55. Table 7, "Communicants or Members in Cities having a Population of 100,000 to 500,000," ibid., 98-99; Table 11, "Communicants or Members in Cities having a Population of 25,000 to 100,000," ibid., 112-15. Religious studies tend to be sympathetic and uncritical. See such accounts as W. W. Barnes, *The Southern Baptist Convention, 1845-1953* (Nashville, 1954); Paul N. Garber, *The Methodists Are One People* (Nashville, 1939); Carter Woodson, *The History of the Negro Church* (1921; rpr. Washington, 1945), John W. Cromwell, "First Negro Churches in the District of Columbia," *Journal of Negro History* 7 (January 1922):64-106.

56. Some of the more comprehensive studies have been done on Jews. See Isaac Fein, *The Making of an American Jewish Community: The History of Baltimore Jewry from 1773 to 1920* (Philadelphia, 1971); Leonard Dinnerstein and Maury Dale Palsson, *Jews in the South* (Baton Rouge, 1973); Eli N. Evans, *The Provincials; A Personal History of Jews in the South* (New York, 1973); Myron Berman, *Richmond's Jewry: Shabbat to Shockoe, 1796-1976* (Charlottesville, 1979); Steven Hertzberg, *Strangers within the Gate City: The Jews of Atlanta, 1845-1915* (Philadelphia, 1978).

57. Wilma Dykeman, *Tennessee: A Bicentennial History* (New York, 1975), 163.

58. See Woodward, *Origins of the New South*, 60-64; Monroe Lee Billington, *The American South: A Brief History* (New York, 1971), 277-81; *Report of the Commissioner of Education, 1880: Report of the Secretary of Interior,* vol. 3 (Washington, 1882).

59. Quoted in Gaston, *New South Creed*, 104.

60. Billington, *American South*, 278-79. See also Edgar Knight, *The Influence of Reconstruction on Education in the South* (1913; rpr. New York, 1969).

61. Table II, "School Statistics of Cities Containing 7,500 Inhabitants and over, from Replies to Inquiries by the United States Bureau of Education," *Report of the Commissioner of Education,* 7, 61, 420-62.

62. See Howard N. Rabinowitz, "Half a Loaf: The Shift from White to Black Teachers in the Negro Schools of the Urban South, 1865-1890," *Journal of Southern History* 40 (November 1974):565-94. Additional material can be found in Rabinowitz, *Race Relations*, 152-81.

63. *Report of the Commissioner of Education,* 62 (Atlanta), 62 (Savannah), 8 (Mobile).

64. Quoted in Eaton, *Old South Civilization*, 163.

65. Ibid., 107-9; Woodward, *Origins of the New South*, 436-37; Billington, *American South*, 285.

66. Table IX, "Statistics of Universities and Colleges for 1880," *Report of the Commissioner of Education,* 640-75. There are numerous college histories, most of which are long, detailed, and short on analysis. Many are cited in Cunningham, "The Southern Mind since the Civil War," in Arthur S. Link and Rembert W. Patrick, eds., *Writing Southern History: Essays in Historiography in Honor of Fletcher M. Green* (1965; rpr. Baton Rouge, 1967), 383-409. They tend to emphasize the exploits of educational bureaucrats and to downplay the role of students and faculty.

67. Quoted in King, *Great South*, 608.

68. *Report of the Commissioner of Education,* 640-75. See Frederick Chambers, "Histories of the Black Colleges and Universities," *Journal of Negro History* 57 (July 1972):270-75.

69. Grady, *New South*, 146.

4. Railroads Are Talismanic Winds

1. See "The Natural Laws of Commerce," *Western Journal* 1 (April 1848):173-77, for a typical statement of the importance of geography in building commercial systems.

2. Both quotations are from Philip S. Foner, *Business and Slavery: The New York Merchants and the Irrepressible Conflict* (Chapel Hill, 1941), 12, 13.

3. "Mississippi Valley Railroad," *Western Journal and Civilian* 9 (November 1852):14.

4. The standard survey on southern railroading in the last half of the nineteenth century is John F. Stover, *The Railroads of the South, 1865-1900: A Study in Finance and Control* (Chapel Hill, 1955). The 1850s are covered on pages 3-14. See also Robert S. Cotterill, "Southern Railroads, 1850-1860," *Mississippi Valley Historical Review* 10 (March 1924):396-405.

5. Eugene Alvarez, *Travel on Southern Antebellum Railroads, 1828-1860* (University, Ala., 1974), 27-28.

6. Stover, *Railroads of the South,* 11.

7. See the appropriate sections of Edward Hungerford, *The Story of the Baltimore and Ohio Railroad, 1827-1927,* 2 vols. (New York, 1928).

8. See Stover, *Railroads of the South,* 15-22.

9. Quoted in ibid., 16-17.

10. Quoted in ibid., 22.

11. See ibid., 23-58.

12. There is good material on the politics of railroading in C. Vann Woodward, *Origins of the New South, 1877-1913,* A History of the South, vol. 9 (Baton Rouge, 1951), 1-22.

13. Stover, *Railroads of the South,* 61. See John Doster, "Trade Centers and Railroad Rates in Alabama, 1873-1885: The Cases of Greenville, Montgomery, and Opelika," *Journal of Southern History* 18 (May 1952):169-92.

14. Stover, *Railroads of the South,* 96.

15. See ibid., 99-122.

16. The Richmond Terminal provided proof that New South propagandists could organize business activities. See Maury Klein, *The Great Richmond Terminal: A Study in Businessmen and Railroad Strategy* (Charlottesville, 1970), viii-x.

17. See John F. Stover, "Southern Ambitions of the Illinois Central Railroad," *Journal of Southern History* 20 (November 1954):499-510, and his *History of the Illinois Central Railroad* (New York, 1975).

18. The most recent history of the line is Maury Klein, *History of the Louisville and Nashville Railroad* (New York, 1972). Two other histories of the line are John L. Kers, *The Louisville and Nashville: An Outline History* (New York, 1933); Kincaid Herr, *The Louisville and Nashville Railroad, 1850-1963* (Louisville, 1963).

19. See Hungerford, *Baltimore and Ohio Railroad.*

20. Quoted in *Social Statistics of Cities,* 2:76 (Portsmouth), 81 (Richmond), 136 (Chattanooga), 159 (Atlanta).

21. See Leonard P. Curry, *Rail Routes South: Louisville's Fight for the Southern Market, 1865-1872* (Lexington, 1969).

22. Quoted in Woodward, *Origins of the New South,* 7.

23. See Milton Reizenstein, *The Economic History of the Baltimore and Ohio Railroad,* Johns Hopkins University Studies in Historical and Political Science, Fifteenth Series, vols. 7-8 (Baltimore, 1897).

24. An older book of value is Ulrich P. Phillips, *A History of Transportation in the Eastern Cotton Belt to 1860* (New York, 1913). Other materials useful in studying southern railroad patterns include Jesse C. Burt, Jr., "Four Decades of the Nashville, Chattanooga and St. Louis Railway, 1873-1916," *Tennessee Historical Quarterly* 9 (June 1950):99-132; Samuel Derrick, *Centennial History of South Carolina Railroad* (Columbia, 1930); and Richard Price, *Georgia Railroads and the West Point Route* (Salt Lake City, 1962).

25. *Social Statistics of Cities,* 2:15 (Baltimore), 57 (Alexandria), 31 (Washington), 54 (Georgetown), 80 (Richmond), 66 (Norfolk), 76 (Portsmouth), 93 (Wilmington), 98 (Charleston), 176 (Savannah), 194 (Mobile), 268-69 (New Orleans).

26. Ibid., 2:24 (Baltimore), 293 (New Orleans), 180 (Savannah), 103-4 (Charleston), 69 (Norfolk), 197 (Mobile), 94 (Wilmington).

27. Ibid., 1:593 (New York), 149-51 (Boston), 836 (Philadelphia), 2:812 (San Francisco).

28. The formative stages of New Orleans' commercial develpment are covered in John G. Clark, *New Orleans, 1718-1812: An Economic History* (Baton Rouge, 1970), esp. 299-329. See also Lawrence H. Larsen, "New Orleans and the River Trade: Reinterpreting the Role of the Business Community," *Wisconsin Magazine of History* 61 (Winter 1977- 78):112-24; Robert M. Brown, "The Mississippi River as a Trade Route," *Bulletin of the American Geographical Society of New York* 38 (1906):347-54; *Social Statistics of Cities*, 2:251-55. Statistics on the movement of grain can be found in many places, including John G. Clark, *The Grain Trade in the Old Northwest* (Urbana, 1966). A detailed table, "Receipts of Flour and Grain at New Orleans from 1832 to 1862," appears in "The Grain Trade of the United States and Tables on the World's Wheat Supply and Trade," Bureau of Statistics, Department of the Treasury, *Monthly Summary of Commerce and Finances, January, 1900*, n.s., no. 7 (Washington, 1900). Despite the narrow title, this is a very detailed monographic history of the grain trade in the United States, based on statistics compiled primarily by federal agencies.

29. Frederick Jackson Turner, *The United States, 1830-1850: The Nation and Its Sections* (1935; rpr. New York, 1962), 220-22; *Social Statistics of Cities*, 2:252.

30. "The Grain Trade of the United States," 1962, 1969.

31. William M. Burwell, "The Commercial Future of the South," *DeBow's Review* 30 (February 1861):147.

32. "The Grain Trade of the United States," 1959; *Social Statistics of Cities*, 2:253-64; "The Mouths of the Mississippi," *DeBow's Review* 17 (July 1854):15-25; Walter M. Lowrey, "Navigational Problems at the Mouth of the Mississippi River, 1698-1880" (Ph. D. dissertation, Vanderbilt University, 1956); Walter M. Lowrey, "The Engineers and the Mississippi," *Louisiana History* 5 (Summer 1964):223-56.

33. In 1851-52 the surplus reaching New Orleans was worth $180 million. Of this amount, cotton furnished over $48 million, sugar and molasses nearly $16 million, pork and its products about the same amount, and tobacco over $7 million. Receipts for corn, flour, and wheat came to $5.5 million (Turner, *United States, 1830-1850*, 220).

34. Fredrick Marcel Spletstoser, "Back Door to the Land of Plenty: New Orleans as an Immigrant Port, 1800-1860," 2 vols. (Ph.D. dissertation, Louisiana State University, 1978), 1:205-14. See also John G. Clark, "New Orleans and the River: A Study in Attitudes and Responses," *Louisiana History* 8 (Spring 1967):117-36; Walter Parker, "Facilities of the Port of New Orleans," *Annals of the American Academy of Political and Social Science* 86 (November 1919):188-98; Gary Bolding, "Change, Continuity and Commercial Identity of a Southern City: New Orleans, 1850-1950," *Louisiana Studies* 14 (Summer 1975):161-78; A. L. Kohlmeier, *The Old Northwest as the Keystone of the Arch of the American Federal Union: A Study in Commerce and Politics* (Bloomington, Ind., 1938); Henry C. Hubbart, *The Older Midwest, 1840-1880* (New York, 1936).

35. "Competition of the Gulf and Atlantic Ports," *DeBow's Review* 24 (January 1858): 47-48. The city steadily lost ground owing to the rise in quality of northeastern ports and their distributing systems. Imports through New Orleans totaled $17 million in 1835, $8 million in 1842, and $9.8 million in 1845 (*Social Statistics of Cities*, 2:256).

36. R. B. Way, "The Commerce of the Lower Mississippi in the Period 1830-1860," *Mississippi Valley Historical Review* Extra Number (July 1920):57-68. See also Frank H. Dixon, *A Traffic History of the Mississippi River System*, National Waterways Commission, Doc. 11 (Washington, 1909).

37. U.S. Congress, Senate, *Report of Israel D. Andrews on the Trade and Commerce of the British North American Colonies, and upon the Trade of the Great Lakes and Rivers*, Senate Executive Document 112, 32d Cong., 1st sess., Serial 622, p. 343. This is the classic account of the effects of transportation developments on urbanization in the first half of the nineteenth century. See also Gerald M. Gibson, "Israel DeWolf Andrews: Perceptive Bureaucrat" (M.A. thesis, University of Missouri-Kansas City, 1976).

38. Valuable material on New Orleans can be found in Arthur Harrison Cole, *Wholesale Commodity Prices in the United States, 1700-1861* (Cambridge, Mass., 1938), 65-76, 170-79.

39. See James Cairns, "The Response of New Orleans to the Diversion of Trade from the Mississippi River, 1845-1860" (M.A. thesis, Columbia University, 1950); Erastus P. Puckett, "The Attempt of New Orleans to Meet the Crisis of Her Trade with the West," *Mississippi Valley Historical Review*, Extra Number (February 1923):481-95.

40. The best work on the railroads of antebellum Louisiana is Merl E. Reed, *New Orleans and the Railroads: The Struggle for Commercial Empire, 1830-1860* (Baton Rouge, 1966). The characteristics of the leaders and their sometime alliance with rural slaveholders in Louisiana politics are covered in Robert W. Shugg, *Origins of the Class Struggle in Louisiana: A Social History of White Farmers and Laborers during Slavery and after, 1840-1875* (1939; rpr. Baton Rouge, 1968), 121-56.

41. Quoted in Shugg, *Origins of the Class Struggle*, 108. See also Harry Howard Evans, "James Robb, Banker and Pioneer Builder of Ante-Bellum Louisiana," *Louisiana Historical Quarterly* 33 (January 1940): 170-258; Ottis Clark Skipper, "J.D.B. DeBow, the Man," *Journal of Southern History* 10 (November 1944): 404-23.

42. *Social Statistics of Cities*, 2:225. During most of the 1850s the loans outstanding of New Orleans' banks fluctuated between $13 million and $24 million ("The Banks and Insurance Companies of New Orleans," *DeBow's Review* 25 [November 1858]: 561).

43. Reed, *New Orleans and the Railroads*, 68-80, 128-30. See also James P. Baughman, "The Evolution of Rail-Water Systems of Transportation in the Gulf Southeast, 1836-1890," *Journal of Southern History* 34 (August 1968):351-81. The quote is from *Social Statistics of Cities*, 2:265.

44. In part, the Great Northern aimed at countering the threat of the Mobile and Ohio Railroad. In 1852 an official of the Mobile and Ohio made a speech on how much trade it would bring to Mobile. DeBow reprinted it for the edification of the New Orleans business community (J. Childs, "Railroad Progress and the Mobile and Ohio Road," *DeBow's Review* 12 [February 1852]:203-4). See Stover, *Illinois Central*, 18-19, 80, 170-71.

45. Reed, *New Orleans and the Railroads*, 108-20. See also Marshall Gautreau, "The New Orleans, Opelousas and Great Western Railroad" (M.A. thesis, Louisiana State University, 1955).

46. "The Grain Trade of the United States," 1960-61.

47. Lawrence H. Larsen, "Chicago's Midwest Rivals: Cincinnati, St. Louis, and Milwaukee," *Chicago History: The Magazine of the Chicago Historical Society* 5 (Fall 1976):141-51. There is valuable material in Wyatt Belcher, *The Economic Rivalry between St. Louis and Chicago, 1850-1880* (New York, 1947); and Richard Wade, *The Urban Frontier: Pioneer Life in Early Pittsburgh, Cincinnati, Lexington, Louisville, and St. Louis* (Chicago, 1959).

48. "The Grain Trade of the United States," 1961.

49. Ibid., 1959, 1961-62.

50. Ibid., 1979-82.

51. Ibid., 1979.

52. Ibid., 1875-78, 1884-88. See also George Rogers Taylor and Irene D. Neu, *The American Railroad Network* (Cambridge, Mass., 1956), 29-30.

53. Edward King, *The Great South*, ed., W. Magruder Drake and Robert R. Jones (1879; rpr. Baton Rouge, 1972), 52.

54. Quoted in Paul M. Gaston, *The New South Creed: A Study in Southern Mythmaking* (New York, 1970), 65.

55. Henry W. Grady, *The New South* (New York, 1890), 223.

56. Quoted in Roger L. Ransom and Richard Sutch, *One Kind of Freedom: The Economic Consequences of Emancipation* (Cambridge, Eng., 1977), 150. This book contains an excellent analysis of the economic problems that afflicted southern agriculture.

57. Quoted in ibid., 149. See Jacqueline P. Bull, "The General Merchant in the Economic History of the New South," *Journal of Southern History* 18 (February 1952):37-59.

58. *Report of Israel D. Andrews*, 749.

59. Weymouth T. Jordan, *Ante-Bellum Alabama: Town and Country*, Florida State University Studies, no. 27 (Tallahassee, 1957).

60. Grady, *New South*, 191-92.

61. Table VI, "Manufactures of 100 Principal Cities, by Totals: 1880," *Report of the Manufactures of the United States, Tenth Census of the United States, 1880* (Washington, 1883), 2:379-80.

62. Table VI, "Manufactures of 100 Principal Cities, by Specified Industries: 1880," ibid., 383-443. There are two Table VIs, back to back, in the census. The same information on specified industries can also be found under the appropriate cities in the *Social Statistics of Cities*. All the manuscript census schedules for products of industry for cities over 8,000 population in 1880 have been destroyed.

63. Norris Preyer, "Why Did Industrialism Lag in the Old South?" *Georgia Historical Quarterly* 55 (Fall 1971):378-96, stresses the strongly held belief in the South and elsewhere that the factory system was dangerous to democratic institutions. Southern firms had trouble competing with those from the North. See Carrol H. Quenzel, "The Manufacture of Locomotives and Cars in Alexandria in the 1850s," *Virginia Magazine of History and Biography* 62 (April 1954):181-89. Northern competition also hurt the South Carolina iron industry. See Ernest M. Lander, Jr., "The Iron Industry in Ante-Bellum South Carolina," *Journal of Southern History* 20 (August 1954):337-55; and Raymond L. Cohn, "Local Manufacturing in the Antebellum South and Midwest," *Business History Review* 54 (Spring 1980):80-91.

5. Joy Brightens Her Face

1. M. B. Hillyard, *The New South: A Description of the Southern States, Noting Each State Separately, and Giving Their Distinctive Features and Most Salient Characteristics* (Baltimore, 1887), 57. The optimistic mood of the New South spokesmen is conveyed in Holland Thompson, *The New South* (New Haven, 1919).

2. Rollin G. Osterweis, *Romanticism and Nationalism in the Old South* (New Haven, 1949), is the basic work on southern romanticism. He elaborated earlier themes in a later book, *The Myth of the Lost Cause, 1865-1900* (New York, 1973).

3. The basic work on the convention movement remains Herbert Wender, *Southern Commercial Conventions, 1837-1859*, John Hopkins University Studies in Historical and Political Science, series 48, no. 4 (Baltimore, 1930). See also Frederick Jackson Turner, *The United States, 1830-1850: The Nation and Its Sections* (1935; rpr. New York, 1962). David R. Goldfield, *Urban Growth in the Age of Sectionalism: Virginia, 1847-1861* (Baton Rouge, 1977), shows how the major cities of the Old Dominion competed against each other. There is excellent material in such works as Ulrich P. Phillips, *A History of Transportation in the Eastern Cotton Belt to 1860* (New York, 1913), and Merl E. Reed, *New Orleans and the Railroads: The Struggle for Commercial Empire, 1830-1860* (Baton Rouge, 1966), but a need exists for comprehensive state studies on urban rivalries and aspirations in the antebellum South.

4. Quoted in William Best Hesseltine, *Confederate Leaders in the New South* (1950; rpt. Westport, Conn., 1970), 28, 32.

5. Quoted in Paul M. Gaston, *The New South Creed: A Study in Southern Mythmaking* (New York, 1970), 187 (Grady), 96 (Watterson), 82 (Edmonds).

6. Henry Grady, *The New South* (New York, 1890), 182.

7. Quoted in Gaston, *New South Creed*, 96.

8. Quoted in C. Vann Woodward, *Origins of the New South, 1877- 1913. A History of the South*, vol. 9 (Baton Rouge, 1951), 145-46.

9. Leadership is a difficult subject to assess. Historically, community power brokers have tended to operate behind the scenes. The problems are discussed in an insightful article, David C. Hammack, "Problems in the Historical Study of Power in the Cities and Towns of the United States, 1800-1960," *American Historical Review* 83 (April 1978):323-49. Material on leaders is scattered throughout old local histories, particularly in their accompanying biographical volumes. The few economic histories of individual southern towns are more helpful in piecing together leadership groups. Among these are Constance McLaughlin Green, *Washington*, 2 vols. (Princeton, 1962-63); Thomas J. Wertenbaker, *Norfolk: Historic Southern Port*, ed. Marvin Schlegel (1931; rpr. Durham, 1962); Gerald Capers, *The Biography of a Rivertown: Memphis, Its Heroic Age* (Chapel Hill, 1939). Some business or trade combinations existed. The Louisville and Nashville Railroad dominated Louisville in the early days of the New South. There is an excellent discussion of the railroad's role in George R. Leighton, *Five Cities: The Story of Their Youth and Old Age* (New York, 1939), 60-74. See also L. Tuffly Ellis, "The New Orleans Cotton Exchange: The Formative Years, 1871-1880," *Journal of Southern History* 38 (November 1973):545-64; Maury Klein, *The Great Richmond Terminal: A Study in Businessmen and Business Strategy* (Charlottesville, 1970); Hesseltine, *Confederate Leaders in the New South;* Eugene J. Watts, *The Social Bases of City Politics: Atlanta, 1865-1903* (Westport, Conn., 1978); Carl V. Harris, *Political Power in Birmingham, 1871-1921* (Knoxville, 1977); Richard J. Hopkins, "Status, Mobility, and Dimensions of Change in a Southern City: Atlanta, 1870-1910," in Kenneth T. Jackson and Stanley F. Schultz, eds., *Cities in American History* (New York, 1972), 216-31.

10. Quoted in Woodward, *Origins of the New South*, 130.

11. Ibid., 7; *Dictionary of American Biography*, s.v., "Duke, Basil Wilson,"; Basil Wilson Duke, *Reminiscences of Basil W. Duke, C.S.A.* (Garden City, 1911).

12. Quoted in J. R. Killick, "The Transformation of Cotton Marketing in the Late Nineteenth Century: Alexander Sprunt and Son of Wilmington, N.C., 1866-1956," *Business History Review* 55 (Summer 1981):143-69. The quote is on p. 147. All the material on Alexander Sprunt and Son is from this excellent article.

13. There is information on these firms in Edward King, *The Great South*, ed. W. Magruder Drake and Robert R. Jones (1879; rpr. Baton Rouge, 1972), 53 (Hilliard, Summers and Company), 373 (Columbus Manufacturing Company), 582 (Petersburg cotton manufactories).

14. Grady, *New South*, 213.

15. The rise of Kansas City is told in A. Theodore Brown and Lyle W. Dorsett, *K.C.: A History of Kansas City, Missouri* (Boulder, 1978).

16. T. Harry Williams argued that the Redeemers placed economics ahead of race in *Romance and Realism in Southern Politics* (Athens, 1961). There is an excellent account of the character of the New South leadership on the state level in Woodward, *Origins of the New South*, 1-22. See also Eugene J. Watts, "Property and Politics in Atlanta, 1865-1903," *Journal of Urban History* 3 (May 1977):295-322; William J. Cooper, Jr., *The Conservative Regime: South Carolina, 1877-1890* (Baltimore, 1968); Grady McWhiney, *Southerners and Other Americans* (New York, 1973), 133-37; William Ivy Hair, *Bourbonism and Agrarian Protest: Louisiana Politics, 1877-1900* (Baton Rouge, 1961). A good summary of the historiography of the Redemption can be found in Paul M. Gaston, "The 'New South,' " in Arthur S. Link and Rembert W. Patrick, eds., *Writing Southern History: Essays in Historiography in Honor of Fletcher M. Green* (1965; rpr. Baton Rouge, 1967), 316-36. See also Howard R. Rabinowitz, "From Reconstruction to Redemption in the Urban South," *Journal of Urban History* 2 (February 1976):169-94.

17. Quoted in Woodward, *Origins of the New South*, 15.

18. Quoted in ibid., 1 (*Jackson Clarion*), and Gaston, "The 'New South," 324.

19. Hillyard, *New South*, 8.

20. The best studies of the origins of modern city government are Jon C. Teaford's two books, *The Municipal Revolution in America, 1650-1825* (Chicago, 1975); and *City and Suburb: The Political Fragmentation of Metropolitan America, 1850-1970* (Baltimore, 1979). See also the sections on city government in Carl Bridenbaugh, *Cities in the Wilderness: The First Century of Urban Life in America* (1938; rpr. New York, 1955).

21. The occupation of Memphis is discussed in Capers, *Biography of a Rivertown*. For New Orleans see Gerald Capers, *Occupied City: New Orleans under the Federals, 1862-1865* (Lexington, 1965). The government established by Federal authorities in Nashville went into receivership in 1869 (Eleanor Graham, ed., *Nashville: A Short History of Selected Buildings* [Nashville, 1974], 31. Augusta experienced a very mild occupation, during which the Union commander restored order and became a community hero (Florence Corley, *Confederate City: Augusta, Georgia, 1860-1865* [Columbia, 1960], 93-98).

22. Albion Winegard Tourgée, *Fool's Errand* (New York, 1880), 83. See also Otto H. Olsen, *Carpetbagger's Crusade: The Life of Albion Winegard Tourgée* (Baltimore, 1965).

23. The ill-fated territory of the District of Columbia and Alexander Shepherd's activities are discussed in Constance McLaughlin Green, *Washington*, Vol. 1; *Village and Capital, 1800-1878* (Princeton, 1962), 339-62. See also Charles N. Glaab and A. Theodore Brown, rev. by Charles N. Glaab, *A History of Urban America* (1967; rpr. New York, 1976), 193-94; Constance McLaughlin Green, *American Cities in the Growth of the Nation* (1957; rpr. New York, 1965), 228-41. Two classic studies of the condition of urban government in the United States are James Bryce, *The American Commonwealth* (New York, 1888), and Lincoln Steffens, *Shame of the Cities* (New York, 1904).

24. Quoted in Green, *Washington* 1: 347.

25. *Social Statistics of Cities*, 2:191 (Mobile), 199 (Montgomery), 211 (Little Rock), 27 (Georgetown and Washington), 157 (Atlanta), 163 (Augusta), 169 (Macon), 173, (Savannah), 111 (Covington), 117 (Lexington), 122 (Louisville), 131 (Newport), 213 (New Orleans), 3 (Baltimore), 209 (Vicksburg), 93 (Wilmington), 95 (Charleston), 105 (Columbia), 135 (Chattanooga), 140 (Memphis), 151 (Nashville), 53 (Alexandria), 60 (Lynchburg), 65 (Norfolk), 71 (Petersburg), 75 (Portsmouth), 79 (Richmond). One southern city had a city income tax on merchants in the antebellum period; see J. David Griffin, "Savannah's City Income Tax," *Georgia Historical Quarterly* 50 (September 1969):173-76. For a survey of local government politics see Michael J. Schewel, "Local Politics in Lynchburg, Virginia, in the 1880s," *Virginia Magazine of History and Biography* 89 (April 1981):170-80.

26. *Social Statistics of Cities*, 2:725 (Des Moines), 530 (Quincy).

27. Table VI, "Analysis of the Outstanding Bonded Debt of Cities, Towns, etc., Having 7,500 or More Inhabitants for which Bonds were Issued," *Report on Valuation, Taxation, and Public Indebtedness, Tenth Census of the United States, 1880* (Washington, 1884), 7:684-85 (Alabama and Arkansas), 686-87 (District of Columbia and Georgia), 688-89 (Kentucky, Louisiana, and Maryland), 692-93 (Mississippi), 694-95 (North Carolina), 696-97 (South Carolina), 698-99 (Tennessee and Virginia).

28. Ibid., 684 (California).

29. The most comprehensive study of postbellum racial problems in southern cities is Howard Rabinowitz, *Race Relations in the Urban South, 1865-1890*, Urban Life in America Series (New York, 1978). A standard work is C. Vann Woodward, *The Strange Career of Jim Crow* (New York, 1955). The lot of blacks in the pre–Civil War North is treated in Leon Litwack, *North of Slavery* (Chicago, 1961).

30. David Macrae, *The Americans at Home*, 2 vols. (Edinburgh, 1870), 2:219.

31. A fine case study is Terry L. Seip, "Municipal Politics and the Negro: Baton Rouge, 1865-1880," in Mark T. Carleton, Perry H. Howard, and Joseph B. Parker, eds., *Readings in Louisiana Politics* (Baton Rouge, 1975), 242-66. See also John T. O'Brien, "Reconstruction in Richmond: White Restoration and Black Protest, April-June 1865," *Virginia Magazine of History and Biography* 89 (July 1981): 259-91.

32. The two quotes are from Seip, "Municipal Politics," 243, 246.

33. Quoted in ibid., 248.

34. Quoted in ibid., 250. A controversial study with an admitted point of view claims that a major thrust of white southern life has been to keep blacks in a docile state: Lawrence J. Friedman, *The White Savage: Racial Fantasies in the Postbellum South* (Englewood Cliffs, N.J., 1970).

35. Rabinowitz, *Race Relations*, 97-124.

36. The quotes are in ibid., 100 (Nashville), 106 (Atlanta).

37. Table XXV, "Dwellings, Families, and Population in 100 Principal Cities: 1800," *Statistics of the Population of the United States, Tenth Census of the United States, 1880* (Washington, 1883), 1:670-71.

38. Quoted in Clement Eaton, *The Waning of the Old South Civilization, 1860-1880s,* Mercer Univ. Lamar Memorial Lectures No. 10 (Athens, Ga., 1968), 152.

39. King, *Great South*, 350.

40. Quoted in William B. Hesseltine and David L. Smiley, *The South in American History* (Englewood Cliffs, N.J., 1960), 7. John W. Reps, *The Making of Urban America* (Princeton, 1965), 90-91.

41. The Atlantic Coast cities' topography is covered in *Social Statistics of Cities*, 2:15 (Baltimore), 32 (Washington and Georgetown), 57 (Alexandria), 67 (Norfolk), 76 (Portsmouth), 99 (Charleston), 176 (Savannah).

42. King, *Great South*, 471.

43. The piedmont towns are discussed in *Social Statistics of Cities*, 2:81 (Richmond), 71 (Petersburg), 62 (Lynchburg), 107 (Columbia), 165 (Augusta).

44. King, *Great South*, 718.

45. Ibid., 697. The "New West" cities' topography is covered in *Social Statistics of Cities,* 2:118-19 (Lexington), 123 (Louisville), 153 (Nashville), 112-13 (Covington), 132 (Newport). For Cumberland see *Encyclopedia Americana: International Edition,* s.v., "Cumberland."

46. *Social Statistics of Cities*, 2:195.

47. Quoted in ibid., 2:214.

48. The interior cities' topography is covered in ibid., 2:159 (Atlanta), 170 (Macon), 136 (Chattanooga), 200 (Montgomery), 143 (Memphis), 211-12 (Little Rock), 209-11 (Vicksburg), For Columbus see *Encyclopedia Americana*, s.v., "Columbus."

49. King, *Great South*, 287.

50. Ibid., 110-14 (Williamsburg), 240-62 (Washington). Excellent studies of planning in the District of Columbia are Frederick Gutheim, *Worthy of the Nation: The History of Planning for the National Capital* (Washington, 1977); and John W. Reps, *Monumental Washington: The Planning and Development of the Capital Center* (Princeton, 1967). See also *Social Statistics of Cities,* 2:87; John W. Reps, *Tidewater Towns: City Planning in Colonial Virginia* (Charlottesville, 1972). Valuable background information can be found in Lewis Mumford, *The City in History: Its Origins, Its Transformations, and Its Prospects* (New York, 1961).

51. Reps, *Making of Urban America*, 81-87.

52. Quoted in John W. Reps, *Town Planning in Frontier America* (1965; rpr. Columbia, 1980), 165-66.

53. *Social Statistics of Cities*, 2:789 (Sacramento), 800 (San Francisco), 817 (Stockton).

54. Ibid., 2:3 (Baltimore), 53 (Georgetown), 65 (Norfolk), 75 (Portsmouth), 93 (Wilmington), opposite 95 (Charleston), 79 (Richmond), 71 (Petersburg), 60 (Lynchburg), 105 (Columbia), 163 (Augusta), 111 (Covington), 131 (Newport), 117 (Lexington), 151 (Nashville), 135 (Chattanooga), 157 (Atlanta), 169 (Macon), 199 (Montgomery), 140 (Memphis), 209 (Vicksburg), 211 (Little Rock). For Columbus and Cumberland see *Encyclopedia America*, s.v., "Columbus" and "Cumberland."

55. See Albert Fein, *Frederick Law Olmsted and the American Environmental Tradition*

(New York, 1972). In the 1830s and 1840s landscaped cometeries had captured the public imagination. This may have helped set the stage for the movement. A Swedish visitor wrote about a cemetery in Macon, "Wandering on through the solitary park I came to the banks of a river which ran in gentle windings between banks as beautiful, and as youthfully verdant as we, in our youth, imagine the Elysian fields. On my side of the river I beheld white marble monuments glancing forth from amid the trees, speaking of the city of the dead" (Fredrika Bremer, *The Homes of the New World: Impressions of America,* trans. Mary Howith, 3 vols. [London, 1853], 1:332).

56. For a concise account of the City Beautiful movement see Glaab and Brown, *Urban America,* 233-36.

57. *Social Statistics of Cities,* 2:58 (Alexandria), 67 (Norfolk), 76 (Portsmouth), 133 (Newport), 137 (Chattanooga), 113 (Covington), 201 (Montgomery).

58. Ibid., 2:177 (Savannah), 100 (Charleston), 160 (Atlanta), 170 (Macon), 107 (Columbia), 274-75 (New Orleans).

59. Quoted in ibid., 2:195.

60. Quoted in ibid., 2:18-19.

61. Ibid., 2:39-40.

62. Ibid., 37-39. See *An Omnibus of the Capitol,* House of Representatives Doc. 412, 2d ed., 86 Cong., 2d sess. (Washington, D.C., 1959).

63. A basic study of architectural trends is James Marston Fitch, *American Building: The Forces That Shape It* (1948; rpr. New York, 1977). See also Christopher Tunnard and Henry Hope Reed, *American Skyline: The Growth and Form of Our Cities and Towns* (New York, 1955); Vincent Scully, *American Architecture and Urbanism* (New York, 1969); Thomas A. Tallmadge, *The Story of Architecture in America* (New York, 1936); Talbot F. Hamlin, *Greek Revival Architecture in America* (New York, 1944).

64. Architectural and inconographic studies of individual southern cities have generally tended to appeal to popular audiences. Typical are the older William Casey, *An Architectural Monograph: Charleston Doorways, Entrance Motives from a South Carolina City,* White Pine Series, vol. 14, monograph 81 (New York, 1928), and the newer Franklin Garrett, *Yesterday's Atlanta,* Seeman's Historic Cities Series, no. 8 (Miami, 1974). Of more use from a scholarly standpoint are Everett B. Wilson, *Early Southern Towns* (South Brunswick, N.J., 1967); James Bonner, "Plantation Architecture of the Lower South on the Eve of the Civil War," *Journal of Southern History* 11 (August 1945):370-88; Henry Forman, *Architecture of the Old South: The Medieval Style, 1585-1850* (Cambridge, Mass., 1948).

65. The Tennessee statehouse is discussed in Clayton B. Dekle, "The Tennessee State Capitol," *Tennessee Historical Quarterly* 25 (Fall 1966):213-38. For the Chattanooga station see Gilbert E. Govan, "The Chattanooga Union Station," *Tennessee Historical Quarterly* 29 (Winter 1970-71):372-78. The Baltimore City Hall is described in *Social Statistics of Cities,* 2:17-18. Frank E. Vandiver, ed., *The Idea of the South: Pursuit of a Central Theme* (Chicago, 1964), 52, says the Kimball House was built by a corrupt northern opportunist. See Keith L. Bryant, "Cathedrals, Castles, and Roman Baths: Railroad Station Architecture in the Urban South," *Journal of Urban History* 2 (February 1976):195-230. Actually, Victorian and Gothic styles were English imports. In the mid-nineteenth century, during a period of rapid urbanization, British architects fought a battle of styles, moving away from Georgian to more eclectic forms (Asa Briggs, *Victorian Cities* [New York, 1963], 43).

66. Lewis Mumford, *The South in Architecture* (New York, 1941), 81, 102, 122. See also Woodward, *Origins of the New South,* 163.

67. *Social Statistics of Cities,* 2:19 (Baltimore), 125 (Louisville), 275 (New Orleans), 144 (Memphis), 82 (Richmond), 40 (Washington), 165 (Augusta), 67-68 (Norfolk), 62 (Lynchburg), 160 (Atlanta), 137 (Chattanooga).

68. Hugh F. Rankin, "The Colonial South," in Link and Patrick, *Writing Southern*

History, 21. For a history of the theater in an individual town see Sarah Sprott Morrow, "A Brief History of the Theater in Nashville," *Tennessee Historical Quarterly* 30 (Summer 1971):178-89.

69. See the provocative study by Gunther Barth, *City People: The Rise of Modern City Culture in Nineteenth-Century America* (New York, 1980). Dale A. Somers, *The Rise of Sports in New Orleans, 1850-1900* (Baton Rouge, 1972), is useful.

70. Herbert J. Doherty, Jr., has noted that although there were many "southern minds" in the antebellum period, cities were the cultural centers of the antebellum South. "Much of the more rarified cultural activity—such as art, *belles lettres*, literary criticism, music and the theater, and liberal theological speculation—was carried on almost exclusively in the urban centers," he wrote. "Foremost were Baltimore, Richmond, Charleston, and New Orleans, while towns such as Savannah, Natchez, and Nashville assumed secondary importance" (Herbert J. Doherty, Jr., "The Mind of the Antebellum South," in Link and Patrick, *Writing Southern History*, 198-223; the quote is on page 199). See such accounts as F. Garvin Davenport, *Cultural Life in Nashville on the Eve of the Civil War* (Chapel Hill, 1941); Joseph G. Tregle, Jr., "Early New Orleans Society: A Reappraisal," *Journal of Southern History* 18 (February 1952):20-36.

6. Fearless in Discharge of Their Duties

1. Charles N. Glaab and A. Theodore Brown, rev. by Charles N. Glaab, *A History of Urban America* (1967; rpr. New York, 1976), 12-13. See also Carl Bridenbaugh, *Cities in the Wilderness: The First Century of Urban Life in America* (1938; rpr. New York, 1955). For a fascinating account of the origins of "modern" urban services see G. T. Salisbury, *Street Life in Medieval England* (1939; rpr. Totowa, N.J., 1975).

2. *Social Statistics of Cities*, 2:16. This compilation, bringing together tens of thousands of primary sources, contains a detailed and panoramic view of urban services in the South and the rest of the nation. The compiler George Waring, Jr., wrote in his Letter of Transmittal, 20 February 1885, in the front of part 1, "Although published at this late day, the report relates only to the condition of cities treated of in the census year (1880). It is believed that for that year it presents an accurate statement of their condition so far as relates to the subjects dscussed."

3. Excellent material on street surfaces can be found in Winston A. Walden, "Nineteenth Century Street Pavements" (M.A. thesis, University of Missouri-Kansas City, 1967). See also Blake McKelvey, *The Urbanization of America: 1860-1915* (New Brunswick, 1963), 88-89; Clay McShane, "Transforming the Use of Urban Space: A Look at the Revolution in Street Pavements, 1880-1924," *Journal of Urban History* 5 (May 1979): 279-307; George A. Soper, *Modern Methods of Street Cleaning* (New York, 1909).

4. *Social Statistics of Cities*, 2:32-33 (Washington), 272 (New Orleans), 99 (Charleston), 159-60 (Atlanta), 143-44 (Memphis), 132 (Newport). An attempt in 1871 to pave Pennsylvania Avenue in Washington with wooden blocks was a failure (David L. Lewis, *District of Columbia: A Bicentennial History* [New York, 1976]).

5. *Social Statistics of Cities*, 2:58 (Alexandria), 67 (Norfolk), 272 (New Orleans), 113 (Covington), 143 (Memphis), 176 (Savannah), 99 (Charleston).

6. Ibid., 2:170.

7. Ibid., 2:124 (Louisville), 58 (Alexandria), 165 (Augusta), 62 (Lynchburg), 72 (Petersburg), 99 (Charleston), 170 (Macon), 176 (Savannah), 272 (New Orleans).

8. Lawrence H. Larsen, "Nineteenth-Century Street Sanitation: A Study of Filth and Frustration," *Wisconsin Magazine of History* 52 (Spring 1969): 239-47. There is valuable information in Soper, *Street Cleaning*, 7-22. Otto L. Bettmann, *The Good Old Days—They Were Terrible* (New York, 1974), approached the subject from an entertaining and popular standpoint.

9. Larsen, "Street Sanitation," 244.

10. Frederick Law Olmsted, *A Journey in the Seaboard Slave States, with Remarks on Their Economy* (New York, 1859), 137-38.

11. McKelvey, *Urbanization of America*, 88-89.

12. *Social Statistics of Cities*, 2:121 (Lexington), 149 (Memphis), 59 (Alexandria), 68 (Norfolk), 115 (Covington), 171 (Macon), 108 (Columbia), 102 (Charleston), 161 (Atlanta), 179 (Savannah), 287-88 (New Orleans). The quotes are from this source.

13. Ibid., 2:21-22 (Baltimore), 84 (Richmond), 102 (Charleston), 64 (Lynchburg), 94 (Wilmington), 108 (Columbia), 171 (Macon), 149 (Memphis), 288 (New Orleans). The quotes are from this source.

14. Ibid., 2:22 (Baltimore), 46 (Washington), 59 (Alexandria), 102 (Charleston), 197 (Mobile). The quotation is from this source.

15. Ibid., 2:115 (Covington), 21 (Baltimore), 68 (Norfolk), 108 (Columbia), 128 (Louisville), 149 (Memphis), 288 (New Orleans). The quotation is from this source. There is excellent material on national developments in Martin V. Melossi, *Garbage in the Cities: Refuse, Reform, and the Environment, 1880-1980* (College Station, Tex., 1981).

16. *Social Statistics of Cities*, 2:46.

17. The movement toward professionalism is covered in Stanley K. Schultz and Clay McShane, "To Engineer the Metropolis: Sewers, Santiation, and City Planning in Late-Nineteenth-Century America," *Journal of American History* 65 (September 1978): 389-411. See the appropriate sections of John Fairlie, *Municipal Administration* (New York, 1901); Charles Zueblin, *American Municipal Progress* (1902; rpr. New York, 1916).

18. *Social Statistics of Cities*, 2:64 (Lynchburg), 69 (Norfolk), 73 (Petersburg), 107 (Columbia), 195 (Mobile), 121 (Lexington), 167 (Augusta), 171 (Macon).

19. Quoted in ibid., 2:201.

20. Quoted in idid., 2:19.

21. Quoted in C. Vann Woodward, *Origins of the New South, 1877-1913*, A History of the South, vol. 9 (Baton Rouge, 1951), 227-28.

22. *Social Statistics of Cities*, 2:144-48; Glaab and Brown, *History of Urban America*, 155-56.

23. Quoted in *Social Statistics of Cities*, 2:145. See also Appendix I, "Sanitary Survey of Memphis, Tenn.," U.S. Congress, House of Representatives, *Annual Report of the National Board of Health, 1879*, House Executive Document 10, 46th Cong., 2d sess., 237-62.

24. *Dictionary of American Biography*, s.v., "Waring, George Edward"; James W. Cassedy, "The Flamboyant Colonel Waring," *Bulletin of the History of Medicine* 36 (March-April 1962): 163-76. Waring was the compiler of the *Social Statistics of Cities*. See Joel A. Tarr, "The Separate vs. Combined Sewer Problem: A Case Study in Urban Technology Design Choice," *Journal of Urban History* 5 (May 1979): 308-39.

25. Quoted in *Social Statistics of Cities*, 2:146-47. See John H. Ellis, "Memphis' Sanitary Revolution, 1880-1890," *Tennessee Historical Quarterly* 23 (March 1964): 59-72.

26. Quoted in *Social Statistics of Cities*, 2:22.

27. Ibid., 2:109 (Columbia), 134 (Newport), 289 (New Orleans), 179 (Savannah), 167 (Augusta), 202 (Montgomery), 84 (Richmond). The quotations are from this source.

28. Ibid., 2:22 (Baltimore), 46 (Washington), 64 (Lynchburg), 102 (Charleston), 109 (Columbia).

29. Quoted in ibid., 2:73.

30. The primary study of waterworks is Nelson Blake, *Water for the Cities: A History of the Water Supply Problem in the United States* (Syracuse, 1956). See also Walter G. Elliott, "Report on the Water-Supply of Certain Cities in the United States," *Reports on the Water-Power of the United States, Tenth Census of the United States, 1880*, vol. 17, pt. 2 (Washington, 1887), 1-272. *Social Statistics of Cities*, 2:76 (Portsmouth), 119 (Lexington), 99 (Charleston), 137 (Chattanooga), 144 (Memphis), 201 (Montgomery), 67 (Norfolk), 273 (New Orleans).

31. Frederick Behlendorff, "Recollections of a Fortyeighter," *Deutsche Ameribanncke Geschechts Blatter* 4 (1915): 322-23. See also Joel A. Tarr, James Mclurler, and Terry F. Yosie, "The Development and Impact of Urban Wastewater Technology: Changing Concepts of Water Quality Control, 1850-1930," in Martin V. Melosi, ed., *Pollution and Reform in American Cities, 1870-1930* (Austin, 1980), 68-69.

32. *Social Statistics of Cities,* 2:64 (Lynchburg), 69 (Norfolk), 84 (Richmond), 109 (Columbia), 115 (Covington), 134 (Newport), 167 (Augusta), 179 (Savannah), 161 (Atlanta), 139 (Chattanooga).

33. Ibid., 2:160 (Atlanta), 67 (Norfolk).

34. Ibid., 2:58 (Alexandria), 67 (Norfolk), 76 (Portsmouth), 72 (Petersburg), 99 (Charleston), 107 (Columbia), 113 (Covington), 125 (Louisville), 137 (Chattanooga), 165 (Augusta), 119 (Lexington), 144 (Memphis), 160 (Atlanta), 170 (Macon), 274 (New Orleans), 177 (Savannah).

35. Table 1, "General Financial Exhibit: 1880," *Report on the Agencies of Transportation in the United States, Including the Statistics of Railroads, Steam Navigation, Canals, Telegraphs, and Telephones, Tenth Census of the United States, 1880* (Washington, 1883), 4: 18-23.

36. *Social Statistics of Cities,* 2:72 (Petersburg), 76 (Portsmouth), 107 (Columbia), 170 (Macon), 119 (Lexington), 201 (Montgomery), 32 (Washington), 17 (Baltimore), 124 (Louisville), 273 (New Orleans), 62 (Lynchburg), 67 (Norfolk), 99 (Charleston), 138 (Chattanooga), 195 (Mobile), 165 (Augusta), 160 (Atlanta). See also Frank Rowsone, Jr., *Trolley Car Treasury: A Century of American Streetcars, Horsecars, Cable Cars, Interurbans, and Trolleys* (New York, 1956); E. Merton Coulter, *The South during Reconstruction,* A History of the South, vol. 8 (Baton Rouge, 1947), 263.

37. *Social Statistics of Cities,* 2:32 (Washington), 81 (Richmond), 176 (Savannah), 99 (Charleston), 144 (Memphis), 165 (Augusta), 201 (Montgomery), 160 (Atlanta).

38. Ibid., 2:120 (Lexington), 114-15 (Covington), 133 (Newport), 161 (Atlanta), 108 (Columbia), 202 (Montgomery), 138 (Chattanooga), 148 (Memphis). See Richard J. Hopkins, "Public Health in Atlanta: The Formative Years, 1865-1879," *Georgia Historical Quarterly* 53 (September 1969):287-304; John H. Ellis, "Business and Public Health in the Urban South during the Nineteenth Century: New Orleans, Memphis, and Atlanta," *Bulletin of the History of Medicine* 44 (May-June 1970):197-212.

39. *Social Statistics of Cities,* 2:20-21 (Baltimore), 44-45 (Washington), 127-28 (Louisville). The quotes are from this source. For a model code that was not fully put into practice see *Code of the Board of Health of the District of Columbia, 1871* (Washington, 1872).

40. See, for example, U.S. Congress, Senate, *Quarantine System on Southern and Gulf Coasts,* Senate Executive Document 9, 42d Cong., 3d sess., Serial 1545.

41. *Social Statistics of Cities,* 2:285-86.

42. Appendix B, "Havana Yellow Fever Commission," *Annual Report of the National Board of Health, 1879,* 33-73.

43. Quoted in *Social Statistics of Cities,* 2:287.

44. Quoted in ibid., 2:286. See also Donald Everett, "The New Orleans Yellow Fever Epidemic of 1853," *Louisiana Historical Quarterly* 33 (October 1950):380-405.

45. "First Report of the Committee on Public Hygiene of the American Medical Association," *Transactions of the American Medical Association* 2 (Philadelphia 1849):443-44; David R. Goldfield, "The Business of Health Planning, Disease Prevention in the Old South," *Journal of Southern History* 42 (November 1976):557-70, argues that urban boosterism retarded reforms.

46. See Jo Ann Corrigan, "Yellow Fever in New Orleans: Abstractions and Realities," *Journal of Southern History* 25 (August 1959):339- 55; Jo Ann Corrigan, "Privilege, Prejudice, and Strangers' Disease in Nineteenth-Century New Orleans," *Journal of Southern History* 36 (November 1970):568-78; Appendix L, "Annual Report for 1882 of Stanford E. Challe, M.D., Supervising Inspector, National Board of Health at New Orleans, La., "

U.S. Congress, Senate, *Annual Report of the National Board of Health: 1882*, Senate Executive Document 5, 47th Cong., 2d sess., 498-99.

47. *Social Statistics of Cities*, 2:281-86. The quotation is from this source. See also Elizabeth Wisner, *Public Health Administration in Louisiana* (Chicago, 1930).

48. Quoted in *Social Statistics of Cities*, 2:286-87.

49. Table LXIV, "Approximate Life Tables for Certain States and Cities," *Report on the Mortality and Vital Statistics of the United States, Tenth Census of the United States, 1880* (Washington, 1886), 12:777 (Baltimore), 780 (Charleston), 783 (New Orleans), 773 (District of Columbia), 781 (Chicago), 782 (Cincinnati), 787 (St. Louis), 784-85 (New York), 788 (San Francisco).

50. Table XLIV, ibid. 777 (Baltimore), 780 (Charleston), 783 (New Orleans), 773 (District of Columbia).

51. *Social Statistics of Cities*, 2:66 (Norfolk), 30-31 (Washington), 158 (Atlanta), 106 (Columbia), 80 (Richmond), 72 (Petersburg), 164 (Augusta), 123 (Louisville), 175 (Savannah), 15 (Baltimore). See E. Merton Coulter, "The Great Savannah Fire of 1820," *Georgia Historical Quarterly* 23 (March 1939):1-27; John B. Clark, Jr., "The Fire Problem in Kentucky, 1778-1865: A Case History of the Ante-Bellum South," *Register of the Kentucky Historical Society* 51 (April 1953):97-122.

52. *Social Statistics of Cities*, 2:139 (Chattanooga). The quotations are from this source.

53. Reading, Pennsylvania, for example, a city of 43,278 in 1880, had a volunteer fire department. All members were unpaid, including the chief engineer (ibid., 1:880).

54. Ibid., 2:74 (Petersburg), 179 (Savannah), 103 (Charleston), 128-29 (Louisville), 23-24 (Baltimore).

55. Quoted in ibid., 2:50.

56. Ibid., 2:23.

57. Quoted in ibid., 2:129.

58. Ibid., 2:47 (Washington), 292 (New Orleans), 23 (Baltimore), 103 (Charleston), 162 (Atlanta), 203 (Montgomery), 167 (Augusta), 139 (Chattanooga), 172 (Macon), 134 (Newport), 69 (Norfolk), 508-9 (Chicago), 528 (Peoria), 649 (Fond du Lac), 681 (Oshkosh). The evolution of police systems in America is covered in Fairlie, *Municipal Administration;* Raymond Fosdick, *American Police Systems* (New York, 1920); James F. Richardson, *Urban Police in the United States* (Port Washington, N.Y., 1974).

59. *Social Statistics of Cities*, 2:139 (Chattanooga), 167 (Augusta), 172 (Macon), 179 (Savannah), 103 (Charleston), 59 (Alexandria), 197 (Mobile), 162 (Atlanta), 149 (Memphis), 203 (Montgomery), 23 (Baltimore), 69 (Norfolk).

60. Quoted in ibid., 2:292.

61. Ibid., 2:103 (Charleston), 69 (Norfolk), 121 (Lexington), 179 (Savannah), 292 (New Orleans), 210 (Vicksburg).

62. Ibid., 2:69 (Norfolk), 167 (Augusta), 172 (Macon).

63. Ibid., 2:23 (Baltimore), 49 (Washingon), 103 (Charleston), 149 (Memphis), 167 (Augusta), 162 (Atlanta), 69 (Norfolk), 197 (Mobile), 172 (Macon), 121 (Lexington), 139 (Chattanooga), 203 (Montgomery), 210 (Vicksburg). For a comparison with antebellum times see Richard H. Haunton, "Law and Order in Savannah, 1850-1860," *Georgia Historical Quarterly* 56 (Spring 1972):1-24. In Montgomery, several voluntary organizations—the True Blues, the Rifles, and Cadets, and the Dragoons—helped keep slaves and free Negroes under surveillance (Virginia Van der Veer Hamilton, *Alabama: A Bicentennial History* [New York, 1977]).

64. Quoted in Albert Bushnell Hart, *The Southern South* (New York, 1910), 217. For an extreme view see Lawrence J. Friedman, *The White Savage: Racial Fantasies in the Postbellum South* (Englewood Cliffs, N.J., 1970), 140-42.

65. Quoted in Howard N. Rabinowitz, *Race Relations in the Urban South, 1865-1890* (New York, 1978), 53-54; *Alexandria Weekly Town Talk*, 18 June 1892.

66. Rabinowitz, *Race Relations*, 40-46, 278.

67. *Social Statistics of Cities*, 2:47.

68. Table CXXVI, "Police Statistics for 1880 of Cities in the United States having 5,000 or more Inhabitants," *Report on the Defective, Dependent, and Delinquent Classes of the Population of the United States, Tenth Census of the United States, 1880* (Washington, 1888), 21:566-74.

69. Rabinowitz, *Race Relations*, 52-54. See also Howard N. Rabinowitz, "The Conflict between Blacks and the Police in the Urban South," *Historian* 34 (November 1976):62-76.

70. *Report on the Defective, Dependent, and Delinquent Classes*, 566-74.

71. From the 1840s until the 1870s, Gallatin Street in the French Quarter had no legitimate businesses. See Herbert Ashbury, *The French Quarter: An Informal History of the New Orleans Underworld* (New York, 1938).

7. The Promise of Her Great Destiny

1. The Birmingham, Chattanooga, and Roanoke quotations are from C. Vann Woodward, *Origins of the New South, 1877-1913*, A History of the South, vol. 9 (Baton Rouge, 1951), 137-38.

2. The quotes are from ibid., 138.

3. *Alexandria Daily Town Talk*, 23 May 1884.

4. Woodward, *Origins of the New South*, 138.

5. Ibid., 137.

6. Henry Grady, *The New South* (New York, 1890), 162.

7. See Robert F. Fries, *Empire in Pine: The Story of Lumbering in Wisconsin, 1830-1900* (Madison, 1951); Agnes M. Larsen, *History of the White Pine Industry in Minnesota* (Minneapolis, 1949).

8. Henry C. Haskell, Jr., and Richard B. Fowler, *City of the Future: A Narrative History of Kansas City, 1850-1950* (Kansas City, 1950), 59-67.

9. Robert P. Porter, et al., "Progress of the Nation," *Total Population, Eleventh Census of the United States, 1890*, vol. 1, pt. 1 (Washington, 1895), lxvi.

10. "Totals for States and Industries," *Report on Manufacturing Industries in the United States at the Eleventh Census: 1890, Eleventh Census of the United States, 1890*, vol. 6, pt. 1 (Washington, 1895), 3-8.

11. Ibid., pt. 2, *Social Statistics of Cities*, xiv, 38, 330, 62, 478. With some exceptions, most new industry went to established towns (Edd Winfield Park, "Southern Towns and Cities," in W. T. Couch, ed., *Culture in the South* [Chapel Hill, 1934], 501-18). See also T. Lynn Smith, "The Emergence of Cities," in Rupert B. Vance and Nicholas J. Demerath, *The Urban South* (Chapel Hill, 1954), 33.

12. A standard account remains C. Vann Woodward, *The Strange Career of Jim Crow* (New York, 1955). Even as the South made an inward turn an optimist predicted the "complete social unification" of the country (Philip A. Bruce, *The Rise of the New South* [Philadelphia, 1905], 435). See also Broadus Mitchell and George Mitchell, *The Industrial Revolution in the South* (Baltimore, 1930); Ethel M. Armes, *The Story of Coal and Iron in Alabama* (Birmingham, 1910).

13. All histories of the South and on national developments in this period treat the agrarian revolt in the South. There are a large number of works on southern and northern Populists, most of which totally ignore any connections with urbanization or pre–Civil War developments. An exception is Stanley B. Parsons, *The Populist Context: Rural versus Urban Power on a Great Plains Frontier* (Westport, Conn., 1973). Most of the more recent scholars of the movement use the Populists to grind their own ideological axes. See Lawrence Goodwyn, *Democratic Promise: The Populist Revolt in America* (New York, 1976); Robert C. McMath, Jr., *Populist Vanguard: A History of the Southern Farmers' Alliance*

(Chapel Hill, 1976); Michael Schwartz, *Radical Protest and Social Structure: The Southern Farmers' Alliance and Cotton Tenancy, 1880-1890* (New York, 1976). A useful summary is John D. Hicks, *The Populist Revolt* (Minneapolis, 1931). The literature of the movement in the South is surveyed in Allen J. Going, "The Agrarian Revolt," in Arthur S. Link and Rembert W. Patrick, eds., *Writing Southern History: Essays in Historiography in Honor of Fletcher M. Green* (1965; rpr. Baton Rouge, 1967), 362-82; Patrick E. McLear, "The Agrarian Revolt in the South: A Historiographical Essay," *Louisiana Studies* 12 (Summer 1973):443-63. See also C. Vann Woodward, *Tom Watson: Agrarian Rebel* (New York, 1938).

14. Paul Gaston states, "To many it seemed that the Jim Crow system was a natural addition and reassuring guarantee of the safety of those standards celebrated in the New South myth, and institutionalization of ideas already approved as right. Thus, at the opening of the new century several fundamental patterns had been established: the incipient New South creed rationalized the abandonment of Reconstruction and the inauguration of the Redeemer regimes in the 1870's; the mature doctrine undermined the first menacing reform movement designed to overhaul that order in the 1890's; the Jim Crow system was added as an insurance measure; and the New South myth, fully articulated, offered a harmonizing and reassuring world view to conserve the essential features of the status quo. The New South movement itself was simultaneously ended" (Paul M. Gaston, *The New South Creed: A Study in Southern Mythmaking* [New York, 1970], 220-21).

15. Table 5, "Aggregate Population of Cities, Towns, Villages, and Buroughs having 2,500 Inhabitants or more in 1890, with Population for 1880 and Increase during the Decade," *Compendium of the Eleventh Census: 1890, Eleventh Census of the United States, 1890,* vol. 1, pt. 1 (Washington, 1892), 442-52.

16. Gunther Barth, *Instant Cities: Urbanization and the Rise of San Francisco and Denver* (New York, 1975); Lawrence H. Larsen, *The Urban West at the End of the Frontier* (Lawrence, 1978).

17. Grady, *New South,* 162.

18. *Alexandria Daily Town Talk,* 30 March 1883.

19. *Compendium of the Eleventh Census,* 442-52.

20. Flagler was an associate of Florida entrepreneur Henry Bradley Plant, who at the time of his death in 1899 controlled through the Plant System fourteen railroads and several steamship companies. See Woodward, *Origins of the New South,* 297-99; John F. Stover, *The Railroads of the South, 1865-1900: A Study in Finance and Control* (Chapel Hill, 1955), 268-70, 281.

21. Grady, *New South,* 265.

22. "Progress of the Population," xxviii.

23. *Alexandria Daily Town Talk,* 30 September 1883.

24. Woodward, *Origin of the New South,* 136.

25. "Progress of the Nation," lxix. A commonly held misconception in studying nineteenth-century urban population figures is that they are for the governmental unit. Actually, the figures are for census tracts. They frequently extend beyond a city's boundaries, taking in built-up sections outside the actual city limits. Thus the people living in the hastily constructed black shantytowns constructed just outside many southern cities during Reconstruction show up on the rolls as residents of the city rather than of the county. Of course, sprawling subdivisions were a different matter, as illustrated by Knoxville.

26. Quoted in Woodward, *Origins of the New South,* 126-27. An excellent essay on Birmingham's fortunes before the conclusion of the Great Depression of the 1930s is George R. Leighton, *Five Cities: The Story of Their Youth and Old Age* (New York, 1939), 100-139.

Essay on Sources

This bibliographical essay is included for three purposes: to acquaint readers with the sources that have been most useful in pursuing the study of urban history, to provide ideas for further directions in research, and to provide guidelines for those who wish to extend their general knowledge of southern urban history. Only a representative portion of the vast number of materials consulted in the preparation of this book are listed here, primarily those that were most extensively drawn upon and cited. All sources are cited in full in the notes.

Gathering the data used in writing this study took over a decade. Almost all the sources are traditional in nature: scholarly monographs, articles in professional journals, published federal documents, contemporary commentaries, unpublished materials, travel accounts, newspapers, and local histories. Given the broad nature of this study, it was impossible to gather data systematically. The contemporary article on the river passes into the Gulf of Mexico below New Orleans, "The Mouths of the Mississippi," *DeBow's Review* 17 (July 1854):15-25, was found while I was doing research on an entirely different subject. The quotations on the New South from the Alexandria, Louisiana, *Town Talk* were furnished by a colleague. Material on federal attitudes toward the impact of disease in New Orleans came to light while I was doing research at the National Archives in Washington, D.C., on an unrelated project and using the records of the National Board of Health and the Marine Hospital Service. One of the many satisfying parts of research is when one unexpectably finds valuable material on a subject while working on an entirely different topic. This is bound to happen to the student of nineteenth-century southern urban history. Although scholars have never totally ignored the role of cities in the history of the South, they have not viewed them as a central theme in the section's development. Rich materials exist on southern urbanization, but they are spread through a wide variety of primary and secondary sources. A major need exists for a detailed and analytical bibliography of sources about the urban history of Dixie.

The broad contours of city building in the South are readily discernible. Useful surveys that fit the southern picture into larger patterns are Bayrd Still, *Urban America: A History with Documents* (Boston, 1974), and Charles N. Glaab and A. Theodore Brown, rev. by Charles N. Glaab, *A History of Urban America*, 2d ed. (New York, 1976). Carl Bridenbaugh, *Cities in the Wilderness: The First Century of Urban Growth in America* (1938; rpr. New York, 1955), is a rich source on the origins of southern towns. General histories of the American South contain scattered information. Of particular value for the post-Reconstruction years is William B. Hesseltine and David L. Smiley, *The South in American*

History (Englewood Cliffs, N.J., 1960). This work has valuable insights on the relationship between national economic developments and northern penetration of the southern urban economy. E. Merton Coulter, *The South during Reconstruction, 1865–1877,* A History of the South, vol. 8 (Baton Rouge, 1947), contains a pioneering suggestive essay on southern urbanization in the 1870s.

The few existing theoretical essays or anthologies dealing with the meaning and significance of southern urban history are of excellent quality. David R. Goldfield, *Cotton Fields and Skyscrapers: Southern City and Region, 1607–1980* (Baton Rouge, 1982), attempts to develop a synthesis for the history of the urban South. His bold, stimulating, and provocative analysis stands as a starting point for studying city building in Dixie. A straightforward compilation, Blaine A. Brownell and David R. Goldfield, eds., *The City in Southern History: The Growth of Urban Civilization in the South,* National University Publications Interdisciplinary Urban Series (Port Washington, N.Y., 1977), referred to hereinafter as *The City in Southern History,* contains several original scholarly essays. Two chapters of background value in this work are Carville Earle and Ronald Hoffman, "The Urban South: The First Two Centuries," and Brownell and Goldfield, "Pursuing the American Urban Dream: Cities in the Old South." Another essay, Howard N. Rabinowitz, "Continuity and Change: Southern Urban Development, 1860–1900," traces the growth of the urban network. Two pieces by Leonard P. Curry, "Urbanization and Urbanism in the Old South: A Comparative View," *Journal of Southern History* 40 (February 1974):43-60, and a pamphlet, *Urban Life in the Old South* (St. Louis, 1976), conclude that the Old South had a significant urban dimension. T. Lynn Smith, "The Emergence of Cities," in Rupert B. Vance and Nicholas J. Demearth, eds., *The Urban South* (Chapel Hill, 1954), shows how the South steadily lost ground relative to the rest of the nation. Blaine Brownell argues that urbanization in the South differed from that in other parts of the country in "Urbanization in the South: A Unique Experience," *Mississippi Quarterly* 26 (Spring 1973):105-20. See also his book, *The Urban Ethos in the South, 1920-1930* (Baton Rouge, 1975). David R. Goldfield, "The Urban South: A Regional Framework," *American Historical Review* 86 (December 1981):1009-34, takes a somewhat similar view, claiming that southern city building was "urbanization without cities."

Students of nineteenth-century southern ubanization have not made sufficient use of contemporary printed federal documents. Most of these are difficult to peruse because of antiquated methods of organization, small print, bureaucratic prose, and lack of indexes. Many depositories do not have complete runs either in printed, photo, or machine form of the federal serial set, the state papers, or the census. Moreover, indexes of documents, such as *McKee's Compilations,* are vexing to employ and hard to find. Still, if used judiciously and with an element of caution in relying upon them as "official" sources, federal documents are of value in nineteenth-century urban research.

A primary source of special importance is a remarkable survey, George E. Waring, Jr., comp., "The Southern and the Western States" and "The New England and the Middle States," *Report on the Social Statistics of Cities, Tenth Census of the United States, 1880,* vols. 9 and 10, pts. 1 and 2 (Washington, 1886-87). At the time he directed the project, Waring was a member of the National Board of Health and one of the nation's leading experts on the relationship between urban sanitation and public health. Thousands of individuals from all around the country, including historians, provided the information that resulted in the *Social Statistics of Cities*. George W. Cable, the controversial author of *The Creoles of Louisiana* (New York, 1884), was the author of a fifty-four-page account of the history of New Orleans. Most of the contributors, however, were appointed or elected local officials. Although the vast number are anonymous, they included R. T. Scowden, the city engineer of Louisville, and Edward Fenner, vice-president of the Auxiliary Sanitary Association of New Orleans.

Much of the material in the *Social Statistics of Cities* is in monographic rather than statistical form. There are few of the detailed numerical tables usually associated with census compilations. The "Tabulated Index of Cities and Subjects" indicates the wide range of information included: cemeteries, climate, commerce and navigation, distance chart, drainage, financial condition, fire department, garbage, gas, history, infectious diseases, inspection, interments, location, manufactures, markets, monuments, municipal cleansing, parks, penal reformatory, charitable and healing institutions, places of amusement, police, population by decades, and by present division, public buildings, railroads, sanitary authority, schools and libraries (public), streets, topography, tributary country, watercourses, harbors, etc., and waterworks. The data enable a modern researcher to obtain information that otherwise would be very difficult if not impossible to find. Most city governments, lacking storage capacity, throw out "housekeeping" records at frequent intervals, sometimes at the end of each fiscal year. Until recently few historical depositories have attempted to collect routine city records. The *Social Statistics of Cities* is a unique and invaluable source to all students of the American city of the late nineteenth century. The hundreds of pieces of information, ranging from the cost ($40,000) to build the city waterworks in Columbia, South Carolina, to the detail that the police in Chattanooga, Tennessee, carried clubs and pistols, provide the raw data that enable the historian to develop interpretations based on specific evidence.

Information is included on 222 of the 228 cities in the United States that had populations of 10,000 or more in 1880. At least some data are included on all the major southern cities except Columbus, Georgia, and Cumberland, Maryland. Census experts had incorrectly projected that those two cities would have less than 10,000 inhabitants in 1880. Because of their regional importance in Florida, there are sections on Jacksonville and Pensacola, even though their populations in 1880 were under 8,000. Unfortunately, Waring kept custody of all the manuscript materials for the *Social Statistics of Cities*. Apparently, they have been destroyed, a great loss to researchers.

The *Tenth Census of the United States, 1880,* was the most comprehensive compilation attempted up until that time, a response to congressional desire for a survey of the progress of the nation during its first hundred years. Statisticians presented persuasive arguments that the gathering of vast amounts of detailed material would enable scholars to use "aggregates," leading to a reinterpretation of the national experience and the role of the common people in building the nation. The twenty-four volumes in the census contain everything from material on projected model homes for workers in paternalistic communities to figures on cotton production in every county in the country.

Several of the volumes are indispensable in studying southern cities in the Gilded Age. Vital statistics on blacks, natives, foreign-born, females, males, and workers can be found throughout the *Statistics of the Population of the United States*, vol. 1 (Washington, 1883). Of special usefulness are Table IX, "Population, as Native and Foreign-born, of Cities and Towns of 4,000 Inhabitants and Upward: 1880 and 1870," pp. 447-56; Table VI, "Population, by Race, of Cities and Towns of 4,000 Inhabitants and Upward: 1880 and 1870," pp. 416-25; Table XVI, "Foreign-born Population of Fifty Principal Cities, Distributed According to Place of Birth, among the Various Foreign Countries: 1880," pp. 538-41; Table XV, "Native Population of Fifty Principal Cities Distributed According to States and Territories of Birth: 1880," pp. 536-37; Table XXXV, "Number of Persons in Fifty Principal Cities Engaged in Each Class of Occupation with Distinction of Age and Sex and of Nativity: 1880," p. 885.

Other volumes cover a variety of essential subjects. There are tabulations on railroads and telephone companies in the *Report on the Agencies of Transportation in the United States, Including the Statistics of Railroads, Steam Navigation, Canals, Telegraphs, and Telephones*, vol. 4 (Washington, 1883): Table II, "Index to Physical Characteristics of Railroads," pp. 627-35; Table I, "General Financial Exhibit: 1880," pp. 18-23. Extensive industrial statistics can be found in the *Report of the Manufactures of the United States*, vol. 2 (Washington, 1883). An important register is Table VI, "Manufactures of 100 Principal Cities, by Totals: 1880," pp. 379-80. Another Table VI in the same volume is "Manufactures of 100 Principal Cities, by Specified Industries: 1880," pp. 384-443. There is a compilation of police statistics in the *Report on the Defective, Dependent, and Delinquent Classes of the Population of the United States*, vol. 21 (Washington, 1888), Table CXXXVI, "Police Statistics for 1880 of Cities in the United States having 5,000 or more Inhabitants," pp. 566-74. Information on waterworks is in Walter G. Elliott, "Report on the Water-Supply of Certain Cities in the United States," *Reports on the Water-Power of the United States*, vol. 17, pt. 2 (Washington, 1887). Vital statistics on birth and death ratios are included in the *Report on the Mortality and Vital Statistics of the United States*, vol. 12 (Washington, 1886), Table LXIV, "Approximate Life Tables for Certain States and Cities," pp. 773-83.

The tables of contents in the various census volumes are confusing. Furthermore, out-of-date typefaces, difficult-to-use indexes, small print, and confusing tabulations complicate the use of the documents. From more than twenty years of experience, I have found that working with any materials printed by the federal government in the late nineteenth century requires a high degree of patience and perseverance.

Federal documents from the *Eleventh Census of the United States* were of great help in writing about southern cities in the Gilded Age. The *Report on Statistics of Churches in the United States*, vol. 9 (Washington, 1894), has the best available religious tabulations. (Attempts to take a religious census in 1880 failed because of faulty methodology.) Table 1, "Summary of Denominations for 124 Cities, by Cities," p. 91, shows the number of organizations, church edifices, value of church property, and members. Two other tables give numbers of communicants by denominations: Table 7, "Communicants or Members in Cities having a Population of 100,000 to 500,000," pp. 98-99; Table 11, "Communicants or Members in Cities having a Population of 25,000 to 100,000," pp. 112-15. These tables, which are in small type, with the statistics spread in long rows across two pages, are difficult to use, and it would have been helpful if the tables had been combined. Much easier to use are the comparative manufacturing statistics contained in *Report on Manufacturing Industries in the United States at the Eleventh Census, 1890*, pts. 1 and 2 (Washington, 1895). See also *Compendium of the Eleventh Census, 1890*, vol. 1, pt. 1 (Washington, 1892); and *Population*, vol. 1, pt. 2 (Washington, 1892). The *Compendium* Table 5, "Aggregate Population of Cities, Towns, Villages, and Bouroughs having 2,500 Inhabitants or more in 1890, with Population for 1880 and Increase during the Decade," pp. 442-452, is valuable.

A variety of other federal documents contain helpful information. A detailed source for educational statistics is the Report of the Secretary of the Interior, *Report of the Commissioner of Education, 1880*, vol. 3 (Washington, 1882). This compilation has educational statistics for important cities and material on educational programs and practices for both white and black schools, provided by local officials. U.S. Congress, House of Representatives, *Annual Report of the National Board of Health, 1879*, House Executive Document 10, 46th Cong., 2d sess., has valuable data on sanitary conditions. Basic to understanding the forces in the economy that enabled Baltimore to garner a significant portion of the post–Civil War grain trade, at the same time that New Orleans' relative share declined, is "The Grain Trade of the United States and Tables on the World's Wheat Supply and Trade," Bureau of Statistics, Department of the Treasury, *Monthly Summary of Commerce and Finances, January, 1900*, n.s., no. 7 (Washington, 1900). Despite the limited scope of the title, this lengthy report has historical tables and a lengthy economic analysis on the evolution of the nineteenth-century American grain trade. A unique report, produced in the 1850s to help Congress determine the advisability of a Canadian reciprocity treaty, includes considerable information on the southern cotton economy and New Orleans trade in particular. It is U.S. Congress, Senate, *Report of Israel D. Andrews on the Trade and Commerce of the British North American Colonies, and upon the Trade of the Great Lakes and Rivers*, Senate Executive Document 112, 32d Cong., 1st sess., Serial 622. Andrews was a foreign service officer and expert on internal and external trade patterns. See Gerald M. Gibson, "Israel DeWolf Andrews: Perceptive Bureaucrat" (M.A. thesis, University of Missouri-Kansas City, 1976).

Some basic federal documents have been reproduced as National Archives and Record Service microfilm T publications. All existing manuscript population schedules are available in this form. Unfortunately, many sheets are missing for Cumberland and Columbus, making it impossible to determine how many females lived in those towns in 1880. This information does not appear in the printed census. It is also vexing that the 1890 federal manuscript census schedules were destroyed in a fire. Fortunately, the printed volumes are sufficiently detailed to provide an overall view of the characteristics of the United States in 1890.

Rich materials exist on the New South movement. Henry Grady stated his case in his valedictory, *The New South* (New York, 1890). A need remains for a comprehensive biography of Grady. The best available at this time is Raymond Nixon, *Henry Grady: Spokesman of the New South* (New York, 1943). Henry Watterson, *The Compromises of Life* (New York, 1903), attempted to sum up his own career. The choice of a title reveals much about the man. Biographies of the Louisville editor include Isaac Marcosson, *"Marse Henry": A Biography of Henry Watterson* (New York, 1951); Joseph Wall, *Henry Watterson: Reconstructed Rebel* (New York, 1956). Walter Hines Page's career is admirably told in John Milton Cooper, Jr., *Walter Hines Page: The Southerner as American, 1855-1918* (Chapel Hill, 1977). The importance of newspapers to the New South movement is shown in Thomas D. Clark, "The Country Newspaper: A Factor in Southern Opinion, 1865–1930," *Journal of Southern History* 14 (February 1948): 3-33.

Of great importance in understanding the complex philosophical strains that led to the New South concept is Paul M. Gaston, *The New South Creed: A Study in Southern Mythmaking* (New York, 1970). It contains an excellent bibliography. The basic work on the period in general is C. Vann Woodward, *Origins of the New South, 1877–1913,* A History of the South, vol. 9 (Baton Rouge, 1951). Neither author viewed the men of the New South in the mainstream of American urban development. Both deplored what they saw as cynical attempts to exploit the race issue and to persuade white southerners to adopt Yankee ways under the guise of progress. Gaston wrote, "Admirable in its vision, the New South creed had been manipulated through most of its history by men who served the region poorly, and the hold it gained over the American mind had obstructed more frequently than it had promoted achievement of its ideas" (p. 245). Woodward attacked the term itself. "If it were possible," he said, "to dispense with a phrase of such wide currency, I would not use the name 'New South' except to designate an ill-defined group of Southerners. . . . Disinfected as much as possible, the term 'New South' will be used in the following pages without its slogan—like connotations" (p. ix-x). The duality about the value of cities that has permeated the southern experience has also bothered many southern historians. For a summary of the roots of the New South, see Sheldon Hackney, "Origins of the New South in Retrospect," *Journal of Southern History* 38 (May 1972):191-216.

Several conceptual essays, interpretations, and compilations are of considerable help in placing the urban South in perspective. Within a larger context, C. Vann Woodward, *The Burden of Southern History* (1960; rpr. Baton Rouge, 1968), contains ten essays that selectively deal with the southern experience. Of special significance are the first two, "The Search for Southern Identity" and "The Historical Dimension." Twelve Southerners, *I'll Take My Stand: The South and the Agrarian Tradition* (New York, 1930), launched a classic attack on the trend toward industry in the South, ignoring the section's urban traditions. Carl N. Degler, *Place over Time: The Continuity of Southern Distinctiveness* (Baton Rouge, 1977), also discounted the South's urban antecedents. He wrote, "Or how can one generalize about the rise of industry and the spread of urbanization in the last century without recognizing that those social developments were not, for the South, nineteenth-century phenomena?" (p. 127). An important intellectual history, W. J. Cash, *The Mind of the South* (New York, 1941), argued that the incessant needs of the "peculiar institution" gave rise to a philosophy of caste. Although V. O. Key, Jr., *Southern Politics in State and Nation*

(New York, 1949), concentrates on twentieth-century politics, it is essential reading. Other works of use include J. Isaac Copeland, ed., *Democracy in the Old South and Other Essays by Fletcher Melvin Green* (Nashville, 1969); Grady Mc-Whiney, *Southerners and Other Americans* (New York, 1973); Benjamin Burks Kendrick and Alex Mathews Arnett, *The South Looks at Its Past* (Chapel Hill, 1935); William H. Nichols, *Southern Tradition and Regional Progress* (Chapel Hill, 1960); Harriet Chappell Owsley, ed., *The South: Old and New Frontiers: Selected Essays of Frank Lawrence Owsley* (Athens, Ga., 1969); Henry Savage, Jr., *Seeds of Time: The Background of Southern Thinking* (New York, 1959); Donald Davidson, ed., *Selected Essays and Other Writings of John Donald Wade* (Athens, Ga., 1966); T. Harry Williams, *Romance and Realism in Southern Politics* (Athens, Ga., 1961); Frank E. Vandiver, ed., *The Idea of the South: Pursuit of a Central Theme* (Chicago, 1964); and Dewey W. Grantham, Jr., ed., *The South and the Sectional Theme since Reconstruction* (New York, 1967). Almost all these studies of the southern experience ignore urbanization as a factor in sectional development.

Certain other works have valuable insights that relate, sometimes directly and at others indirectly, to the study of urbanization. Of fundamental importance in understanding regionalism is William Best Hesseltine, "Regions, Classes and Sections in American History," *Journal of Land and Public Utilities Economics* 1 (February 1944):35-44. An influential study that attempted to sum up the meaning of the South, W. T. Couch, ed., *Culture in the South* (Chapel Hill, 1934), has a number of essays that touch upon urban and industrial concerns. One of the essays represents an early attempt, if not the first, to establish a framework for understanding the southern city. It is Edd Winfield Parks, "Southern Towns and Cities," 501-18. Park, an English professor, concluded that although southern cities were distinct from one another, an "amazing homogeneity of the people" set them apart from those in the North. A suggestive summary, which views the New South movement as a limited attempt by a few individuals to sell out the South to make money, relates postbellum to antebellum concerns, demonstrating the continuity of southern history: Clement Eaton, *The Waning of the Old South Civilization, 1860-1880's*, Mercer University Lamar Memorial Lectures, No. 10 (Athens, Ga., 1968). One of the first efforts to establish a basis for analyzing the South touches throughout on urban subjects. It is Albert Bushnell Hart, *The Southern South* (New York, 1910). William Best Hesseltine, *Confederate Leaders in the New South* (1950; rpr. Westport, Conn., 1970), shows how many war leaders moved easily into urban leadership positions. A number of the contributions to Arthur S. Link and Rembert W. Patrick, eds., *Writing Southern History: Essays in Historiography in Honor of Fletcher M. Green* (1965; rpr. Baton Rouge, 1967), include historiographical essays that relate to urban themes. Especially valuable is Paul M. Gaston, "The 'New South,' " 316-36. Taken together, the many works that delineate a structure for the study of the South provide an excellent and intellectually exciting starting point for understanding the role of cities.

The forces that affected the course of Dixie's urban network and the response by southern cities in the antebellum period are amplified in a number of studies. The story of an old land artery, which at one time loomed large in southern plans, is detailed in popular fashion in Philip D. Jordan, *The National Road*, American Travel Series (Indianapolis, n.d.). Robert Greehalgh Albion,

The Rise of New York Port [1815-1860] (New York, 1939), covers the decisions made in 1817 by New York entrepreneurs. The reaction of the city's rivals is analyzed in Julius Rubin, *Canal or Railroad? Imitation and Innovation in the Response to the Erie Canal in Philadelphia, Baltimore, and Boston, Transactions of the American Philosophical Society,* n.s., vol. 51, pt. 3 (Philadelphia, 1961). Baltimore businessmen felt so threatened that they started a railroad to the West in advance of proven technology. The plans unfold in Edward Hungerford, *The Story of the Baltimore and Ohio Railroad, 1827-1927,* 2 vols. (New York, 1928). Two important works on Baltimore's internal improvement schemes are Milton Reizenstein, *The Economic History of the Baltimore and Ohio Railroad,* John Hopkins University Studies in Historical and Political Science, Fifteenth Series, vols. 7-8 (Baltimore, 1897); James Livingood, *The Philadelphia–Baltimore Trade Rivalry, 1780-1860* (Harrisburg, 1947). An older book, Edward Ingle, *Southern Sidelights: A Picture of Social and Economic Life in the South a Generation before the War* (New York, 1896), discusses some of the geographical obstacles faced by the Atlantic ports. The strategies followed by the Virginia cities are discussed in David R. Goldfield, *Urban Growth in the Age of Sectionalism: Virginia, 1847-1861* (Baton Rouge, 1977). See also Thomas Armstrong, "Urban Vision in Virginia: A Comparative Study of Antebellum Fredericksburg, Lynchburg, and Saunton" (Ph.D. dissertation, University of Virginia, 1974). David R. Goldfield, "Urban-Rural Relations in the Old South: The Example of Virginia," *Journal of Southern History* 42 (February 1976): 146-68, stresses the mutual concerns of planters and merchants in the emerging commercial system. Background information can be found in David T. Gilchrist, ed., *The Growth of the Seaport Towns, 1790-1825* (Charlottesville, 1967).

The impact of New York's rise on the South is analyzed in a standard work, Philip S. Foner, *Business and Slavery: The New York Merchants and the Irrepressible Conflict* (Chapel Hill, 1941). Two ill-digested works are less satisfactory. They are by geographer Allan R. Pred, contributions to the Harvard Studies in Urban History, *Urban Growth and Circulation of Information: The United States System of Cities, 1790-1840* (Cambridge, Mass., 1973), and *Urban Growth and City-Systems in the United States, 1840-1860* (Cambridge, Mass., 1980). Pred uses mathematical equations to draw conclusions about urban systems from data on such subjects as shipments of shoes from Boston to Charleston. Much remains to be done on antebellum economic relations between the South and the Northeast.

The rise of the Midwest and the impact on southern hopes and aspirations is expanded upon in a number of sources. John G. Clark, *The Grain Trade in the Old Northwest* (Urbana, 1966), details the growth and mechanics of the trade. Charles N. Glaab and Lawrence H. Larsen, "Neenah-Menasha in the 1870's," *Wisconsin Magazine of History* 52 (Autumn 1968):19-34, has material on the westward movement of the grain industry. Early settlement patterns and the beginning of the shift of important cities from the South to Midwest are outlined in Richard Wade, *The Urban Frontier: Pioneer Life in Early Pittsburgh, Cincinnati, Lexington, Louisville, and St. Louis* (Chicago, 1959). Cincinnati's southern ties are dealt with in David Kelley Jackson, ed., *American Studies in Honor of William Kenneth Boyd* (1940; rpr. Freeport, N.Y., 1968). Basic to understanding the growth of an urban network in the Midwest is Wyatt Belcher, *The Economic Rivalry between St. Louis and Chicago, 1850-1880* (New York, 1947). See also J. Christopher Schnell, "Chicago versus St. Louis: A Reassessment of the Great Rivalry," *Missouri Historical Review* 71 (April 1977):245-65; Lawrence H. Larsen, "Chicago's Midwest Rivals: Cincinnati, St. Louis, and Milwaukee," *Chicago History: The Magazine of the Chicago Historical Society* 5 (Fall 1976):141-51. A major work on the rise of sections remains Frederick Jackson Turner, *The United States, 1830-1850: The Nation and Its Sections* (1935; rpr. New York, 1962). Neil Primm, *St. Louis: Lion of the Valley* (Boulder, 1981), shows the shift of St. Louis from a southern to a midwestern city. Other studies of value are A. L. Kohlmeier, *The Old Northwest as the Keystone of the Arch of the American Union* (Bloomington, Ind., 1938); Henry C. Hubbart, *The Older Middle West, 1840-1880* (New York, 1936). Even so, much remains to be written on the economic, political, and social forces that led to the South's loss of the Midwest trade.

More has been done on the response of New Orleans to the crisis in the upper Mississippi River Valley than on any other southern city. The Crescent City's early economic development is detailed in John C. Clark, *New Orleans, 1718-1812: An Economic History* (Baton Rouge, 1970). Problems with the river route are analyzed by a number of scholars, including Robert M. Brown, "The Mississippi River as a Trade Route," *Bulletin of the American Geographical Society of New York* 38 (1906):347-54; R. B. Way, "The Commerce of the Lower Mississippi in the Period 1830-1860," *Mississippi Valley Historical Review*, Extra Number (July 1920):57-68; Frank H. Dixon, *A Traffic History of the Mississippi River System*, National Waterways Commission, Doc. 11 (Washington, 1909); Walter M. Lowrey, "Navigational Problems at the Mouth of the Mississippi River, 1698-1880" (Ph.D. dissertation, Vanderbilt University, 1956); Walter M. Lowrey, "The Engineers and the Mississippi," *Louisiana History* 5 (Summer 1964):223-56. The reaction of New Orleans to its growing plight is surveyed in many accounts, including G. W. Stephens, "Some Aspects of Early Intersectional Rivalry for the Commerce of the Upper Mississippi Valley," *Washington University Studies* 10 (1923):277-300; John G. Clark, "New Orleans and the River: A Study in Attitudes and Responses," *Louisiana History* 8 (Spring 1967):117-36; Gary Bolding, "Change, Continuity, and Identity of a Southern City: New Orleans, 1850-1950," *Louisiana Studies* 14 (Summer 1975):161-78; James Cairns, "The Response of New Orleans to the Diversion of Trade from the Mississippi River, 1845-1860" (M.A. thesis, Columbia University, 1950); Erastus P. Puckett, "The Attempt of New Orleans to Meet the Crisis of Her Trade with the West," *Mississippi Valley Historical Review*, Extra Number (February 1923):481-95. The poor port facilities in New Orleans were stressed in Walter Parker, "Facilities of the Port of New Orleans," *Annals of the American Academy of Political and Social Science* 86 (November 1919):188-98.

The shift of community aspirations to a regional strategy has come under increasing investigation. Lawrence H. Larsen, "New Orleans and the River Trade: Reinterpreting the Role of the Business Community," *Wisconsin Magazine of History* 61 (Winter 1977-78):112-24, emphasizes the impact of transportation costs. The basic monograph on the city's railroad strategy is Merl E. Reed, *New Orleans and the Railroads: The Struggle for Commerical Empire, 1830-1860* (Baton Rouge, 1966). Two other articles on the subject are Harry Howard Evans, "James Robb, Banker and Pioneer Builder of Ante-Bellum Louisiana," *Louisiana Historical Quarterly* 33 (January 1940):170-258; James P. Baughman, "The Evolu-

tion of Rail-Water Systems of Transportation in the Gulf Southeast, 1836-1890,"
Journal of Southern History 34 (August 1968):351-81. See also Ottis Clark Skipper,
"J.D.B. DeBow, the Man," *Journal of Southern History* 10 (November
1944):404-23. The characteristics of New Orleans and Louisiana leaders can be
found in Robert W. Shugg, *Origins of the Class Struggle in Louisiana: A Social
History of White Farmers and Laborers during Slavery and After, 1840-1875* (1939; rpr.
Baton Rouge, 1968). A broader study has valuable economic information:
Arthur Harrison Cole, *Wholesale Commodity Prices in the United States, 1700-1861*
(Cambridge, Mass., 1938). The attempts of other southern towns to counter
changed conditions in the Midwest constitute a fruitful area of research.

Local histories of varying content and quality are available for all thirty of
the southern cities that had 10,000 or more people in 1880. Most are long and
poorly organized. The majority are "day-by-day" chronicles, without any
analytical structure. Only the most indefatigable and resolute of readers have
ever read one from end to end. In many instances the authors, untrained in
historical methods, were enthusiastic amateurs or local leaders. The emphasis
placed on events contains valuable insights on concerns at given points in
community development. Later histories of the same town frequently draw
directly and heavily on earlier ones, thus indicating a shift from promotional
concerns to a need to document historical roots and so on. All the local histories
produced after 1865 place great emphasis on the Civil War, which should give
scholars interested in delineating new breaking points for southern history
reason to pause. Usually, accompanying biographical volumes, sometimes
called "mug books," have sketches of the lives of leaders. In an era in which few
newspapers printed obituaries, these biographies can be of immense value in
piecing together the contours of a community power structure. If used correctly, local histories are some of the most valuable sources available for urban
research. They contain a wide variety of information on such subjects as
population trends, social life, and economic developments that for the most
part are unavailable elsewhere. Indeed, what they leave out—few contain data
on the black community—illustrates attitudes and conditions. To sum up, the
local histories dispute the assertion of some leading scholars that the South has
little in the way of an urban past.

Several of the local histories are old enough to qualify as primary sources.
They include *Baltimore: Past and Present, with Biographical Sketches of Its Represen-
tative Men . . .* (Philadelphia, 1881); Charles Todd, *The Story of Washington: The
National Capital* (New York, 1889); Benjamin Cassedy, *The History of Louisville
from Its Earliest Settlement till the Year 1852* (Louisville, 1852); De Saussure and J.
L. Dawson, *Census of the City of Charleston, for the Year 1848: Exhibiting the
Condition and Prospects of the City, Illustrated by Many Statistical Details, prepared
under the Authority of the City Council* (Charleston, 1849); H. W. Burton, *History of
Norfolk, Virginia: A Review of Important Events and Incidents Which Occurred from
1736 to 1877; Also a Record, Personal Reminiscences and Political, Economical, and
Curious Facts* (Norfolk, 1874); Samuel Mordecai, *Virginia, Especially Richmond in
By-gone Days, with a Glance at the Present, Being Reminiscences and Last Words of an
Old Citizen,* 2d ed. (Richmond, 1860); Margaret Couch Cabell, *Sketches and
Recollections of Lynchburg* (Richmond, 1858); George Ranck, *History of Lexington,
Kentucky: Its Early Annals and Recent Progress, Including Biographical Sketches and*

Personal Reminiscences of the Pioneer Settlers, Notices of Prominent Citizens, etc. etc. (Cincinnati, 1872); James Davis, *The History of Memphis* (Memphis, 1873); John Butler, *Historical Record of Macon and Central Georgia* (1879; rpr. Macon, 1950); *Past, Present, and Future of Chattanooga, Tennessee, "The Industrial Center of the South": Its Superior Resources and Advantages, and the Inducements It Offers for Capital and Labor in Farming, Manufacturing, Mining, and Commerce* (Chattanooga, 1885); Edward Clarke, *Illustrated History of Atlanta, Containing Glances at Its Population, Business, Manufactures, Industries, Institutions . . . and Advantages Generally, with Nearly One Hundred Illustrations, and a Lithographic Map of the City* (Atlanta, 1878). Local libraries invariably have copies of books on their individual cities, but few depositories boast complete runs. Even then, they are frequently classified as reference books or as parts of special collections. Consequently, to the vexation of scholars, they do not circulate.

There are many local histories of more recent vintage. Representative examples include Charles Hirschfield, *Baltimore, 1870-1900: Studies in Social History* (Baltimore, 1941); Sherry Olson, *Baltimore: The Building of an American City* (Baltimore, 1980); William Stevens, *Washington: the Cinderella City . . .* (New York, 1943); Isabella McMeekin, *Louisville: The Gateway City* (New York, 1946); Lyle Saxon, *Fabulous New Orleans, Louisiana . . .* (Chicago, 1928); Harriet Leiding, *Charleston: Historic and Romantic* (Philadelphia, 1931); John P. Little, *History of Richmond* (Richmond, 1933); Marshall Butt, *Portsmouth under Four Flags, 1752-1881* (Portsmouth, 1961); Nettie Voges, *Old Alexandria: Where America's Past Is Present* (McLean, Va., 1975); William Christian, *Lynchburg and Its People* (Lynchburg, 1935); Jesse Burt, *Nashville: Its Life and Times* (Nashville, 1959); Ira Richards, *Story of a Rivertown: Little Rock in the Nineteenth Century* (Benton, Ark., 1969); *Montgomery, City of Progress: Yesterday and Today* (Montgomery, 1937); Etta Blanchard Worsley, *Columbus on the Chattahoochee* (Columbus, 1950); Helen Kohn Hennig, ed., *Columbia: Capital City of South Carolina, 1786-1936* (Columbia, 1936); Zella Armstrong, *The History of Hamilton County and Chattanooga, Tennessee*, 2 vols. (Chattanooga, 1931-40); Walter Cooper, *Official History of Fulton County* (Atlanta, 1934); Caldwell Delaney, *The Story of Mobile* (Mobile, 1953); Betsy Fancher, *Savannah: A Renaissance of the Heart* (Garden City, 1976). Every decade or so, an enthusiastic amateur brings the Mobile story, the Richmond story, or the Altanta story up to date. The continuing attempt to document the history of cities by their citizens has been an ongoing part of the American experience and of community building.

There are far too few analytical urban biographies of southern cities. Those that exist are of high quality. Thomas J. Wertenbaker, *Norfolk: Historic Southern Port*, edited by Marvin Schlegel (1931; rpr. Durham, 1962), is one of the earliest studies of a city undertaken by a professional historian. Another pioneering effort is Gerald Capers, *The Biography of a Rivertown: Memphis, its Heroic Age* (Chapel Hill, 1939). Capers has excellent material on the destructive yellow fever epidemics of the 1870s. He concludes that they retarded the city's growth by several decades. Constance McLaughlin Green, *Washington*, vol. 1, *Village and Capital, 1800-1878* (Princeton, 1962), and *Washington*, vol. 2, *Capital City, 1879-1950* (Princeton, 1963), explores the history of the nation's capital in thorough and readable fashion. *Atlanta: A City of the Modern South*, American Guide Series (1942; rpr. St. Clair Shores, Mich., 1973), draws together important aspects of Atlanta's history. So does *New Orleans City Guide*, American Guide Series (Boston, 1938); *Washington: City and Capital*, American Guide Series (Washington, 1937). Less successful is an attempt to do an analytical history of a city by a noted newspaper editor: Virginius Dabney, *Richmond: The Story of a City* (Garden City, 1976).

A small number of books and articles delineate specific themes that indicate something about urban development. An interpretive study, Harry M. Ward and Harold E. Greer, Jr., *Richmond during the Revolution, 1775-83* (Charlottesville, 1977), shows the impact of the Revolution on the city's future growth. Joy J. Jackson, *New Orleans in the Gilded Age* (Baton Rouge, 1969), emphasizes political themes. A recent partial biography of Baltimore in antebellum times, Gary Browne, *Baltimore in the Nation, 1789-1861* (Chapel Hill, 1980), emphasizes the role of noneconomic forces in building the Monumental City. Two articles in the *Georgia Historical Quarterly* that place a medium-sized city in perspective during antebellum days are James H. Stone, "Economic Conditions in Macon, Georgia, in the 1830s," 54 (Summer 1970):209-25; and Bowling Gates, "Macon, Georgia, Inland Trading Center, 1826-1836," 55 (Fall 1971):365-77. Of special note are the essays, "An American Museum Piece" (Louisville) and "The City of Perpetual Promise" (Birmingham), in George R. Leighton, *Five Cities: The Story of Their Youth and Old Age* (New York, 1939). His harsh appraisal of the motives of the business community, written against the backdrop of the Great Depression, represents an early attempt to escape from the chronological approach in writing about a city. Several decades later, there is a definite need for studies of southern cities that selectively study and draw conclusions about the main components of their development.

More books have been written on southern cities in the Civil War than upon any other aspect of their histories. Many are autobiographical or "potboilers," which emphasize the sensational and the role of individuals. A few are scholarly, many times overly technical. Typical are some of the books written about Vicksburg. Two accounts written by participants in the events are Mary Loughborough, *My Cave Life in Vicksburg: With Letters of Trial and Travail* (Little Rock, 1882); and Osborn Oldroyd, *A Soldier's Story of the Siege of Vicksburg* (Springfield, Ill., 1885). A semischolarly popular account is Adolph Hoehling and the editors of *Army Times*, *Vicksburg: 47 Days of Siege* (Englewood Cliffs, N.J., 1969). A scholarly monograph that covers more than simply the siege is Peter Walker, *Vicksburg: A People at War, 1860-1865* (Chapel Hill, 1960). Technical studies include John Milligan, *Gunboats Down the Mississippi* (Annapolis, 1965); William Everhart, *Vicksburg National Park, Mississippi*, National Park Service Historical Handbook Series no. 2 (Washington, 1954). Representative books on the Civil War experience in other cities include J. Winston Coleman, *Lexington during the Civil War* (Lexington, 1938); Catherine Copeland, *Bravest Surrender: A Petersburg Patchwork* (Richmond, 1961); Marvin Lucas, *Sherman and the Burning of Columbia* (College Station, 1976); Samuel Carter III, *The Siege of Atlanta, 1864* (New York, 1973); Noah Brooks, *Washington in Lincoln's Time* (New York, 1895); and Earl Schenck Miers, ed., *When the World Ended: The Diary of Emma LeConte* (New York, 1957), which is about Columbia. An account that places the occupation of a major southern city in perspective is Gerald M. Capers, *Occupied City: New Orleans under the Federals, 1862-1865* (Lexington, Ky., 1965). Unlike many of the studies of cities in the Civil War, two on Augusta emphasize the larger consequences: Florence Corley, *Confederate City: Augusta, Georgia, 1860-1865* (Columbia, 1960); Barry Fleming, *Autobiography of a City in Arms: Augusta, Georgia, 1861-1865* (Augusta, 1975). So far, despite a plethora of books, no one has produced a synthesis on the southern city in the Civil War. The studies on Civil War cities point up the importance attached to the period. Unfortunately, no similar body of material is available on a variety of the other areas fundamental to understanding the roots of southern urbanization in the Gilded Age.

Histories of immigration that touch on urban subjects are few and far between. A few general studies, some very dated, have information that relates to the South. Some of these are Stephen Byrne, *Irish Emigration to the United States: What It has Been, and What It Is* (New York, 1873); Albert Faust, *The German Element in the United States,* 2 vols. (New York, 1912); Carl Wittke, *We Who Built America: The Saga of the Immigrant* (Cleveland, 1939); Stanley C. Johnson, *A History of Emigration from the United Kingdom to North America, 1763-1912* (London, 1913). Valuable general material can be found in Stephen Thernstrom, ed., *Harvard Encyclopedia of American Ethnic Groups* (Cambridge, Mass., 1980). A state study with good data on Baltimore Germans is Dieter Cunz, *The Maryland Germans: A History* (1948; rpr. Port Washington, N.Y., 1972). Two useful articles in the *Louisiana Historical Quarterly* on Germans are Robert T. Clark, "Reconstruction and the New Orleans German Colony," 23 (April 1940):501-24; and Bob Cyrus Rauchle, "The Political Life of the Germans in Memphis, 1848-1900," 28 (Summer 1968):165-75. The basic study of the role of the Irish in a major city is Earl Niehaus, *The Irish in New Orleans, 1800-1860* (Baton Rouge, 1965). Darrell Overdyke, *The Know-Nothing Party in the South* (Baton Rouge, 1950), illustrates the adverse reaction of southern nativists to immigrant groups. Fredrick Marcel Spletstoser, "Back Door to the Land of Plenty: New Orleans as an Immigrant Port, 1820-1860," 2 vols. (Ph.D. dissertation, Louisiana State University, 1978), covers the influx of immigrants into New Orleans and the diffusion of many of them throughout the Mississippi River Valley. The study of immigrant groups in southern cities and their impact on institutions remains a fertile field of investigation.

The role of blacks in antebellum and postbellum cities has attracted increasing attention. The pioneer study on urban slavery before the Civil War remains Richard Wade, *Slavery in the Cities: The South, 1820-1860* (New York, 1964). Claudia Dale Golden, *Urban Slavery in the American South, 1820-1860: A Quantitative History* (Chicago, 1976), has detailed and complex data. Leonard P. Curry, *The Free Black in Urban America, 1800-1850: The Shadow of the Dream* (Chicago, 1981), contains valuable material on urban blacks in the upper South and Louisville in particular. Robert S. Starobin, *Industrial Slavery in the Old South* (New York, 1970), deals with an important but neglected subject. More has been done on urban free Negroes. Useful articles, all in the *Journal of Negro History,* include L. P. Jackson, "Free Negroes of Petersburg, Virginia," 12 (July 1927):365-88; E. Horace Fitchett, "The Origin and Growth of the Free Negro Population of Charleston, South Carolina," 26 (October 1941):421-37; Dorothy Provine, "The Economic Position of Free Blacks in the District of Columbia," 58 (January 1973):61-72. See also Ira Berlin, *Slaves without Masters: The Negro in the*

Antebellum South (New York, 1974). A few studies touch on the Gilded Age. John W. Blassingame, *Black New Orleans, 1860-1880* (Chicago, 1973); Constance M. Green, *The Secret City: A History of Race Relations in the Nation's Capital* (Princeton, 1967); and Robert E. Perdue, *The Negro in Savannah, 1865-1900* (New York, 1973), show how blacks established stable communities after the Civil War. See also Dale Somers, "Black and White in New Orleans: A Survey of Urban Race Relations, 1865-1900," *Journal of Southern History* 40 (February 1974):19-42. Unlike many other areas, a valuable synthesis covers major concerns of urban blacks in the Gilded Age: Howard N. Rabinowitz, *Race Relations in the Urban South, 1865-1890*, History of Urban America Series (New York, 1978). A well-researched study with a point of view, Lawrence J. Friedman, *The White Savage: Racial Fantasies in the Postellum South* (Englewood Cliffs, N.J., 1970), rasies provocative points about race relations. For a more balanced account see Howard N. Rabinowitz, "The Conflict between Blacks and the Police in the Urban South," *Historian* 34 (November 1976):62-76. A basic work is C. Vann Woodward, *The Strange Career of Jim Crow* (New York, 1955). A case study that addressed important aspects of white racial concerns is Terry L. Seip, "Municipal Politics and the Negro: Baton Rouge, 1865-1900," in Mark T. Carleton, Perry H. Howard, and Joseph B. Parker, eds., *Readings in Louisiana Politics* (Baton Rouge, 1975), 242-66. More case studies are needed on black and white relationships in the postbellum urban South.

Because of the nature of the subject, the impact of religious institutions on southern cities is a difficult area with which to deal. Ray Allen Billington, *The Protestant Crusade, 1800-1860: A Study of the Origins of American Nativism* (New York, 1938), contains data on the reaction of certain southern sects to immigrants. Edwin McNeill Poteat, Jr., "Religion in the South," in Couch, ed., *Culture in the South*, 248-69, stresses the South's fundamentalist tenets. Hunter D. Farish, *The Circuit Rider Dismounts: A Social History of Southern Methodism, 1865-1900* (Richmond, 1938), and Rufus B. Spain, *At Ease in Zion: Social History of the Southern Baptists, 1865-1900* (Nashville, 1967), have limited material on the transition of a frontier religion to urban values. Kenneth K. Bailey, "Southern White Protestants at the Turn of the Century," *American Historical Review* 68 (April 1963):618-35, is a helpful analysis. Charles Reagan Wilson, "The Religion of the Lost Cause: Ritual and Organization of the Southern Civic Religion, 1865-1920," *Journal of Southern History* 46 (May 1980):219-38, contains valuable material that illustrates the link between the Confederacy and civic religion in the cities of the New South. Sympathetic assessments of religious organizations include W. W. Barnes, *The Southern Baptist Convention, 1845-1953* (Nashville, 1954); Paul N. Garber, *The Methodists Are One People* (Nashville, 1939); Carter Woodson, *The History of the Negro Church* (1921; rpr. Washington, 1945); and John M. Cromwell, "First Negro Churches in the District of Columbia," *Journal of Negro History* 7 (January 1922):64-106. Various studies of a more general nature touch upon the Jewish religious experience. Among them are Isaac Fein, *The Making of an American Jewish Community: The History of Baltimore Jewry from 1773 to 1920* (Philadelphia, 1971); Leonard Dinnerstein and Maury Dale Palsson, *Jews in the South* (Baton Rouge, 1973); Eli N. Evans, *The Provincials: A Personal History of Jews in the South* (New York, 1973); Myron Berman, *Richmond's Jewry: Shabbat to Shockoe, 1796-1976* (Charlottesville, 1979); Steven

Hertzberg, *Strangers within the Gate City: The Jews of Altanta, 1845-1915* (Phila-delphia, 1978). So far, scholars have barely touched the surface in studying the southern urban religious experience.

Hardly any studies of note are available on urban education in the South in the Gilded Age. An older work, Edgar Knight, *The Influence of Reconstruction on Education in the South* (1913; rpr. New York, 1969), has some useful background material. Howard N. Rabinowitz, "Half a Loaf: The Shift from White to Black Teachers in the Negro Schools of the Urban South, 1865-1890," *Journal of Southern History* 40 (November 1974):565-94, although limited in scope, deals with an important subject. Frederick Chambers, "Histories of Black Colleges and Universities," *Journal of Negro History* 57 (July 1972):270-75, is essentially a list. Horace H. Cunningham, "The Southern Mind since the Civil War," in Link and Patrick, *Writing Southern History,* 383-409, is a stimulating account. Chapter 7, "Education," in Rabinowitz, *Race Relations in the Urban South,* has much useful material. In general, the educational experience has to be pieced to-gether from a variety of secondary and primary sources. A scholar has yet to write a basic book on education and its philosophical relationship to the Lost Cause and the New South.

Although much has been written about the South's rich cultural traditions, little of it touches directly upon the Gilded Age. Two books by Rollin G. Osterweis, *Romanticism and Nationalism in the Old South* (New Haven, 1949), and *The Myth of the Lost Cause, 1865-1900* (New York, 1973), place southern roman-ticism in perspective. Sarah Sprott Morrow, "A Brief History of the Theater in Nashville," *Tennessee Historical Quarterly* 30 (Summer 1971):178-89, shows how during Reconstruction the legitimate theater declined, replaced by minstrel and variety shows. Herbert J. Doherty, Jr., "The Mind of the Antebellum South," in Link and Patrick, *Writing Southern History,* emphasizes the growing importance of cultural activities. Dale A. Somers, *The Rise of Sports in New Orleans, 1850-1900* (Baton Rouge, 1972), explores a neglected aspect of urban social history. For background data see F. Garvin Davenport, *Cultural Life in Nashville on the Eve of the Civil War* (Chapel Hill, 1941); Joseph G. Tregle, Jr., "Early New Orleans Society: A Reappraisal," *Journal of Southern History* 18 (February 1952):20-36. No one has as yet tested in the South the provocative views on urban culture contained in Gunther Barth, *City People: The Rise of Modern City Culture in Nineteenth-Century America* (New York, 1980). Barth contends that such agencies as baseball teams, apartment houses, and depart-ment stores were of crucial importance as urban value givers.

Excellent but limited amounts of material are readily available on the South's contributions to city planning. The most comprehensive data, relating southern developments to national themes, can be found in a basic work, John W. Reps, *The Making of Urban America* (Princeton, 1965). Other studies by Reps that deal with southern planning themes are *Town Planning in Frontier America* (1965; rpr. Columbia, 1980); and *Monumental Washington: The Planning and Development of the Capital Center* (Princeton, 1967). An excellent study on the District of Columbia is Frederick Gutheim, *Worthy of the Nation: The History of Planning for the National Capital* (Washington, 1977). Albert Fein, *Frederick Law Olmsted and the American Environmental Tradition* (New York, 1972), places the City Beautiful movement in a national context. Fundamental to any study of urban planning is Lewis Mumford, *The City in History: Its Origins, Its Trans-formations, and Its Prospects* (New York, 1961).

Many works exist on various phases of southern urban architecture. Basic studies of architectual trends that place the South within the traditions of building in America include James Marston Fitch, *American Building: The Forces That Shape It* (1948; rpr. New York, 1977); Christopher Tunnard and Henry Hope Reed, *American Skyline: The Growth and Form of Our Cities and Towns* (New York, 1955); Vincent Scully, *American Architecture and Urbanism* (New York, 1969); Thomas A. Tallmadge, *The Story of Architecture in America* (New York, 1936); Talbot F. Hamlin, *Greek Revival Architecture in America* (New York, 1944). Most studies of individual southern cities are intended for popular audiences. Typical are the older William Casey, *An Archetectural Monograph: Charleston Doorways, Entrance Motives from a South Carolina City,* White Pine Series, vol. 14, monograph 81 (New York, 1928), and the newer Franklin Garrett, *Yesterday's Atlanta,* Seeman's Historic Cities Series, no. 8 (Miami, 1974). Of more scholarly quality are Everett B. Wilson, *Early Southern Towns* (South Brunswick, N.J., 1967); James Bonner, "Plantation Architecture of the Lower South on the Eve of the Civil War," *Journal of Southern History* 11 (August 1945):370-88; and Henry Forman, *Architecture of the Old South: The Medieval Style, 1585-1850* (Cambridge, Mass., 1948). For characteristic studies of individual buildings see *An Omnibus of the Capitol,* House of Representatives, Doc. 412, 2d ed., 86th Cong., 2d sess. (Washington, 1959); Clayton B. Dekle, "The Tennessee State Capitol," *Tennessee Historical Quarterly* 25 (Fall 1966):213-38; Gilbert E. Govan, "The Chattanooga Union Station," *Tennessee Historical Quarterly* 29 (Winter 1970-71):327-78; and Keith L. Bryant, "Cathedrals, Castles, and Roman Baths: Railroad Station Architecture in the Urban South," *Journal of Urban History* 2 (February 1976):195-230. Given the growing interest in architectural roots and the establishment in many cities of preservation agencies, the future bodes well for a steady stream of contributions documenting southern urban designs. An example is Eleanor Graham, ed., *Nashville: A Short History and Selected Buildings* (Nashville, 1974).

A number of scholarly studies detail the roots of southern industrialism. Broadus Mitchell, *William Gregg: Factory Master of the Old South* (Chapel Hill, 1928), and Fletcher M. Green, "Duff Green: Industrial Promoter," *Journal of Southern History* 2 (February 1936):29-42, draw succinct conclusions about two of the Old South's important exponents of industrialism. A number of sources make it clear that there was interest in the antebellum South in manufacturing. Among them are Herbert Collins, "The Idea of a Cotton Textile Industry in Ante-Bellum North Carolina, 1870-1900," *North Carolina Historical Quarterly* 34 (July 1927):358-92; Herbert Collins, "The Southern Industrial Gospel before 1860," *Journal of Southern History* 12 (August 1946):383-402; Robert S. Cotterill, "The Old South to the New," *Journal of Southern History* 15 (February 1949):3-8; Diffee W. Standard and Richard Griffin, "The Cotton Textile Industry in Ante-Bellum North Carolina," *North Carolina Historical Review* 34 (January 1957):15-37; 34 (April 1957):131-66; and Weymouth T. Jordan, *Ante-Bellum Alabama: Town and Country,* Florida State University Studies, no. 27 (Tallahassee, 1957). Problems with northern competition are discussed in Ernest M. Lander, Jr., "The Iron Industry in Ante-Bellum South Carolina," *Journal of Southern*

History 20 (August 1954):337-55, and Carrol H. Quenzel, "The Manufacture of Locomotives and Cars in Alexandria in the 1850s," *Virginia Magazine of History and Biography* 62 (April 1954):181-89. Norris Preyer, "Why Did Industrialism Lag in the Old South?" *Georgia Historical Quarterly* 55 (Fall 1971):378-96, notes the fears expressed by some observers that the factory system threatened democratic institutions. Raymond L. Cohn, "Local Manufacturing in the Antebellum South and Midwest," *Business History Review* 54 (Spring 1980):80-91, found many similarities between early midwestern and southern frontier manufacturing. Charles D. Dew, *Ironmaker for the Confederacy: Joseph R. Anderson and the Tredegar Iron Works* (New Haven, 1966), is an outstanding business history. Broadus Mitchell, *The Rise of Cotton Mills in the South*, John Hopkins University Studies in Historical and Political Science, ser. 39, no. 2 (Baltimore, 1921), traces the rise of an important industry. For promotional activities see Ethel M. Ames, *The Story of Coal and Iron in Alabama* (Birmingham, 1910), and Patrick J. Hearden, *Independence and Empire: The New South's Cotton Mill Campaign, 1865-1901* (DeKalb, Ill., 1982). Broadus Mitchell and George Mitchell, *The Industrial Revolution in the South* (Baltimore, 1930), concluded that industrialization threatened southern institutions. Chapter 5, "The Industrial Evolution," in Woodward, *Orgins of the New South*, 107-39, lucidly analyzes the rise of industry. No one as yet has written a general account of manufacturing in the South of the Gilded Age and its social impact. The appropriate census volumes remain the primary source of detailed information on industrial growth.

There is a large body of literature on southern railroads. Eugene Alvarez, *Travel on Southern Antebellum Railroads, 1828-1860* (University, Ala., 1974), is a well-written and fascinating excursion into practical aspects of social history. Merl E. Reed, *New Orleans and the Railroads: The Struggle for Commercial Empire, 1830-1860* (Baton Rouge, 1966), is fundamental to understanding New Orleans' railroad strategy. See also Marshall Gautreau, "The New Orleans, Opelousas and Great Western Railroad" (M.A. thesis, Louisiana State University, 1955). Robert S. Cotterill, "Southern Railroads, 1850-1860," *Mississippi Valley Historical Review* 10 (March 1924):396-405, surveys the growth of the network in the decade in which railroading passed out of its formative years. John F. Stover, *The Railroads of the South, 1865-1900: A Study in Finance and Control* (Chapel Hill, 1955), is the standard work on southern railroad policy. Stover shows the shift of control to outside interests. Maury Klein, *The Great Richmond Terminal: A Study in Businessmen and Railroad Strategy* (Charlottesville, 1970), traces the growth of a powerful railroad combination. Leonard P. Curry, *Rail Routes South: Louisville's Fight for the Southern Market, 1865-1872* (Lexington, 1969), deals with a period crucial to Louisville's metropolitan aspirations. Richard Price, *Georgia Railroads and the West Point Route* (Salt Lake City, 1962), draws conclusions about the significance of an important east-west connecting link. A technical study on a very important subject is John Doster, "Trade Centers and Railroad Rates in Alabama, 1873-1885: The Cases of Greenville, Montgomery, and Opelika," *Journal of Southern History* 18 (May 1952):169-92. George Rogers Taylor and Irene D. Neu, *The American Railroad Network* (Cambridge, Mass., 1956), though national in scope, has valuable traffic information on the South. Although much of value has been done, more first-rate studies of railroad strategy are needed. No general study exists that relates the growth of the railroad network to concerns of southern urbanization and nationalism. Herbert Wender, *Southern Commercial Conventions, 1837-1859*, Johns Hopkins University Studies in Historical and Political Science, series 48, no. 4 (Baltimore, 1930), makes clear that many antebellum statesmen considered railroads and cities of great importance to the rise of southern nationalism.

Some southern railroads have been the subject of biographies. Several of the studies are of use in relationship to city building in the Gilded Age. These include Hungerford, *Baltimore and Ohio Railroad;* John F. Stover, *History of Illinois Central Railroad* (New York, 1975); Maury Klein, *History of the Louisville and Nashville Railroad* (New York, 1972); John L. Kers, *The Louisville and Nashville: An Outline History* (New York, 1933); Kincaid Herr, *The Louisville and Nashville Railroad, 1850-1963* (Louisville, 1963); Jesse C Burt, Jr., "Four Decades of the Nashville, Chattanooga and St. Louis Railway, 1873-1916," *Tennessee Historical Quarterly* 9 (June 1950):99-132; and Samuel Derrick, *Centennial History of South Carolina Railroad* (Columbia, 1930). Unfortunately, few of these and other studies touch directly upon urbanization activities. Such information has to be ferreted out by researchers.

The state of southern agriculture had a tremendous impact on city building in the postbellum South. Roger L. Ransom and Richard Sutch, *One Kind of Freedom: The Economic Consequences of Emancipation* (Cambridge, Eng., 1977), comprehensively describes and evaluates the problems faced by southern agrarians. John D. Hicks, *The Populist Revolt* (Minneapolis, 1931), remains a useful summary. For surveys of Populist literature see Allen J. Going, "The Agrarian Revolt," in Link and Patrick, *Writing Southern History,* 362-82; Patrick E. McLear, "The Agrarian Revolt in the South: A Historiographical Essay," *Louisiana Studies* 12 (Summer 1973):443-63. An excellent biography of an agrarian leader is C. Vann Woodward, *Tom Watson: Agrarian Rebel* (New York, 1938). Reactions at the state level are discussed in William J. Cooper, Jr., *The Conservative Regime: South Carolina, 1877-1890* (Baltimore, 1968); William Ivy Hair, *Bourbonism and Agrarian Protest: Louisiana Politics, 1877-1900* (Baton Rouge, 1961). Current concerns of those involved in a debate over Populism have not touched directly on urban themes. Representative are Lawrence Goodwyn, *Democratic Promise: The Populist Movement in America* (New York, 1976); Robert C. McMath, Jr., *Populist Vanguard: A History of the Southern Farmers' Alliance* (Chapel Hill, 1976); and Michael Schwartz, *Radical Protest and Social Structure: The Southern Farmers' Alliance and Cotton Tenancy, 1880-1890* (New York, 1976). A valuable addition to the literature of agrarian protest would be a study relating farmers' concerns to the capabilities of the banking sructure in the South.

Too few students have written accounts relating to municipal concerns in southern cities. A variety of general studies have some value for the story in the South. For streets see Winston A. Walden, "Nineteenth Century Street Pavements" (M.A. thesis, University of Missouri-Kansas City, 1967); Clay McShane, "Transforming the Use of Urban Space: A Look at the Revolution in Street Pavements, 1880-1924," *Journal of Urban History* 5 (May 1979):279-307; George A. Soper, *Modern Methods of Street Cleaning* (New York, 1909); Lawrence H. Larsen, "Nineteenth-Century Street Sanitation: A Study of Filth and Frustration," *Wisconsin Magazine of History* 52 (Spring 1969):239-47; and Otto L. Bettmann, *The Good Old Days—They Were Terrible* (New York, 1974). Disposal problems are dealt with in Martin V. Melossi, *Garbage in the Cities: Refuse, Reform, and the Environment, 1880-1980* (College Station, Tex., 1981); Stanley K. Schultz and Clay McShane, "To Engineer the Metropolis: Sewers, Sanitation, and City Planning in Late-Nineteenth-Century America," *Journal of American History* 65 (September 1978):389-411; Joel A. Tarr, "The Separate vs. Combined Sewer Problem: A Case Study in Urban Technology Design Choice," *Journal of Urban History* 5 (May 1979):308-39; and Martin V. Melossi, ed., *Pollution and Reform in American Cities, 1870-1930* (Austin, 1980). Nelson Blake, *Water for the Cities: A History of the Water Supply Problem in the United States* (Syracuse, 1956), is basic. Two books by Jon C. Teaford, *The Municipal Revolution in America, 1650-1825* (Chicago, 1975), and *City and Suburb: The Political Fragmentation of Metropolitan America, 1850-1970* (Baltimore, 1979), show the technical evolution of city government. Howard N. Rabinowitz, "From Reconstruction to Redemption in the Urban South," *Journal of Urban History* 2 (February 1976):169-94, demonstrates how Democrats in several cities made only halfhearted attempts to capture black votes, leaving Republicans open to charges of being the "Negro party." General surveys of government include two old but still valuable studies: Charles Zueblin, *American Municipal Progress* (1902; rpr. New York, 1916); and John Fairlie, *Municipal Admministration* (New York, 1901). Frank Rowsone, Jr., *Trolley Car Treasury: A Century of American Streetcars, Horsecars, Cable Cars, Interurbans, and Trolleys* (New York, 1956), has some useful information. Raymond Fosdick, *American Police Systems* (New York, 1920), and James F. Richardson, *Urban Police in the United States* (Port Washington, N.Y., 1974), cover police systems. These representative studies give an indication of the general direction of municipal research.

A small number of articles represent starting points for further research on southern municipal services. A pioneering piece on city taxes is J. David Griffin, "Savannah's City Income Tax," *Georgia Historical Quarterly* 50 (September 1969):173-76. John H. Ellis, "Memphis Sanitary Revolution, 1880-1890," *Tennessee Historical Quarterly* 23 (March 1964):59-72, describes the Memphis reform program. Eugene J. Watts, "Property and Politics in Atlanta, 1865-1903," *Journal of Urban History* 3 (May 1977):295-322, shows how city officials favored property interests. Two background pieces on fire protection are E. Merton Coulter, "The Great Savannah Fire of 1820," *Georgia Historical Quarterly* 23 (March 1939):1-27; and John B. Clark, Jr., "The Fire Problem in Kentucky, 1778-1865: A Case History of the Ante-Bellum South," *Register of the Kentucky Historical Society* 51 (April 1953):97-122. Richard H. Haunton, "Law and Order in Savannah, 1850-1860," *Georgia Historical Quarterly* 56 (Spring 1972):1-24, provides a unique look at law enforcement problems in late antebellum times. The condition of municipal systems is an important indication of urbanization. Great opportunities for significant case studies await scholars in this difficult-to-research area of investigation. The ground for the urban South in the Gilded Age has hardly been touched.

Several thorough studies enrich the material that touches upon public health problems in the South. Richard J. Hopkins, "Public Health in Atlanta: The Formative Years, 1865-1879," *Georgia Historical Quarterly* 3 (September 1969):287-304; John H. Ellis, "Business and Public Health in the Urban South during the Nineteenth Century: New Orleans, Memphis, and Atlanta," *Bul-*

letin of the History of Medicine 44 (May-June 1970):197-212; and David R. Gold-field, "The Business of Health Planning, Disease Prevention in the Old South," *Journal of Southern History* 42 (November 1976):557-70, all have valuable data relating health problems to larger themes. The serious visitations of yellow fever that inflicted New Orleans and the community response are dealt with in Donald Everett, "The New Orleans Yellow Fever Epidemic of 1853," *Louisiana Historical Quarterly* 33 (October 1950):380-405; Jo Ann Corrigan, "Yellow Fever in New Orleans: Abstractions and Realities," *Journal of Southern History* 25 (August 1959):339-55; and Jo Ann Corrigan, "Privilege, Prejudice, and Strang-ers' Disease in Nineteenth-Century New Orleans," *Journal of Southern History* 36 (November 1970):568-78. More research and analysis are needed on the impact of disease upon southern urbanization, from both practical and the-oretical standpoints.

Few analytical studies have been done on urban entrepreneurs in the South in the Gilded Age. A starting point for those interested in community leaders is David C. Hammack, "Problems in the Historical Study of Power in the Cities and Towns of the United States, 1800-1960," *American Historical Review* 83 (April 1978):323-49. William Best Hesseltine, *Confederate Leaders in the New South* (1950; rpr. Westport, Conn., 1970); Eugene J. Watts, *The Social Bases of City Politics: Atlanta, 1865-1903* (Westport, 1978); Carl V. Harris, *Political Power in Birmingham, 1871-1921* (Knoxville, 1977); and Robert J. Hopkins, "Status, Mobi-lity, and Dimensions of Change in a Southern City: Atlanta, 1870-1910," in Kenneth T. Jackson and Stanley K. Schultz, eds., *Cities in American History* (New York, 1972), 216-31, have valuable data. Klein, *Great Richmond Terminal*, is essential readng. L. Tuffly Ellis, "The New Orleans Cotton Exchange: The Formative Years, 1871-1880," *Journal of Southern History* 38 (November 1973):545-64, surveys an important institution. J. R. Killick, "The Transforma-tion of Cotton Marketing in the Late Nineteenth Century: Alexander Sprunt and Son of Wilmington, N.C., 1866-1956," *Business History Review* 55 (Summer 1981):143-69, is a model study of an innovative business activity. The great voids in southern business history are hard to justify, given the emphasis placed on promoting manufacturing and northern ties by the leaders of the New South movement.

No history of a southern state has a central theme built around urbaniza-tion, although some of the volumes of the bicentennial series published under the auspices of the American Association for State and Local History have information relating to urbanization. Louis B. Rubin, Jr., *Virginia: A Bicentennial History* (New York, 1977), contains data on local antebellum rivalries. Good material on blockade running in the Civil War and the start of cotton manufac-turing can be found in William S. Powell, *North Carolina: A Bicentennial History* (New York, 1977). Virginia Van der Vees Hamilton, *Alabama: A Bicentennial History* (New York, 1977) has significant information on early Montgomery. David L. Lewis, *District of Columbia: A Bicentennial History* (New York, 1976), is useful. All the state compilations done as part of the Works Project Administra-tion's American Guide Series have valuable data on important cities and ur-banization trends. *Virginia: A Guide to the Old Dominion* (New York, 1940), is especially good on Portsmouth, promotional rivalries, and the rise of the tobacco industry. Interesting facts about transportation and cities run through

Georgia: A Guide to Its Towns and Countryside (Athens, 1940). Antebellum urban transportation plans are surveyed in *Maryland: A Guide to the Old Line State* (New York, 1940). *Mississippi: A Guide to the Magnolia State* (New York, 1938) details early economic developments. *Arkansas: A Guide to the State* (New York, 1941) studies educational patterns. *Kentucky: A Guide to the Bluegrass State* (New York, 1939) is a fine treatment of commercial growth. Thomas D. Clark, *Kentucky: Land of Contrast* (New York, 1968), summarizes urban ethnic problems in Louisville. In general, the vast number of state histories published in the United States contain little material on the urbanization process. An uninformed reader would never know that the nation had cities.

Some of the many available contemporary travel accounts helped to understand the urban components of the nineteenth-century South. Of special value is Edward King, *The Great South,* edited by W. Margruder Drake and Robert R. Jones (1879; rpr. Baton Rouge, 1972). King's "Great South" articles were published in *Scribner's Monthly* in 1873 and 1874. He made a comprehensive examination of southern life, which stressed urban progress. The editors of *The Great South* conclude, "King's work was unquestionably the most thorough treatment of the South since Frederick Law Olmsted's analysis of the slave states in the 1850s. It is manifestly impossible to preserve or embalm a people, a region, or an era of history, but Edward King, as had Olmsted before him, achieved the next best thing in presenting a remarkably sensitive and vivid picture of the American South in an important period of its history" (p. xxii). Frederick Law Olmsted, *A Journey in the Seaboard Slave States, with Remarks on Their Economy* (New York, 1859), had observations on garbage removal practices in Norfolk. President Thomas Jefferson commented on Norfolk's prospects in an interview described in John Melish, *Travels through the United States of America in the Years 1806 and 1807, and 1809, 1810, and 1811, Including an Account of Passages betwixt America and Britain, and Travels through Various Parts of Great Britain, Ireland and Upper Canada,* 2 vols. (Philadelphia, 1818). See also David Macrae, *The Americans at Home,* 2 vols. (Edinburgh, 1870).

Many contemporary articles are of worth in considering the evolution of southern cities in relation to regional concerns. Some of the useful articles in *DeBow's Review* are Ellwood Fisher, "The North and the South," 7 (September 1849):264; William M. Burwell, "Virginia Commercial Convention," 12 (January 1853):30; J. D. B. DeBow, "Contests for the Trade of the Mississippi Valley," 3 (February 1847):98; Jesup W. Scott, "The Great West," 15 (July 1853):51-53; George Fitzhugh, "Washington City and Its Characteristics," 24 (June 1858):502-3; William M. Burwell, "The Commercial Future of the South," 30 (February 1861):147; "Competition of the Gulf and Atlantic Ports," 24 (January 1858):47-48; "The Banks and Insurance Companies of New Orleans," 25 (November 1858):561; J. Childs, "Railroad Progress and the Mobile and Ohio Road," 12 (February 1852):203-4. Typical mid-nineteenth-century statements that emphasize the importance of geography in the construction of transportation systems can be found in the *Western Journal.* They are "The Natural Laws of Commerce," 1 (April 1848):137-77; and "A System of Internal Improvement for the West," 2 (January 1849):1-8. "Mississippi Valley Railroad," *Western Journal and Civilian* 9 (November 1852):14, speculates on the location of the site of a possible great city along the lower Mississippi River. "Commercial Delusions—

Speculations," *American Review* 71 (October 1845):341-57, is a participant's account of the frenzied activities that featured early speculation in the Midwest. Numerous articles in the *Manufacturers Record* stress the themes embodied in the New South creed.

Certain other older items were of special use. Hinton Rowan Helper, *The Impending Crisis of the South: How to Meet It* (New York, 1857), usually thought of as the book that stimulated the slavery controversy, contributed to the debate over whether the South required a great commercial city. Albion Winegard Tourgée, *A Fool's Errand* (New York, 1880), is an entertaining but embittered semifictional account of southern life by a former carpetbagger. Insights on urban sanitation concerns are illustrated in "First Report of the Committee on Public Hygiene of the American Medical Association," *Transactions of the American Medical Association*, vol. 2 (Philadelphia, 1849). For a typical promotional work see M. B. Hillyard, *The New South: A Description of the Southern States, Noting Each State Separately, and Giving Their Distinctive Features and Most Salient Characteristics* (Baltimore, 1887). James Bryce, *The American Commonwealth* (New York, 1888), and Lincoln Steffens, *Shame of the Cities* (New York, 1904), though general in scope, are of use in understanding city government in the South. These and other accounts add richness to the materials needed to pursue the study of the urban South in the Gilded Age.

Index